The Action Française

Edward R. Tannenbaum

Assistant Professor of History

Rutgers, The State University

JOHN WILEY AND SONS, INC. NEW YORK LONDON

The

Action

Française

Die-hard Reactionaries in

Twentieth-Century France

Library of Congress Catalog Card Number: 62-16159
Printed in the United States of America

To My Parents

Preface

This book is about a particular group of Frenchmen in the twentieth century. Most of these people belonged to the Action Française at one time or another, some supported kindred and rival movements, and there were also nonjoiners who contented themselves with saying "the country is going to the dogs" under its democratic regime. My purpose is to show how these people responded to the world around them and how they justified their behavior. I am concerned with their "ideas" mainly as the intellectual basis for their ideology—that is, a set of rationalizations of interest, sentiment, habit, or belief. The history of reactionary political theories from Rivarol to Charles Maurras has been well covered by other writers. I deal primarily with the use that was made of these theories by men and women who wanted to go on living in the past.

Charles Maurras undoubtedly has his place as a literary critic and champion of stylistic purity along classical lines, but twentieth-century France has produced a dozen writers like him. Émile Faguet, Ferdinand Brunetière, and André Rousseaux—to mention only so-called Rightists—have done as much as he to bolster conservative standards of criticism. The style of Anatole France and Jacques de Lacretelle is just as "pure" as his, and they understand their fellow men far better. Maurice Barrès towers over him as an artist, and his nationalism touches the heart as well as the mind. Only in his attacks on certain weaknesses of democratic society does Maurras stand out among his peers. And it is mainly as a publicist that he is treated in this study.

I disapprove of all individuals and groups that try to achieve their goals, no matter what the cost. None of my best friends is a fascist, Communist, nationalist, or religious fanatic. Yet I believe that a historian can understand people he dislikes, that he can put himself in their places and relive their experiences and still condemn them on moral grounds. Eminent scholars have written about such unsavory topics as Attila, slave traders, the Inquisition, Hitler, and Stalin—and if the Devil himself should someday be proven to be "historical" he will undoubtedly have his biographer. The Frenchmen in the Action Française and the movements that were linked with it at various times were not evil; they simply thought and felt differently than I do. For the sake of understanding them, I have temporarily taken on such attitudes as antisemitism, hatred of the masses, intellectual snobbery, and chauvinism. This Stanislavskyan exercise has not made me alter my judgment of the characters who held these prejudices in real life. I have tried to be fair; I cannot claim to be impartial.

EDWARD R. TANNENBAUM

New Brunswick, New Jersey
March 1962

Contents

1

✤ ✤ ✤ ✤ ✤

Two Frances?

It all began in 1789. In that epic year the triumphant middle classes tried to replace the tottering Old Regime with a society in which all men were free from arbitrary rule and equal before the law. Unfortunately, circumstances in France and Europe during the 1790's prevented the moderates from consolidating their gains and repressing opposition from the Left and the Right. They ultimately turned to Napoleon Bonaparte, who substituted glory for liberty. As long as he piled up military victories his regime seemed to work, but he too failed in the end. Then the people who had opposed the Revolution from the start were ready to lead France back to "the good old days."

Insofar as the parties to this conflict may be reduced to two sides, they may be thought of as the proponents of "aristocratic" and "democratic" forms of community.[1] Both factions

[1] The ideas in this paragraph come from Robert R. Palmer, *The Age of Democratic Revolution*, Vol. I, *The Challenge* (Princeton, New Jersey: Princeton University Press, 1959), p. 22.

had been gaining strength since about 1760, and the Revolution had begun as a clash between them. Thus conservatism and counterrevolution were not merely "reactions" against the Revolution. They were eighteenth-century forces against which the Revolution itself was a reaction. Only toward the close of the century did the term "reactionary" clearly divide those Frenchmen who wanted to restore the Old Regime from those who favored even a limited kind of democracy.

The counterrevolutionary faction had shown its greatest strength in 1793 and had then become relatively inactive under Napoleon—after all, he *had* at least maintained order and made peace with the church. Its ranks included most of the clergy, the nobility, and the peasants in the western and southwestern provinces, as well as individual Frenchmen from all other sections of society. Some of them might have been reluctant to part with the confiscated lands they had bought, but they all wanted the throne restored to the Bourbons. Their program called for a hierarchical class system based on order imposed from above and reinforced by the sanctity of the family. All revolutionary innovations—from social equality to long pants—were to be abolished. The beliefs of the Catholic religion were to be instilled into the young, and the church was to be given back its independent moral and spiritual authority so that it could work with the king in maintaining the old *status quo*.

During the Restoration period these reactionaries succeeded in destroying much that had been accomplished since 1789. They replaced the tricolor with the white flag of the Bourbons, rehabilitated the *émigrés*, and favored the Catholic Church in various ways. Except for a few liberals like the Ducs de Broglie, de Choiseul, and Voyer d'Argenson and the irrepressible Marquis de Lafayette, the hereditary aristocracy backed the policies of the royal ministers. In addition, the best-known political writers of the day, including Joseph de Maistre and Louis de Bonald, preached the doctrine of reaction. To the dismay of the Ultras, Louis XVIII tried to mollify those conservatives who opposed a complete return to the Old Regime, but under his successor no one was "more royalist than the king." For Charles X was an uncompromising counterrevolutionary. He had been the first Bourbon *émigré* in 1789; he became the last one after the Revolution of 1830.

Beginning with Louis Philippe, each new political system that the French tried and abandoned produced another group of Rightists: some of them preferred a constitutional monarchy, others wanted a conservative republic, and, finally, there were the Bonapartists. François Guizot expressed the outlook of the Orleanists by saying that the way to become eligible to vote was to get rich. Adolphe Thiers advocated a somewhat wider suffrage, but under the Second Republic he disenfranchised the poorest third of the adult males and helped the church to regain its monopoly over education. The Bonapartists also moved to the Right during the course of the nineteenth century. Although the Romantic nationalists who sought to revive the Empire in the 1840's were militaristic,[2] many of them were still egalitarian and revolutionary. Napoleon III tried to be all things to all factions, but after his regime collapsed his remaining followers eventually merged with the authoritarian nationalist leagues, which were to form the third section of the French Right under the Third Republic, along with the Legitimist successors of the Ultras and the conservative republicans who were in the Orleanist tradition.[3]

In France, as elsewhere, political movements have reflected traditional and visionary ideologies, real or imagined interests, and changing material conditions. Some of them have

[2] Until 1848 it was the Left that glorified the army, while the conservatives and reactionaries continued to associate it with the defeated Napoleonic regime (Raoul Girardet, *La Société militaire dans la France contemporaine, 1815–1939* [Paris: Plon, 1953], pp. 9–10). The events of June 1848 caused them to reverse this view and to see the military as the defender of order against the "Reds." But the Bonapartists were militarists and nationalists at all times.

[3] René Remond, *La Droite en France de 1815 à nos jours* (Paris: Aubier, 1954), p. 14.

sought to revive outmoded and anachronistic institutions and values; others have been content to preserve the *status quo* or to adapt it to new needs; and there have always been a few who wanted to uproot the existing order and rebuild society according to a utopian blueprint. The attitudes and actions of these people are conventionally called reactionary, conservative, liberal, and radical-revolutionary. Such labels are helpful in suggesting an underlying point of view to the wary observer of human behavior, though they have often been used for rhetorical purposes to sway the unthinking masses and thinking persons in unthoughtful moments.

It is especially difficult to apply these terms to Frenchmen between 1830 and 1870. As one type of regime succeeded another, the same person might change from a radical to a liberal and end as a conservative. Furthermore, industrialization created new economic and social problems that could not be solved merely by changing the constitution or extending the franchise. As early as the 1840's some of the urban workers were already demanding economic as well as political equality. The bourgeois republicans certainly did not share this goal, though many of them were also considered radicals under the July Monarchy and again under the Second Empire. In mid-1848 the typical liberal was an intellectual who wanted a republic and universal suffrage; in the 1860's he might have been an industrialist who opposed government spending and war. The majority of France's peasants were liberals in both respects, but they turned conservative whenever their property was threatened by the Paris "Reds."

All of the Right-wing political movements reasserted themselves in 1870. Just before the Communards were having their brief triumph in the capital, the rest of the country had elected a two-thirds majority of monarchists to the national assembly at Bordeaux. The war with Prussia was still going on, and most Frenchmen had voted for peace, not a king. Besides, the antirepublican delegates were divided among two hundred Legitimists, two hundred Orleanists, and thirty Bonapartists. The greatest hindrance to their unity was the intransigent attitude of the Bourbon pretender, the Comte de Chambord, toward the tricolor and everything that it stood for.

Since a restoration of the king proved to be impossible for the moment, the monarchists in the national assembly tried to set up a regime that would leave the door open for him at some future time. They made Marshal MacMahon president of the republic in 1873 and granted him a large degree of personal power for seven years. Then, in 1875, they adopted a constitution that could operate under a monarchy as well as a republic. Unfortunately for them, MacMahon was unable to impose his will on the chamber of deputies, which asserted its independence in 1877.[4] After the senate also passed into the hands of a republican majority two years later, MacMahon resigned.

The Third Republic was in to stay, but there was still a large antidemocratic minority in the country. It included almost all of the aristocracy and the clergy, a substantial portion of the middle-class conservatives, and peasants who were economically dependent on the landowning nobility or who got their political ideas from their priests. The state administration and the army also remained strongholds of authoritarianism as long as they were manned by people who had been trained under the Second Empire. In 1883 monarchist hopes were aroused momentarily when the death of the Comte de Chambord united many Legitimists with the followers of the Orleanist pretender and again when the conservative parties won a parliamentary majority in the 1885 elections.

Despite these hopeful signs, the royalist movement lost

---

[4] Republican-sponsored demands for leniency toward former Communards played a major role in the reactionaries' determination to destroy representative government in France (Jean T. Joughin, *The Paris Commune in French Politics* [2 vols.; Baltimore: The Johns Hopkins Press, 1955], I, 115).

its vigor. Some of its supporters simply retired from politics and kept in contact with the outside world by reading newspapers like the *Gaulois* or its provincial counterparts.[5] All that was left of their "party" was a small committee subsidized by the Duc d'Orléans. Yet the aristocratic-monarchical view of the world persisted. Its influence virtually disappeared from public life; it lost more of its followers as time went on, but it did not die. It was kept alive in the fashionable salons of Paris, in the châteaux of the country gentry, and in the rectories and seminaries of the Catholic Church. The people whose attitudes and behavior reflected this view called themselves *bien-pensants*; their enemies called them reactionaries.

*

In the late 1880's the *bien-pensants* tried to use General Georges Boulanger in an effort to destroy the Third Republic and install an authoritarian regime. Their role in the campaign to put him in power is significant because it set the pattern for collusion between the traditional reactionaries and the new, antiparliamentary nationalist leagues, which was to plague many democratic countries in the twentieth century. Therefore, it will be examined in some detail.

General Boulanger's main attributes were his habit of talking too much and his handsome appearance on a black horse. While he was minister of war in 1886 he had dismissed four Orleanist princes from the army in accordance with a law prohibiting all pretenders and their direct heirs from serving in France's armed forces. The royalists soon forgave him though, and the current pretender, the Comte de Paris, began making promises to him if he would be his "General Monk." Boulanger was becoming the man of the hour with his talk of *revanche* and constitutional reform. The Parisian masses idolized him, and the Radical Republicans made him their

[5] One of the most notable royalist weeklies, the *Nouvelliste de Bordeaux*, was edited by a future member of the Action Française, the Comte Eugène de Lur-Saluces.

leader. He visited Jérome Bonaparte in Switzerland and agreed to serve him too. Above all, he was *Général Revanche*, the "man" of Paul Déroulède, a minor nationalist poet who headed the League of Patriots.

Déroulède had founded this league in 1882 for the purpose of developing a military spirit in France, preparing Frenchmen morally and physically to be good soldiers, and preserving the cult of *revanche* in the public mind. At first his movement confined its activities to sponsoring athletic contests, military exhibitions, and patriotic rallies. But Déroulède was interested in politics as well as the lost provinces. He wanted a regime that would be directly responsive to the will of the masses through plebiscites. Once he had convinced himself that Boulanger alone could change the system, he began using all the resources of the League of Patriots in an intensive campaign for the general.

Another nationalist writer who backed Boulanger was Maurice Barrès. His emotional and intellectual development was undoubtedly conditioned by the fact that he had been born in the province of Lorraine.[6] Indeed, he once said that during his boyhood his chief thought had been to avoid becoming a German.[7] Barrès had a mystical conception of the French nationality, which he attributed to all people who spoke the language—in some ways it was like Hitler's notion of the *Volksdeutsch* in the 1930's. According to him, there were also local differences in regions where French culture prevailed. "You must recognize the fact that you were made to feel as Lorrainers, Alsatians, Bretons, Belgians, and Jews," he told his readers.[8] Germany's effort to destroy the regional cultural heritage in the French provinces she had annexed prompted Barrès to develop a theory of the "group self" which must preserve itself from foreign influences.[9] By the

[6] Ernst Robert Curtius, *Maurice Barrès und die geistigen Grundlagen des französischen Nationalismus* (Bonn: F. Cohen, 1921), p. 1.
[7] Maurice Barrès, *Mes Cahiers* (4 vols.; Paris: Plon, 1929–1931), I, 14–15.
[8] *Un Homme libre* (Paris: E. Paul, 1912), p. 231.   [9] *Ibid.*, p. 167.

1890's he was already speaking of the struggle between the French "race" and the "alien Jewish race."

Barrès felt uprooted—*déraciné*—when he arrived in Paris. There he devoted himself to extolling the virtues of what he called the "French spirit." This spirit, he maintained, could be revived only through a national effort to wipe out the humiliation of the defeat by Prussia. His solution to the nation's domestic political problems was a strong military leader. Unlike Déroulède, he favored a dictatorship rather than a mass democracy; but both men opposed the bourgeois republic, and they worked together to help General Boulanger overthrow it.

By 1887 Boulanger had become the symbolic chief of most citizens who disliked the existing regime. Some of them opposed its colonial policy and its anticlericalism, others its indifference to demands for constitutional reform. The economic crisis that had begun in 1882 was also causing widespread social unrest among the country's wage earners—especially the two to three hundred thousand who were unemployed. While the Radicals did nothing and the Socialists were weak and divided, Boulanger promised action. His warmongering nationalism offered another kind of "action" to millions of lower middle-class and lower class Frenchmen who were already beginning to feel like outsiders—socially and economically *déracinés*—in an emerging industrial society that seemed to be dominated by greedy capitalists and politicians who were committed to maintaining the *status quo*. For in 1887 Maurice Rouvier formed the first of a new type of "republican defense" coalition consisting of conservatives and moderates. In that same year the miners and metal workers of the Nord elected Boulanger as their representative to the chamber of deputies.[10]

[10] Jacques Néré, "La Crise économique et sociale de 1882 et le mouvement Boulangiste" and "Les Élections Boulangistes dans le Nord" (unpublished doctoral theses, Sorbonne, 1959), *passim*.

The army general staff became impatient with Boulanger's political activities and put him on the retired list just before the 1887 election, but his popularity continued to grow. Most of the Radical politicians turned against him because they feared that he wanted to become a dictator. In spite of their opposition, Boulanger won elections in the Somme and Charente-Inférieure, and in January 1889 he gained the parliamentary seat of the Seine. On the evening after this spectacular victory Déroulède and his other champions tried to persuade the general to march on the presidential palace and set up a new regime. Instead of responding to this appeal, Boulanger continued to drink toasts with his friends and finally went home to bed.

What made this potential Caesar stop at his Rubicon? Charles-Louis de Saulces de Freycinet (who was minister of war at the time) says that he either lacked boldness or was not lacking enough in scruples, that if he had marched with his companions he might well have gained power, since there was confusion among the police, many of whom were sympathetic to him.[11] Although this may have been so, Boulanger certainly knew that the Military Governor of Paris would have called out the army in case of an emergency and that the soldiers would have done what they were told. The Republic may have governed badly, but it defended itself well.

A man with Boulanger's following was an obvious threat to the regime, even after he had refused to storm the Elysée Palace. He went on making provocative speeches in February and March of 1889. At Tours he called for the end of the parliamentary system and demanded a republic of all men of good will, whether monarchists or republicans. This pronouncement led the authorities to prosecute him, along with the leaders of the League of Patriots.

The hapless general fled to Brussels just before his trial,

[11] Charles-Louis de Saulces de Freycinet, *Souvenirs* (2 vols.; Paris: Delagrave, 1912–1913), I, 419–420.

but his supporters continued to campaign for him in France. Among them were duchesses and streetwalkers, habitués of the most fashionable salons and of the gutter, outcasts from the different political parties, and malcontents of every description. At the head of them all, full of dignity, was Baron Mackau, the self-styled representative of order and religion.[12] Large sums were spent for propaganda. Although naïve patriots in the provinces made some contributions, the major part of the money came from rich royalists. The Duchesse d'Uzès alone gave three million francs to the "cause." [13]

Despite this backing, Boulanger was defeated in the local elections of September 1889, and the royalists soon abandoned him. Arthur Meyer, editor of the *Gaulois*, expressed their disappointment and recriminations in the following way: [14]

Our purpose was to take over General Boulanger, to push him to the Right and to rise with him in an attack on universal suffrage. Events made General Boulanger deviate from his original direction, which was altogether illusory.

The League of Patriots was disbanded, Barrès devoted himself to a literary career, and most of the little people who had placed their hopes in Boulanger soon forgot him. Meanwhile, the reactionaries who had tried to use him to overthrow the Republic bided their time.

The Boulanger episode marked a turning point in the distribution of attitudes among French political movements. Like the other monarchists, the Bonapartists had backed the ersatz emperor.[15] When he disappeared, their party declined, and their goals were taken over by the newer nationalist

[12] Édouard Drumont, *Le Testament d'un antisémite* (Paris: E. Dentu, 1891), p. 46.
[13] France, Archives Nationales, *Haute Cour*, F⁷12452, *Police Générale*, June 29, 1899. Also, see *Souvenirs de la Duchesse d'Uzès* (Paris: Plon, 1934), p. 93, in which she says that the Comte Albert de Mun persuaded her to contribute this money to the Boulangist movement.
[14] *Gaulois*, September 23, 1889.
[15] Adrien Dansette, *Du Boulangisme à la révolution Dreyfusienne*, Vol. I: *Le Boulangisme, 1886–1890* (Paris: Perrin, 1938), p. 379.

leagues at the end of the century. As for the Legitimists and
Orleanists, their efforts to use the General had resulted in
disillusionment, though if they had opposed him they might
have lost much of their following as well as their hopes.[16]
Traditionally pacifist, they were to reorient their position
along nationalist lines and champion the goal of *revanche*.
Some of them were even to abandon the dynastic issue.

Boulanger also caused the "government parties" to modify
their views. From the time of MacMahon's resignation until
the Dreyfus Affair, France was governed by a group of men
who called themselves Opportunists in the eighties and Pro-
gressists in the nineties. Its leaders included Jules Ferry,
Maurice Rouvier, Ernest Constans, and Jules Méline. Although they said that public policies should be guided by
technical expediency rather than the defense of ideological
principles, their own thinking reflected the dominant ideology
of the period—positivism. According to these men, the Revolution had attained its permanent structure with the triumph
of the liberal bourgeoisie and the Orleanist Constitution of
1875. Now they wanted to develop the country's economy
and spread enlightenment through public education. They
also felt that building a new colonial empire would side-
track demands for domestic reform, offset the military defeat
of 1870, and create opportunities for economic development
overseas. Then the rise of Boulanger—which seemed to show
the Republic's fragile foundations—made the Opportunists
revise their program. In order to preserve the existing regime,
they decided to abandon their anticlericalism and gain support
from the conservative Catholics.

The Radical Republicans favored a more liberal constitution and *revanche* until the late 1880's, but they gave up both
aims when Boulanger expropriated them. Henceforth they
accepted the single-member constituency and the senate, which
they had previously opposed as limiting the effectiveness of
universal suffrage. They tried to nurture the illusion that they

[16] *Ibid.*

were still Leftists by eventually changing their name to
Radical Socialist and by reviving the issue of anticlericalism.
All the while they were becoming increasingly rigid in their
purely political conception of liberalism. On economic and
social questions they were no longer able to claim that they
had "no enemies to the Left," for the budding syndicalist
and socialist movements were France's true radical-revolution-
aries by the 1890's.

At the other extreme of the political spectrum the reactionaries learned several lessons from the Boulanger fiasco. On
the one hand, they became aware of the dangers of supporting
a man-on-horseback whose public spokesmen did not share
their *bien-pensant* outlook. On the other hand, they discovered that they could hope to overthrow the bourgeois-
democratic regime only by gaining support from a section of
the disgruntled masses. After the 1880's they tried to do this
by adopting nationalist slogans and sponsoring public demonstrations. They continued to plot behind closed doors but
they also invaded the streets.

*

The one reactionary force that remained relatively untouched until the 1880's was the century-old clerical movement. It had first arisen during the Revolution, which had
ceased to protect Catholicism at the expense of other cults
and had disrupted the social bases of the church: the family,
education, and public welfare. Some of the Jacobins had been
actually hostile to Christianity itself. Consequently, many
devout Catholics came to believe that a restoration of the
Old Regime was necessary to the proper functioning of the
church and that the church alone could bring back stability
and order to French society. According to them, neither the
state nor the individual could take its place in this respect.[17]

[17] Waldemar Gurian, *Die politischen und sozialen Ideen des französischen Katholizismus*, 1789–1914 (Munich-Gladbach: Volksvereinsverlag, 1929), pp. 57–60.

Only after the fall of the July Monarchy was the church able to regain its former role in teaching the young. This change was made possible by the Falloux law, which was passed with Thiers's blessing in 1850 and named after the Catholic minister of education. It abolished the monopoly of Napoleon's University of France in higher and secondary schools and permitted the clergy to found colleges of their own. In addition, everything was done to put primary education into the hands of the Catholic teaching orders, and priests were given an active supervisory role in all of its branches. The Falloux law was thus the basis for the church's unusual influence in education until the 1880's. Religious instruction became compulsory in all primary schools under the Second Empire and was provided almost exclusively by monks or nuns.[18]

Although most of the leaders of French Catholicism in the nineteenth century were reactionary and ultramontane, a liberal Catholic movement had appeared in the 1840's under the leadership of a Dominican monk named Lacordaire and Charles Montalembert, a brilliant publicist. These two men wanted the French church to be more independent of papal control than the ultramontanes and they believed that the clergy had to come to grips with the problems of modern society. They also opposed the antibourgeois and antimodern bias of the reactionaries. But the publication of the papal *Syllabus of Errors* in 1864 reinforced the intransigence of the latter, stimulated the growth of Integral Catholicism in opposition to liberalism, and was later to be called "modernism."

The *Syllabus* declared that the church was a complete and perfect society, independent of and superior to all governments, with the exclusive right to educate and the power to use force if necessary. This claim of final authority for the

[18] Merrill L. Hutchins, "The Relations between Church and State in France from 1905–1925" (unpublished Ph.D. dissertation, University of Chicago, 1949), p. 22.

church superseded all theories of national or political sovereignty and condemned the practice of universal suffrage. The *Syllabus* denounced freedom of worship for non-Catholics, as well as freedom of the press and freedom of speech. It denied the right of subjects to refuse obedience to legitimate princes, except when absolved from their oath. Divorce and the belief that a civil contract could constitute a true marriage were also proscribed. Other "errors" listed were the separation of church and state and the suggestion that the removal of the pope's temporal power would serve the church's interests. The last article concluded by saying that it was wrong to believe that "the Roman pontiff can and ought to reconcile himself or compromise with progress, liberalism, and modern civilization."

Beginning with the reign of Napoleon III, one of the leading "integrist" spokesmen was Louis Veuillot, the editor of the weekly *Univers*. In his newspaper he attacked everyone who opposed the supreme authority of Rome, the doctrine of papal infallibility, and the *Syllabus*. Many conservative Catholics wanted an *Ordre Moral* under Marshal MacMahon to be the basis of the political regime after 1871, but Veuillot, the reactionary bishops, and the die-hard Legitimists ruined its chances for success by refusing to compromise on any point. They insisted on destroying everything that had been accomplished since 1789. MacMahon's loss of power to parliament on May 16, 1877, was the death blow to their hopes. Thereafter the laic republicans began to legislate their own reforms.

In the 1880's the positivism of the Opportunists—especially Jules Ferry and his followers—was not merely anticlerical, it was antireligious. As one of them said: "Bismarck made war on the Church. We will make it on God." With this aim in mind, the government tried to abolish religious instruction in the state schools, expel the teaching orders, and establish a compulsory education system that would mold France's children into freethinking, loyal republicans. This program of "laicization" was only partially successful (in 1900 nearly a

third of the school population was still being taught in Catholic schools), and it perpetuated the hostility of millions of
Catholics toward the Republic. As a means of combating anticlericalism, the Augustin Fathers of the Assumption launched
the daily newspaper La Croix in 1883. "They adopted an
aggressive attitude, throwing doubt and suspicion everywhere,
ridiculing the highest public offices, carrying their hatred
of the enemies of the Church to the point of exasperation." [19]

The ideological conflict between positivism and Catholicism
continued into the 1890's, but many republican leaders came
under the influence of a "new spirit" of tolerance and reconciliation toward the church. Freycinet expressed this attitude
to the senate in 1891 when he said: "The cabinet . . . does
not believe that it has received, either from the parliament
or from the country, a mandate to bring about the separation
of the church and the state, or to prepare it." [20] Convinced
that a monarchical restoration was no longer possible in
France, the Vatican welcomed this conciliatory attitude. In
February 1892 Pope Leo XIII urged all Frenchmen to accept
the existing regime and to respect and preserve its institutions.
The ensuing *ralliement* divided French Catholics. The majority remained intransigent, but a number of them abandoned
the royalist cause and began to participate in politics after
years of inactivity.

Many of the *ralliés* moved toward the conservative Center,
where they hoped to be more effective in refashioning the
country's institutional structure in accordance with their own
goals. Though they called themselves Moderates, they were
in complete accord with the social conservatism of the Opportunists and they responded favorably to Jules Méline when
he called for a *rapprochement* in the face of the new enemy
on the Left in the 1890's. For socialism, despite dissension

[19] R. P. Lecanuet, *L'Église de France sous la troisième république*
(Paris: Alcan, 1930), p. 233.
[20] *Journal Officiel de la République Française, débats parlementaires,
Sénat,* December 9, 1891, p. 1078.

in its ranks, was beginning to penetrate the working class, and the anarchists were becoming alarmingly aggressive. The conservative republicans and the *ralliés* united in their efforts to curb these proletarian movements and to resist the income-tax proposals of Léon Bourgeois' Radical cabinet.[21] This Right-Center coalition was committed to the established order, but it harbored potential supporters of future strong men who might try to overthrow the Republic if it ceased to be conciliatory toward the church or if it became too radical politically.

*

The fact that those Rightists who still refused to accept the "principles of 1789" were anything but "moderate" was made evident by the militant form of antisemitism they adopted toward the end of the nineteenth century. Until that time the *bien-pensants* had discriminated against the Jews socially but had not thought of them as political and racial enemies. The stereotyped image of the money-hungry Jew was perpetuated in the writings of Leftists like Proudhon and Zola (in his novel *D'Argent*) as well as Rightists like Balzac and the Comtesse de Ségur. Then Édouard Drumont's book *La France Juive* (which first appeared in 1886) made the image more sinister by charging that "the only one to whom the Revolution was profitable was the Jew." [22] According to Drumont, the immense fortunes of the Jews, their castles and town houses were the spoils of a dominant race from an enslaved race. "Today, thanks to the Jew, money, to which the Christian world used to attach only secondary importance, has become all powerful," said Drumont.[23] This simple-minded explanation of the materialism of modern economic life has always appealed to those classes in France

21 Eugen Weber, "The Right in France: A Working Hypothesis," *American Historical Review*, Vol. LXV, No. 3 (April 1960), 559.
22 *La France juive* (43rd edition, 2 vols.; Paris: E. Dentu, 1886), I, vi.
23 *Ibid.*, p. xiv.

that continued to respond to current conditions with a pre-capitalist outlook.

Drumont sought to attract additional followers to his brand of antisemitism by linking it with nationalism. He was one of the first publicists to identify the Jews with Germany and to accuse them of having betrayed France in 1870.[24] Drumont disapproved of Boulanger for accepting the sponsorship of men of Jewish origin like Arthur Meyer and Alfred Naquet.[25] But he was on fairly good terms with Paul Déroulède by 1890 and said that he had been unjust to him in *La France Juive*.[26] Déroulède was not an antisemite himself, though his anti-German rantings bolstered the development of antisemitism among French nationalists. Maurice Barrès also followed this line. He later wrote that he had admired Drumont from the beginning and that a true nationalist must also be an antisemite.[27]

At the end of *La France Juive* Drumont told his readers that the one figure he had been attempting to describe was that of Christ crucified.[28] Since most of the book had been a condemnation of the Jews as an economic class, this conclusion seemed to be an afterthought, possibly meant to attract those people whom the main attack had not yet convinced. The fact that Drumont frequently wrote articles for *Le Monde*, which was supposedly the semiofficial newspaper of the archbishop of Paris, indicates the close connection between some powerful Catholics and the propagandists for antisemitism. It is highly probable that Drumont consulted his friends at the archdiocese when he wrote his book.

[24] *Ibid.*, p. 372.
[25] In the first public notice of the National Antisemitic League of France on September 5, 1889, he said: "If you vote for Boulanger, you will simply replace the half-blind Jew of Opportunism with the hunched-back Jew of Boulangism"; cited in Alfred Gendrot, *Drumont, La France juive, et la Libre Parole* (Paris: Malfère, 1935), p. 46.
[26] *La Dernière bataille* (Paris: E. Dentu, 1890), p. 138.
[27] Maurice Barrès, *op. cit.*, II, 118.
[28] *Ibid.*, II, 557.

Before 1890 the average Frenchman had no strong feelings concerning the eighty thousand Jews in their country. Except for a small minority of Alsatians, they had been assimilated long before. By the early twentieth century, however, an influx of immigrants from eastern Europe more than doubled the Jewish population in France. The presence of these conspicuous newcomers helped to confirm Drumont's thesis of the "Jewish menace." He was also aided by the Panama scandal, in which two of the principal culprits were Jewish immigrants—Baron Jacques de Reinach and Dr. Cornelius Herz. When he founded his newspaper the *Libre Parole* in 1892, Drumont had a large prospective clientele of reactionaries, clericals, and ex-Boulangists, as well as thousands of small investors who had lost their savings in the defunct Panama Canal Company.

Drumont was an expert polemicist, but he was unsuccessful in uniting the discontented lower classes and the *bien-pensants*. The French National Antisemitic League—which he founded in September 1889—fell apart in less than a year. His only success as an organizer was with a group of packing-house workers in the La Villette district of Paris. The fact that some of their employers were Jews enabled Drumont to relate their antisemitism to an attack on "Jewish capitalism." But it was his partner, the Marquis de Morès, who really tried to mold the antisemites into a protofascist revolutionary movement. Indeed, Maurice Barrès called Morès—whom he admired—"the first National Socialist"; [29] a later commentator added the label "the first storm trooper." [30]

The Marquis de Morès was a young soldier of fortune whose parents belonged to noble Spanish families and whose wife was an American heiress. In 1891 he reorganized Drumont's butchers and a number of other brawny roustabouts

[29] *Scènes et doctrines du nationalisme* (Paris: Juven, 1902), p. 328.
[30] Robert F. Byrnes, *Antisemitism in Modern France*, Vol. I: *The Prologue to the Dreyfus Case* (New Brunswick, New Jersey: Rutgers University Press, 1950), p. 227.

into a gang known as the "Friends of Morès." He outfitted
them with sombreros and purple cowboy shirts—a costume
that had attracted him during his brief experience as a rancher
in North Dakota a few years earlier—thus giving them a
group consciousness resembling that of the storm troopers
of a later era.[31] During the next three years they acquired an
unsavory reputation for street brawling and terrorizing their
opponents. Despite his aristocratic background, Morès was
able to hold the affection of his followers by his lavishness,
his recklessness in dueling, and his mastery in the use of
profanity.

Far more than Drumont, Morès was working toward something that would later be called fascism. Together they ar-
ranged gatherings at which they brought their proletarian
members into contact with French aristocrats. These elegant members of the royalist salons and the Jockey Club believed that they were allied with "right-thinking" working
men in a common effort to lead France out of her humiliation
and back to her former greatness. The butchers, in turn, were
flattered by the presence of these "swells." But by 1894,
Morès had alienated some of his conservative Catholic backers
with his despicable tactics, and even Drumont turned against
him. When he died in 1896, Jules Guérin, a young journalist
and promoter, became the new leader of the "Friends of
Morès." [32]

Meanwhile, the *Libre Parole's* sensational polemics against
everything that was considered Jewish continued to attract
thousands of readers, and the many duels, trials, and scandal-
ous affairs that it publicized incited the public's curiosity
and love of gossip. Drumont also tried to awaken, to deepen,
and to play upon unconscious antisemitic feelings among
ordinary Frenchmen who had no direct contact with Jews.
It is difficult to measure the success of this endeavor, but

[31] *Ibid.*, p. 242.
[32] France, Archives Nationales, *Sureté Générale*, F⁷12459, *Mouvement
antisémitique*, August 16, 1899.

Drumont's newspaper had a large circulation, and he was a prominent national figure.[33]

*

Still, the antisemites, monarchists, and clericals were relatively weak and divided by the late 1890's; only the army remained untouched by republican politics. Many of its officers were narrowly militaristic and antibourgeois. They did not form a separate class—like the Prussian Junkers— based on family tradition, a moral heritage, or a hereditary system of values or duties. Nevertheless, until 1870 this social group was distinguishable by its character as a closed collectivity, its particularism, and its isolation within the national community. Each regiment was virtually a separate entity.[34]

It was the defeat of 1870 and the institution of universal conscription that changed the status of the army in France. During the next two decades millions of people looked to it as the guiding force in the nation's revival. The prestige of gentlemen in epaulettes was higher than at any time in the country's history. Even so, the gap between the officers and the recruits widened in the 1890's as the upper ranks became filled more and more by sons of the old aristocracy and the bien-pensant bourgeoisie.

Many people in these classes came to view the army as both a refuge and an instrument for ridding them of the very regime it was supposed to defend. Between 1830 and 1870 they had been able to retire to their provincial estates and sulk in relative comfort. This form of internal emigration ceased to be possible after the depression of the 1870's and the bad harvests, ruined vines, and foreign competition of

[33] Léon Blum says in his *Souvenirs sur l'Affaire* (Paris: Gallimard, 1935), p. 62, that Drumont occupied an intellectual position in France comparable to that of Charles Maurras on the eve of the First World War.

[34] Girardet, *op. cit.*, pp. 86–87.

the 1880's had weakened the French rural economy. Impoverished noble families could no longer keep up their châteaux, and they wanted their sons to earn a living in one of the traditional services of the state. As politics, diplomacy, the magistrature, and the civil administration were gradually taken over by the republicans, the only acceptable service left was the army (or navy). Here alone the mechanism of promotion escaped the control of the government; here alone could one be among "one's own sort."

It is not difficult to imagine the hopes of French reactionaries for using their remaining bastion for counterrevolutionary ends. Émile Keller, a leading Catholic politician, expressed their feelings in the following way in 1891: [35]

Our most prominent generals and a large number of their subalterns bring honor to themselves by openly showing their religious faith. . . . Today mutilated France belongs to no one. Tomorrow she will give herself to those who will have won back Alsace and Lorraine.

Captain Hubert Lyautey (the future marshal) wrote an article in the *Revue des Deux Mondes* on March 15, 1891, in which he urged army officers to educate their conscripts along authoritarian lines. His views were closely related to those of the Social Catholic movement founded by Bishop Freppel of Angers, the Comte Albert de Mun, and the Marquis René de La Tour du Pin Chambly de la Charce. These people clung to idealized memories of medieval Christianity and corporatism and dreamed of a new paternalistic alliance between the nobility and the masses.

Although not all army officers were of noble origin in the 1890's, the high-ranking ones who were set the tone for the rest. A considerable number of these men had been educated in parochial schools, disliked the Republic, and mistrusted their colleagues from unfamiliar social backgrounds. They carried their prejudices into their professional behavior by

[35] Article in the *Correspondant*, November 1891, cited in Girardet, *op. cit.*, p. 202.

trying to exclude plebeians, freethinkers, and Jews from their ranks. What did these republicans want in the army, since their whole outlook contradicted the principle of unquestioning obedience? And what did these Jews want who imagined that they could abandon the commercial and financial manipulations that were their proper activities in order to pursue a military career? What mercenary thoughts of gain motivated them? These were some of the attitudes of France's typical military leaders—especially in the infantry, cavalry, and intelligence corps—on the eve of the Dreyfus Affair.

When this event became a public issue, the defense of the army was to bring the remnants of the old reactionary Right and the new nationalist leagues into the same camp. The alliance between the miter and the sword was to replace the one between the throne and the altar. *Bien-pensants* who had formerly viewed the army as a creation of the revolutionary period were to join nationalist extremists in defending it. By the end of the nineteenth century the majority of French reactionaries were more militaristic than patriotic, more clerical than religious, and stubbornly opposed to parliamentary institutions. Monarchists had framed the Constitution of 1875, but, since the republicans had taken the regime away from them, some of their successors were ready to overthrow it. They again took up the thread of counterrevolution to guide them out of the labyrinth of modern times and back to their beloved home in the past.

2

❧ ❧ ❧ ❧ ❧ ❧

Captain Dreyfus

Next to the Revolution of 1789, the Dreyfus Affair was to be kept alive in the minds of French reactionaries longer than any other crisis in modern times. It helped them to perpetuate the myth of the "two Frances" until the collapse of Pétain's regime in 1944. The history of the Action Française lies between these two events, each of which involved the alleged treason of an army officer. This movement began its existence by condemning Captain Dreyfus and ended it by defending Marshal Pétain. As the self-designated spokesman for all right-thinking Frenchmen, it continued to call the Dreyfusards the wrong-thinking ones for almost half a century.

*

Although it is beyond the scope of this book to re-examine the details of the Dreyfus Affair,[1] certain common miscon-

[1] Dozens of histories of the case have appeared in the last sixty years. Among the recent ones the following are the most balanced: Jacques

ceptions must be dispelled. There was no battle between good and evil, nor were any of the major protagonists—with the exception of the real traitor, Major Walsin-Esterhazy—unregenerate villains or simon-pure heroes. The officers of the general staff did not arrest Captain Dreyfus[2] in October 1894 because he was a Jew; they honestly suspected him of treason. Some of them were antisemites—including Dreyfus' later defender, Major Picquart—but "the anti-semitic shadow over the case came not from the Army, but from the press."[3] For three years almost everyone accepted in good faith Dreyfus' conviction and his imprisonment on Devil's Island.

The crisis did not reach nationwide proportions until the fall of 1897, when Mathieu Dreyfus' evidence pointing to Esterhazy's guilt persuaded August Scheurer-Kestner, the vice-president of the senate, to join the campaign for a revision of the court-martial's verdict. In response to this demand Albert de Mun made a speech in the chamber of deputies in which he called on the government to "avenge the outraged army by a solemn word."[4] The senators questioned Scheurer-Kestner in a hearing on December 7 and were unimpressed by his plea.[5] But the public was now aroused. Students and

Kayser, *L'Affaire Dreyfus* (Paris: Gallimard, 1946); Nicholas Halasz, *Captain Dreyfus: The Story of a Mass Hysteria* (New York: Simon and Schuster, 1955); Maurice Paléologue, *An Intimate Journal of the Dreyfus Case* (New York: Criterion Books, 1957); and Guy Chapman, *The Dreyfus Case: A Reassessment* (New York: Reynal and Co., 1955), which contains a useful bibliography.

[2] Alfred Dreyfus was born on October 19, 1859. His family owned a cotton-spinning mill in Mulhouse. He was rich, intelligent, and devoted to his wife and children. Aside from them and his military career, he apparently had no other interests. Today he would be called an "organization man." Even his *Lettres d'un innocent*, written during his imprisonment on Devil's Island, show a commonplace imagination. He bore his suffering with courage and dignity, but he recoiled at seeing his named used for any cause, noble or ignoble.

[3] Chapman, *op. cit.*, p. 66.

[4] *Journal Officiel, Chambre des députés*, December 4, 1897, p. 2735.

[5] *Ibid., Sénat*, pp. 1374–1379.

nationalist groups demonstrated against Scheurer-Kestner in the streets. Then, on January 13, 1898, Émile Zola published his famous "J'Accuse" in Clemenceau's newspaper the *Aurore*. In this article Zola accused the army of having convicted Dreyfus in 1894 without sufficient evidence and of having acquitted the traitor Esterhazy, whose trial had just taken place. The officers who were attacked in this article forced the government to prosecute its author.

It was Zola's trial in February 1898 that sparked the first serious antisemitic riots in Paris and brought the intellectuals into the fight (and made them conscious of themselves as a distinct social group for the first time). While Édouard Drumont wrote editorials urging Frenchmen to take the law into their own hands against the Jews and their henchmen, Jules Guérin mobilized his gangs for street demonstrations. Then, on the day after Zola's conviction, a group of writers and scholars—led by Anatole France—founded the League for the Defense of the Rights of Man and the Citizen. The trial itself had taken place in a strained atmosphere with much public pressure coming into play. Even the supposedly neutral daily *Matin* wrote:

> An acquittal will not disarm the belligerents. A condemnation will cut short the dangerous protests in the streets; it will suppress the motives of tumultuous public gatherings. Parisian trade and business, ruined by Zola, will not quickly forgive their lost winter season. With Zola condemned, we shall be able to return to our businesses, our work, and to friendly relations.[6]

Just as Drumont's clamorings in the *Libre Parole* expressed the feeling of many reactionaries, this statement in the *Matin* reflected the view of the conservatives. Both groups were eager to sacrifice the rights of an individual and compromise the democratic process, but for different reasons. The reactionaries faced the situation candidly and took a positive stand; the conservative Parisian merchants refused to admit the existence of an issue and were concerned solely with returning

[6] *Matin*, February 15, 1898.

to "business as usual." Their hope that a quick condemnation of Zola would bring the public off the streets and into their shops was unfulfilled. For after Zola was convicted and went into voluntary exile the supporters of Dreyfus continued their campaign in his behalf, and the antisemitic movement assumed more menacing proportions.

Public agitation in Paris increased, and it eventually spread to the provinces and to North Africa. In many communities Jews were publicly denounced, and their homes were marked off. Elsewhere bands of rowdies threw stones at their store windows and put up signs saying: "Don't buy anything from the Jews!" [7] In Algeria the Jews suffered actual physical violence, and their shops were pillaged.[8] Some frightened businessmen even placed notices in their doorways, which read: "Catholic firm—there are no Jews here." The atmosphere in Algeria was especially explosive because of the resentment of both French and Moslem residents against the fact that the Jews there had been given the privileges of French citizenship by the Crémieux law of 1870. The local authorities in Algiers, led by Mayor Max Régis, invoked extraordinary repressive measures, such as forbidding everyone to employ Jews. At Constantine the municipality decided to deny entrance in the schools to the "Jewish vermin." [9]

In France, itself, the politicians had also entered the Dreyfus controversy. The opposition parties had used it primarily to embarrass the Méline government in early 1898. Then, on August 31, the case took a decisive turn when Colonel Henry, a counterespionage officer, killed himself while awaiting an indictment for having forged documents in the Dreyfus dossier. When the report of his suicide was published the next morning, almost all Parisian dailies accepted the inevitability of revision. Still, it took the politicians and the judges more than four months to consider the means of implementing it.

[7] Jacques Kayser, *op. cit.*, p. 165.
[8] *Libre Parole*, November 14, 1898.
[9] *Ibid.*, December 15, 1898.

Frenchmen became divided into two opposing camps: one clamored for the vindication of an innocent man, the other insisted that the honor of the army and the security of the state were more important. In February 1899 Prime Minister Dupuy got parliament to transfer the handling of the Dreyfus appeal from the criminal chamber of the supreme appellate court (*cour de cassation*) to the three chambers sitting together. Commenting on this arbitrary action, Maurice Paléologue, a high official at the Quai d'Orsay, said:

> Public passions are going to be still more aroused. The abominable dispute is going on; on the one hand, contempt for liberal ideas, appeals to force, offenses against justice; on the other, a progressive darkening of the national conscience and the French mentality. You have to go back to the saddest hours of our history to find a parallel to this tragic discord.[10]

Those Frenchmen who refused to accept the possibility of Dreyfus' innocence and who opposed any change in the decision that had condemned him became the hard core of the anti-Dreyfusard camp, out of which the Action Française developed. Charles Maurras, the movement's future leader, was still a young journalist and literary critic in September 1898 when he wrote a series of articles for the *Gazette de France*, portraying Colonel Henry as a hero. When a prominent Dreyfusard mistakenly accused the deceased officer of being the real traitor, Drumont's *Libre Parole* launched a subscription campaign in mid-December to provide Henry's widow with funds for a libel suit. More than a hundred thousand francs were raised within four weeks.

*

A Comité de l'Action Française had first been launched in April 1898 by Henri Vaugeois, a high school teacher, Mau-

---

[10] Paléologue, *op. cit.*, p. 201. Paléologue was a conservative diplomat and had no love for Jews. He represented the ministry of foreign affairs in all of the principal hearings of the Dreyfus case in 1898 and 1899 and he offers an interesting theory about the true traitors: Esterhazy and two others.

rice Pujo, a hack writer, Colonel de Villebois-Mareul, a professional royalist, and Captain Caplain-Cortambert, Vaugeois' cousin. Just before the May elections these men issued an appeal urging French citizens to fight against the Dreyfusard campaign. Its conclusion read as follows:

True Frenchmen must unite to demand of their representatives of all political beliefs and opinions that they pledge themselves to break all ties with influences that we do not want to designate here by their proper names, but that everybody knows about.

But to defend oneself is not enough, one must live!

After having supported the partisans of a truly French Republic in the electoral struggle, we shall have to reawaken the sense of a French life in the hearts of all. We will encourage all kinds of demonstrations, literary and moral, as well as political.

For this endeavor we appeal to the intelligence and to the hearts of all Frenchmen against intellectualism and sentimentality, which are being used by antinational interests.[11]

But the Dreyfus Affair was not a major issue in the elections, and after the publication of this manifesto the Comité de l'Action Française did nothing further. Maurras says that he was ignorant of its existence before December 1898 and that he first met Vaugeois and Pujo a month later.[12]

Maurras had not remained inactive, though. In September 1898 his friend the Provençal poet Frédéric Amouretti had introduced him to Gabriel Syveton, a history teacher in the *lycée* at Reims, and Louis Dausset, an instructor in the Jesuit-run Collège Stanislas in Paris. Together they tried to form a league of "patriotic intellectuals" in opposition to the Leftist and anticlerical League for the Defense of the Rights of Man.[13] With the help of Maurice Barrès, they succeeded in persuading fifteen thousand people to join their League of the French Fatherland in December 1898.

[11] *Revue de l'Action Française*, I (August 1899), 38.
[12] Charles Maurras, *Au Signe de Flore* (Paris: Collection Hier, 1931), p. 92; Maurras' statement was confirmed to me by Maurice Pujo in a personal interview.
[13] *Ibid.*, p. 85.

The appearance of these leagues emphasized the split in intellectual circles (which was paralleled in other social groups and even within certain families). One example of this division was experienced by the eminent historian and philologist Gaston Paris, who was in the habit of receiving his friends each Sunday in the salon of the Collège de France. The events of the Dreyfus Affair had caused the atmosphere of these gatherings to become strained as early as the spring of 1898. Professor Paris managed to keep them going until the end of the year, but when the League of the French Fatherland was founded Albert Sorel, Paul Bourget, and others who had joined it stayed away.[14]

The newly formed league published the following notice in the *Temps* on January 1, 1899:

Appeal
          The French Fatherland.

The undersigned,
Disturbed to see the most calamitous agitation prolonged and aggravated;
Persuaded that it cannot last any longer without morally compromising the vital interests of the French Fatherland, and notably those interests whose glorious repository is in the hands of the National Army;
Persuaded also that in saying so they express the opinion of France,
Have resolved:
To work within the limits of their professional duty to maintain them by conciliating them with the progress of the ideas, the morals, and the traditions of the French Fatherland,
To unite and to group together above all sectarian spirit in order to act efficaciously in this sense by word, by writings, and by example:
And to fortify the spirit of solidarity that ought to bind together all the generations of a great people.

This appeal was followed by a long list of signatures, including a large section of the French Academy.

[14] Daniel Halévy, "Apologie pour notre passé," *Cahiers de la quinzaine*, Vol. 10, Series 11 (1910), 65.

Beginning on January 4, 1899, the *Temps* published letters from people who had been asked why they had joined the League of the French Fatherland. Many answered that they had thought of it as a movement of conciliation. Professor José-Maria de Hérédia said in his letter that he would like to add the phrase "and respect for justice" to the sentence in the appeal ending with the words "the ideas, the morals, and the traditions of the French Fatherland." The well-known literary critic Ferdinand Brunetière said:

I approve completely of the terms of the Appeal. Each one of the members of the league can have his personal sentiment about the Dreyfus affair. That is not the question. We are joined together to affirm: first, that all the intellectuals, since there are intellectuals, are not on the same side; second, to protest against the attacks on the army, which we consider as the basis, the mainstay of our national unity and grandeur; third, to set up the idea of the Fatherland in opposition to internationalist doctrines.[15]

The historian Albert Sorel said that he was thinking of the future of France in Europe and that he did not want France to be weakened because of internal quarrels.[16] One correspondent supported the league because "French commerce and diplomacy are suffering as a result of the division within the country." [17] Others blamed the recent capitulation to the British at Fashoda on the lack of unity at home.

From the beginning the league was unable to act in a unified fashion for two reasons: its membership was too heterogeneous and most of its leaders would not compromise their principles or condone violence. The majority of them disliked the bourgeois-democratic style of the Third Republic, but the type of government with which they wanted to replace it varied from the plebiscitary democracy of Paul Déroulède to the die-hard royalism of Charles Maurras. Their only common bond was a desire to end the internecine strife surrounding the

[15] *Temps*, January 4, 1899.
[16] *Ibid.*, January 5.
[17] *Ibid.*

Dreyfus Affair and a determination to support the army as the defender of the interests of the fatherland.

During the first two months of 1899 the league lost support from people who felt that it was hindering national reconciliation by its antisemitism and its growing antirepublican bias. At each of its public meetings some *grand seigneur* of letters threatened to leave the stage if a speaker happened to mention the Dreyfusard "syndicate" or the "traitor." [18] Ferdinand Brunetière said in a letter to the *Temps*:

We energetically reject the doctrines of antisemitism and nationalism. We are not the League of Patriots; we are forming a league of patriots. This does not prevent the antisemites and the partisans of M. Déroulède from being received in our midst.[19]

Barrès and Maurras objected to being included in Brunetière's "we." [20] They both wanted to direct the activities of the league along anti-Dreyfusard and antisemitic lines, and Barrès hoped to use it as a medium for spreading his nationalist doctrines. In his speech at its inaugural meeting he said that it should join forces with the followers of Déroulède, the regionalists, and "all those, Catholics or positivists, who want a social discipline." [21] Such an alliance would definitely limit the league's allegedly nonpartisan character. A few weeks later Brunetière, Sorel, Hérédia, and other prominent intellectuals resigned when its semiofficial newspaper, the *Écho de Paris*, condemned Émile Loubet's election as president of the republic.[22]

The literary critic Jules Lemaître was the president of the League of the French Fatherland, and its guiding spirit was his lifelong friend, the Comtesse de Loynes. This ambitious society woman kept a salon on the Left Bank, where Lemaître held court as a kind of Anatole France of the Right. It was

[18] Maurras, *op. cit.*, p. 102.
[19] January 8, 1899.
[20] Barrès, *Scènes et doctrines*, p. 67.
[21] *Ibid.*, p. 73.
[22] *Temps*, February 20, 1899.

there that the real elections to the French Academy were held; [23] it was there that the self-styled "high command of the national resistance" met.[24] Lemaître dictated the policies of the *Écho de Paris*, and Madame de Loynes organized the sensational opening meeting of the league on January 19, 1899, at the Farmers' Hall.[25]

Gabriel Syveton was in charge of the league's finances. He was a burly, sensuous, ambitious man who had recently moved to Paris with his wife and stepdaughter and who lived in a style far above his means.[26] He was friendly with another Paris society woman with political ambitions, Madame Lebaudy, and he got a great deal of money from her for the activities of the league.[27] (Both Madame de Loynes and Madame Lebaudy were to give large sums to the Action Française a few years later.)

* * *

While the anti-Dreyfusard intellectuals were trying to foster patriotism and order through the League of the French Fatherland, the more militant anti-Dreyfusards continued to provoke public disturbances in the winter of 1898–1899. The League of Patriots had been officially disbanded after the flight of Boulanger in 1889, but its leaders had kept in close contact with one another. When Déroulède reorganized it in the fall of 1898, he also founded a newspaper, the *Drapeau*, to broadcast its message. He recruited members among former Boulangists and Bonapartists. Most of these people were clerks in stores and offices, small shopkeepers, and retired noncom-

---

[23] Arthur Meyer, *Ce que je peux dire: la Comtesse de Loynes* (Paris: Plon-Nourrit, 1912), p. 155.
[24] Léon Daudet, *Souvenirs des milieux littéraires, politiques, artistiques, et médicaux* (2 vols., Paris: Nouvelle Librairie Nationale, 1920), p. 487.
[25] Meyer, *op. cit.*, p. 369.
[26] Archives Nationales, *Haute Cour, 1899, F⁷12452, notes policières*, November 8, 1899.
[27] Daudet, *op. cit.*, and Meyer, *op. cit.*, p. 277.

missioned army officers.[28] Déroulède did not want his movement to become antisemitic, but he could not keep his followers from doing so.

Jules Guérin's organization of antisemites had sections in most of the important provincial cities and a newspaper called the *Antijuif*. He received financial backing from aristocratic supporters of the pretender and had several interviews with the Duc d'Orléans in 1898.[29] The League of Antisemitic Youth, with an engineering student named Dubuc as its president,[30] was a subsidiary of Guérin's league. Its purpose seems to have been to incorporate the activities of the younger antisemites into the program of the parent organization.

The strongest of the anti-Dreyfusard organizations was the Royalist Youth Association of André Buffet, with eighteen committees in Paris and thirty-four in the provinces. It claimed thirty thousand active members, and it had more money than the other leagues. The Duc d'Orléans wrote to Buffet in October 1898 [31] telling him to "begin the action and organization we have agreed upon and keep me informed of their progress." He went on to say: "I have decided on a plan that will assure us of the cooperation of many labor unions, not only in Paris, but in all of France." Buffet was to use three hundred thousand francs that he had already received to provoke a general uprising by these unions in the name of the pretender "as soon as a favorable opportunity presents itself."

In December 1898 the pretender was so sure that his "day" was at hand that he had Buffet draw up a list of ministers for his forthcoming government, and he moved from the Bohemian resort of Marienbad to Brussels, where he would be close to the French border. Meanwhile, the Comte Boniface de

---

[28] Evidence presented by the government to the *Haute Cour de Justice* in the fall of 1899, as reported in the *Temps*, November 13, 1899.
[29] *Ibid.*
[30] Archives Nationales, *Police Générale*, F⁷12453, *note policière*, April 29, 1899.
[31] Letter cited in full in the *Temps*, November 13, 1899.

Castellane, one of his agents in Paris, was trying to make a "deal" with Paul Déroulède. This impoverished nobleman had married Anna Gould, and he enjoyed spending her millions. At a dinner party given by Arthur Meyer the count said to the head of the League of Patriots:

We are not seeking the same solution, but we have the same hates and the same disgusts. I do not know if I shall convert you, but you wish to destroy, and so do I. When the problem of reconstruction comes up we shall see who is the better architect. In any case, if ever you need money, let me know, I have a million at your disposal.[32]

Déroulède refused to work with the royalists and decided to "save France and the Republic" himself on February 23, 1899. Félix Faure had died a week earlier, and Émile Loubet had just been elected to succeed him as president of the republic. At the Place de la Nation Déroulède and five hundred of his followers awaited the troops returning from Faure's funeral. When General Roget appeared, Déroulède, Barrès, Marcel Habert, Gabriel Syveton, and Jules Guérin tried to seize the bridle of his horse and persuade him to lead the crowd to the Hotel de Ville and the presidential palace.[33] The general was more concerned with staying in his saddle than with trying to make out what these fanatics were shouting, and, despite their protests, he led his brigade back to its quarters. Undaunted, Déroulède and some of his friends followed the troops into the barracks, still trying to make the general change his mind.

After Déroulède and Habert were arrested that night they admitted that they had expected General Pellieux and not General Roget.[34] General Pellieux was a monarchist. He disliked Déroulède's ideas, but Barrès says that he had agreed to march on the Hotel de Ville and seize it in the name of the antirepublican forces.[35] Déroulède himself blamed the royal-

[32] Meyer, op. cit., p. 369.
[33] Barrès, op. cit., p. 241.
[34] Temps, February 25, 1899.
[35] Barrès, op. cit., p. 237.

ists for changing the plan of march of the troops and claimed that his *coup d'état* had failed because the royalists understood that he would never allow the Republic to come to harm.[36] Actually, the whole scheme had never got off the ground.

*

The failure of Déroulède's *coup* marked a serious setback for those reactionaries who had momentarily united behind the anti-Dreyfusard banner. Soon after his arrest the government imposed small fines on several of the leagues. The League of the French Fatherland was unmolested, but its usefulness as a propaganda medium for the Extreme Right was compromised. In looking for new allies, Henri Vaugeois turned to Charles Maurras, whom he had met in January. The two men quickly became friends and decided to revive the Comité de l'Action Française. They began meeting at the Café Voltaire "in order to found something." [37] In mid-May they created the Action Française Society and began work on a *Bulletin de l'Action Française,* whose first issue appeared in July. (The title was soon changed to the *Revue de l'Action Française.*)

The officers of the Action Française Society were honorary president François de Mahy, a member of the chamber of deputies and a former minister of agriculture and the navy, and acting president Eugène de Cavaignac, who had once been minister of war; Maurice Barrès was vice-president, and Vaugeois served as general secretary.[38] Vaugeois and Caplain-Cortambert tried to raise five hundred thousand francs to found a nationalist republican daily newspaper. Although this effort was unsuccessful,[39] the revitalized Comité de l'Action

[36] *Ibid.*
[37] Maurras, *op. cit.,* p. 121.
[38] Archives Nationales, *Action Française, F⁷12862, Sureté Générale,* May 15, 1899.
[39] *Ibid.*

Française held its first public meeting at the Farmer's Hall in Paris on June 20, 1899, with Mahy presiding. There were only fifteen people in the audience.[40]

In his inaugural speech Vaugeois already showed the influence that Maurras had begun to exert on him. He no longer spoke of the "adversary" as a phantom of ideas, but as a "flesh and blood republican man." [41] Vaugeois supported the Republic for lack of any alternative until he finally accepted royalism. But he and his friends hated the *petit bourgeois* Frenchmen who zealously clung to the ideals of the Revolution, and they were soon to drop the pretense of loyalty to a regime whose institutions and values they loathed.

Vaugeois' first words at the aforementioned meeting concerned the League of the French Fatherland and the "enlightened and ardent patriotism of the illustrious academicians and writers" whom he and his friends had accepted as their leaders. The league, he said, had definitively formulated the protest of the national conscience against the shameful follies that the Dreyfusards wanted it to condone.[42] He then described the Action Française as a group of *franc tireurs*, a spearhead of young comrades who were united by a common sentiment that was especially strong, since they felt it in a variety of ways. Their task, according to Vaugeois, was to clarify and satisfy the needs of the injured patriotic spirit that was being awakened in the hearts of many Frenchmen. The purpose of the present meeting, he said, was not to protest, but to be understood, loved, and, if possible, followed.[43]

He went on to analyze the Jewish, Protestant, and Masonic value-systems, which he called the three sources of evil in France.[44] Vaugeois was particularly vitriolic against the Jews, whom he charged with bringing about the triumph of the

[40] *Ibid.*, June 22, 1899.
[41] *Revue de l'Action Française*, I (July 1899), 17–18.
[42] *Ibid.*, p. 7.
[43] *Ibid.*, p. 9.
[44] *Ibid.*, p. 13.

Dreyfusard cause because they had succeeded in monopolizing the most irresistible social force of modern times—money.[45] Here Vaugeois' antibourgeois and anticapitalist prejudices are clear. Medieval Catholicism had condemned financial manipulations and unfair profits, but the Jews had never been bound by this precept. The Calvinists had emancipated themselves from the idea of the "just price" and had encouraged the accumulation of wealth as a sign of election to grace. In contrast, the intellectuals who founded the Action Française opposed the values of capitalism and bourgeois democracy above all else. Their reasons were somewhat different from those of the old aristocracy and clergy, but their opposition was just as strong. The Dreyfus Affair gave them an opportunity to expose the alleged domination of France by rich Jews and their dupes, the Protestants and Freemasons. From the beginning this idea became one of the cardinal tenets of the Action Française.

Another point in Vaugeois' speech was that France was governed by laws rather than by men. According to him, the situation was all the worse because these laws did not reflect customs or modes of human relations that had been lived through and loved by people of French blood; they were pure ideas. Furthermore, he continued, it was the grievous neutrality of the law that enchanted the Freemasons, Jews, and Protestants. These three groups had in common a mystical mania for abstraction and a taste for empty reasoning and pedantic caviling. Vaugeois charged that the whole Dreyfusian —he distinguished this term, which has a pejorative sense, from Dreyfusard—campaign was nothing but a debauchery of irrefutable logic that led to false conclusions and was ignorant of the facts. This passion for legality was the hideous explosion of the error that had been undermining France for a long time, namely anarchism—the forgetting that human power must be living and personal.[46] Actually, Vaugeois was

[45] *Ibid.*, p. 8.
[46] *Ibid.*, p. 17.

using anarchism—which was the fashionable word at that time for a system one did not like—to describe bourgeois democracy.

From this analysis Vaugeois turned to the problem of what was to be done to save France from the deceptive experience of the regime that represented the selfish *petite bourgeoisie*. He maintained that this political system was as foreign to complete democracy and the true people as it was hostile to aristocracies of birth and elites that had been refined slowly and naturally. What was needed was a few disinterested and energetic men who would devote themselves to the task of reorganizing the Republic and giving it the form and substance of a state. He claimed that only in this way could Frenchmen feel secure from brutal and impulsive measures enforced by a government "controlled by the Dreyfusards and determined to quell all manifestations of patriotism and devotion to the army." [47]

Vaugeois proposed that a national republican party be formed, or reformed, a party that would take up again the optimistic work of the Revolution in the same spirit in which it had been begun. That spirit, he said, "was simply the happy mixture of good sense and moral virtue that had animated the candid smile of our ancestors." Vaugeois chided the *bien-pensant* aristocrats—whom he called "old spoiled children"—who spoke of bringing back Victor Bonaparte or Philippe d'Orléans as they would talk of going to the seashore for a vacation. They did not realize that "the people, who were more serious, were listening." [48] What was essential was to end the regime of government by law and replace it with a government of living heads. "A head is necessary, but I hasten to add that several heads are necessary." [49]

After this speech, Monsieur de Mahy, the new movement's honorary president, declared that he could not associate him-

[47] *Ibid.*, p. 18.
[48] *Ibid.*, p. 20.
[49] *Ibid.*, p. 23.

self with the point about a "head" being necessary and he asserted his loyalty to legal and constitutional methods.[50] Jules Lemaître resigned for the same reason. Mahy wrote Vaugeois a letter a week later, stating that he wanted neither the use of force nor a dictator. Vaugeois assured him that the *raison d'être* of the Action Française was to look for other means than force. He said that he had always been a republican and that he intended to remain one.[51]

But Vaugeois was undoubtedly contemplating an antidemocratic revolution. Although he was to give his allegiance to the royalist pretender two years later, it is interesting to note that the original program of his movement was strikingly close to modern fascism. His desire to "throw out the rascals" who had taken the Republic off its original noble course and to restore the alleged ideals of the founding fathers has a familiar ring. Fortunately, in 1899 France had no leader whose prestige could have attracted nationwide support for a revolt that would have destroyed the rule of law. Besides, other conditions favorable to the rise of fascism—such as an economic depression, a Red scare, or a cold war—were also lacking at that time.

In the second issue of the *Revue de l'Action Française* Vaugeois showed his true colors in an article entitled "Réaction d'abord!" At one point in it he asked: "Is not the Action Française first of all a return to the past, a reaction? We want to render the republic habitable. That is why we shall react first." [52] He declared that he was for reaction first because the "Old France" had fought and was still fighting against the party of the foreigner. His description of himself as "republican, but Frenchman above all" [53] raised the hopes of the handful of *bien-pensants* in the movement. In an obvious attempt to encourage them, he said:

50 Maurras, *op. cit.*, p. 123.
51 *Revue de l'Action Française*, I (July 1899), 29.
52 *Ibid.* (August 1899), p. 5.
53 *Ibid.*, p. 131.

Now, if only those who are profoundly antisemitic are Catholics, royalists, and, as they are called, reactionaries, are we not led, having fought and wanting to fight now a social evil of which Dreyfusism is only a symptom, to denounce purely and simply the republic itself? We think so.[54]

In order to bring about this necessary revolt and reaction, Vaugeois said that his group would deliberately stir up against the existing regime the hoards of hate and contempt that slumber in the hearts of the old French aristocracy. They would also rouse that other moral wealth of France, the simple good sense of the people, its practical intelligence, which demands results and finds no meaning in the three big words inscribed on all public buildings: *Liberté, Égalité, Fraternité.* In addition, the Action Française would appeal to the old-fashioned and well-meaning superstition of French Catholic mothers who hated the freethinking, pedantic teachers in the public primary schools. Finally, according to Vaugeois, the work of the movement could be fruitful only if it had a definite doctrine.[55]

*

While the Action Française was trying to find a formula to save France, the Dreyfus Affair was entering its decisive phase. On June 4, 1899, the supreme appellate court ordered the retrial of Dreyfus by a second court-martial at Rennes. As was to be expected, this news infuriated the nationalists and antisemites. Once again they invaded the streets and organized violent demonstrations. Not even the president of the republic was spared, for an ex-Bonapartist named Baron Christiani hit President Loubet several times with his cane at the opening of the racing season at Auteuil. The elegant spectators in the adjoining boxes hooted Loubet and cheered his assailant on until the police finally arrived on the scene.[56] Then, as the day of the trial approached, Déroulède warned:

[54] *Ibid.*, p. 3.
[55] *Ibid.*, p. 4.
[56] *Temps*, June 6, 1899.

. . . the acquittal of Dreyfus is equivalent to the condemnation of the former minister of war [General Mercier had held this office at the time of Dreyfus' arrest] and the leaders of the army. If the innocence of Dreyfus is demonstrated, no punishment will be too terrible for the ministers who brought charges against him or allowed these charges to be made; all reprisals would be excusable; all kinds of torture would be legitimate. . . . The people of France will have to demand pardon of the people of Israel. . . . If Dreyfus is innocent, the generals are scoundrels.[57]

The government feared that such provocative words might lead to violence at Rennes and spark a nationalist plot to seize power. It is unlikely that any real danger existed, but the understandably nervous officials ordered the police to arrest the leaders of the leagues, placing Déroulède's name at the head of the list. Although the League of the French Fatherland and the Action Française were left intact, the Royalist Youth, the Antisemitic League, and the League of Patriots were permanently dissolved. The Action Française itself could offer no more than a verbal protest at the end of the trial in September.[58]

Dreyfus was found guilty of attempted espionage—with extenuating circumstances(!)—and sentenced to ten years' imprisonment. Déroulède had cannily stated the issue as the military judges saw it: Dreyfus or Mercier. As soldiers, these men could not bring themselves to condemn a senior officer and heap dishonor on the army. It was up to the president of the republic to be merciful. On September 19 President Loubet pardoned Dreyfus and suspended his sentence. He also wanted to reverse the verdict of the court-martial. General Gallifet, the current minister of war, dissuaded him from doing so because he felt that the army and public opinion would oppose such a gesture.

A few die-hard anti-Dreyfusards declared that the new conviction of Dreyfus proved that he was a traitor. In order to save what they could of the situation, they tried to exploit

[57] Cited in Kayser, op. cit., p. 241.
[58] Maurras, op. cit., p. 144.

this judicial half-victory. They were especially worried about the "Jewish revolution" that would wreak vengeance on the army and the church. According to them, the Rennes verdict irrevocably divided France into two camps.[59]

Viewing the "struggle" with the outlook of a Left-Bank intellectual, Vaugeois said that only one of these two camps could survive. "The battle without mercy, the civil and religious war that we have in no way sought, for our part, we accept it. . . . The real conflict begins now." [60] The main opponents of Vaugeois and Maurras were other relatively unknown intellectuals like themselves, particularly Léon Blum and the Natanson brothers, who edited a small magazine called *La Revue Blanche*.[61] For after Dreyfus was pardoned most people considered the case closed and ceased to think about it. Even the majority of the members of the League of the French Fatherland and the Action Française opposed any effort to rehash the proceedings of the Rennes trial.

Despite this lack of support, Vaugeois and Maurras decided to go ahead with their program of "political education." They hoped that in this way they might encourage the kind of action that their colleagues hesitated to take. In November 1899 they published the following notice in their review.

The Dreyfus affair has just shown us the nature of the evil that we are dying of. It is necessary that a new party be formed, indifferent as to persons and means. This party of Old Frenchmen has no fixed program and it is not directed toward the elections. We want to do its advance-guard exploration. Our specifically defined aim is to discover the new party's ideas, and to attempt to form an organization.[62]

Thus the founders of the Action Française saw that only a few die-hard counterrevolutionaries would be interested in

[59] *Ibid.*
[60] *Revue de l'Action Française*, I (September 1899), 158.
[61] *Le Procès de Charles Maurras: compte rendu sténographique* (Paris: Albin Michel, 1946), p. 56.
[62] *Revue de l'Action Française*, I (November 1899), 435.

their efforts at first. They were obscure café intellectuals seeking a following. Their propaganda was to reach a wider audience from time to time later on, but their basic outlook never deviated much from what it had been at the time of the Dreyfus Affair. Throughout its existence the leaders of the movement continued to define most new situations as extensions of the dramatic series of events in which it had originated.

3

❦ ❦ ❦ ❦ ❦ ❦ ❦

Café Intellectuals

During the early 1900's the cafés of Paris and other European cities were the breeding ground of daring new movements in the arts; they also spawned numerous critics who attacked all aspects of contemporary society in their discussion groups and ephemeral reviews. The devastation of the First World War was to make it possible for Mussolini and Lenin —both of whom had formerly frequented the cafés of Zürich —to put their ideas into practice. But before 1914 most Europeans seemed to be supremely confident in a civilization that offered unlimited possibilities for progress. The programs and intrigues of the café intellectuals had little effect on them.

Throughout its history the Action Française reflected the personalities of its founders and the world of cafés and rented rooms in which they lived. Most of these men had virtually no contact with the country's bourgeois and proletarian masses. They began their careers as camp followers of France's academic and artistic armies, but at first they were like mandarins without a state, priests without parishes, and teachers without classes. When they set up shop in the Latin Quarter, students and other café intellectuals like themselves became their main customers. No one exemplified their style of life better than Charles Maurras, who had come to Paris from the small Provençal town of Martigues.

*

Maurras' father was a tax collector under the Second Empire and during the early years of the Third Republic. He was a diligent civil servant with a strong sense of duty.[1] Although he had been loyal to Napoleon III, he had become reconciled to the republican regime at the time of his death in 1874. Like most bureaucrats, he avoided politics and identified himself with whatever authority was in power. Charles, who was only six when his father died, could hardly have remembered much about him. His idealized and secondhand description of him seems calculated mainly to convince himself and his readers that this man was kind and that he often amused his two sons by singing and reading poetry to them.[2]

The mother of these two boys was a pious Catholic and devoted to the royalist cause. She was continually telling them stories about her great grandfather who had been arrested during the Revolution, about clandestine Masses under the Terror, and about her mother who had almost had a stroke when she heard the news of the February revolution in 1848.[3] Since Madame Maurras would not allow her sons to be educated by the hated Republic, she moved from Martigues to nearby Aix-en-Provence, where they could attend a parochial high school.[4] Charles later said that he respected his mother's Christian piety, but he rejected God at an early age and remained an atheist for the rest of his life.

No one can know what inner experiences shaped Maurras'

[1] Maurras, *La Musique intérieure* (Paris: B. Grasset, 1925), p. 3.
[2] Maurras, *Au Signe de Flore* (Paris: Collection Hier, 1931), p. 3.
[3] *Ibid.*, p. 4.
[4] Ade Coudekerque-Lambrecht, *Léon de Montesquiou* (Paris: Nouvelle Librairie Nationale, 1925), p. 44.

personality in his childhood, though the external evidence is certainly suggestive. Here was a homely, sullen, small-town boy being raised by an over-protective mother struggling to make ends meet on a modest pension. He showed intense interest in his studies and decided to prepare for the entrance examinations of the Naval Academy. Then at the age of fourteen he became partially deaf and had to give up this plan. Because of his affliction, he had to accept private tutoring from one of his professors, Abbé Penon, in order to finish high school.[5] This ambitious cleric (he later became the bishop of Moulins) ably guided the intellectual development of his protégé, but he was no emotional substitute for a real father.

Both his personality and his deafness cut young Charles off from the usual camaraderie of teen-age boys. He began to live in a bygone world that he read about in the ancient and seventeenth-century classics. Despite (or perhaps because of) his dependence on his mother and Abbé Penon, he rebelled against their pious outlook. In fact, he expressed contempt for all of the generally accepted ideas of his social milieu. In a later moment of confidence he confessed that he had once gone so far as to deny the validity of geometry.[6] He took pride in being a nonconformist and became bitter and disrespectful when he was criticized for not behaving like other children his age.

Maurras' deafness, his scrawny appearance, and his unsociable habits made him unattractive to most girls. In all the tens of thousands of pages he eventually wrote he rarely spoke of love for a woman (except in Le Mont de Saturne—written when he was past eighty). Both his close associates and his enemies agree that as a man Maurras viewed women with contempt and used them to satisfy his physical needs without expressing the slightest spark of affection for them.[7] He never

[5] Maurras, La Musique intérieure, p. 22.
[6] Maurras, L'Étang de Berre (Paris: E. Champion, 1924), p. 245.
[7] Maurice Pujo and Henri Massis (friends) and Albert Bayet and

married and he seems never to have had a steady mistress. From the time of his childhood he had few playmates and no lovers. Whatever "caused" him to be this way, this was the way he was.

Abbé Penon persuaded Maurras' mother to move to Paris when Charles was seventeen so that he could pursue a literary career. This sensitive young *méridonial* arrived there in December 1885 without fortune, without influence, and with almost no acquaintances. His first reaction to the capital was: "Were Frenchmen still in their homeland in France?" [8] He resented the sight of signs with foreign and Jewish names, which, to him, marred the city's beautiful streets and boulevards. Paris must have seemed unsympathetic to Maurras for many reasons. It was a cold, gray, northern metropolis—brutally different from the sunny Provence—and its inhabitants were impersonal and unfriendly.

Like many uprooted provincials, Maurras judged the behavior of people in unfamiliar contexts according to the standards of expectation he had acquired in a circumscribed and homogeneous environment. He had not thought much about Jews before his arrival in Paris, and he claimed that it was his first impressions of the city that helped him to formulate his particular brand of antisemitism. [9] Hitler, who came from the provincial Austrian town of Linz, responded in the same way

---

Émile Buré (enemies) all told me this in personal interviews. Leon Roudiez, a distinguished American literary critic, says that as a young man Maurras "avait un faible pour les femmes de Paris" (*Charles Maurras jusqu' à l'Action Française* [Paris: André Bonne, 1957], p. 157). But Roudiez's narrative stops just before 1900. The author of a recently published hagiography says that he has seen photographs of Maurras dancing the farandole with the country girls of Provence in the 1930's (Michel Mourre, *Charles Maurras* [Paris: Éditions Universitaires, 1958], p. 22). This is hardly evidence of real affection for women.

[8] Maurras, *Au Signe de Flore*, p. 31.
[9] *Ibid.*

to the cosmopolitan atmosphere of pre-1914 Vienna. This identification of "foreign" with "Jewish" has a two-thousand-year tradition behind it in rural Europe.

Only after he arrived in Paris did Maurras become interested in the history and literature of his native Provence. He nourished this nostalgia by reading the works of Mistral and other poets of the Provençal renaissance. His first essay in literary criticism dealt with these writers. It was praised by the Société des Félibres de Paris and helped to introduce him into this group, which was dominated by a few deputies and senators from the Midi.[10] Within a short time Maurras found a place on the editorial staff of its small monthly review and was invited to its nightly gatherings in a Left-Bank café.

Maurras soon showed his lifelong habit of mixing literature and politics. For he and his friend Frédéric Amouretti wanted to use the revival of the Provençal language as the basis for a federalist regime in which local autonomy and privileges would be restored. Their campaign prompted the majority of the Société des Félibres to oust Maurras and a dozen of his supporters as "reactionaries." These men then formed their own club—the École Parisienne du Félibrige—met in another café, and continued to work for the reconstruction of the nation along federal lines.[11] Maurras was thus a political plotter and a café intellectual in his early twenties.

By the mid-1890's Maurras was producing great quantities of literary criticism and poetry and had joined the École Romane Française of Jean Moréas, Raymond de la Tailhède, Maurice du Plessys, and Ernest Raynaud.[12] These writers wanted to combat what they called "barbarian" influences in French literature and to restore the ancient classics to their place of honor.[13] They reacted most vigorously against nine-

[10] *Ibid.*, p. 33.
[11] *Ibid.*
[12] Maurras, *L'Étang de Berre*, p. 354.
[13] Émile Henriot, *À Quoi rêvent les jeunes gens?* (Paris: H. and E. Champion, 1913), p. 57.

teenth-century German Romanticism. While he was participating in all of these activities, Maurras also contributed articles to Barrès' *Cocarde* and to the royalist newspapers, the *Soleil* and the *Gazette de France*.

The *Gazette* sent Maurras to report on the Olympic games in Athens in 1896. This was the first time he had ever left France, and his trip made a strong impression on him. Aboard ship and in Greece he met many foreigners, especially Englishmen and Germans. He thought that most of them were loud and overbearing, and he asked himself what made England and Germany stronger than France. His answer was that those nations had dynastic monarchies but that France was being corrupted by a democratic regime.[14] He became an avowed monarchist at least a year before the Dreyfus Affair became a public issue.

When the editors of the *Soleil* supported Dreyfus, they persuaded Maurras to stay on (despite his offer to resign), demanding only that he should not speak of the Affair. This sort of agreement was common at that time, even among members of the same family. Maurras was able to continue writing for the *Soleil*,[15] but he felt more at home with the staff of the anti-Dreyfusard *Gazette de France*. It was for this newspaper that he wrote his articles in defense of Colonel Henry's forgery.

Maurras' subsequent activities are discussed elsewhere in this book; we are concerned here with the kind of person he was. During his first years in Paris he continued to educate himself by reading, since his deafness prevented him from attending lectures at the university. He steeped himself in the ancient classics, which helped him to shape his view of the world. While he worshipped the Greek way of life, he dismissed contemporary civilization as contemptible and made little effort to understand it. His personality structure and his acquired attitudes made it easy for him to see Greece as an

[14] *Au Signe de Flore*, p. 47.
[15] *Ibid.*, p. 74.

ideal and to feel oppressed by the environment in which he
lived. Maurras has been described as a modern fatalistic Epi-
curus.[16] He was the archetype of the aesthete, the snob, the
contemner of the masses and of things that are not beautiful.

In his later years Maurras was to occupy himself increasingly with political journalism, but as a young man he was
especially concerned with the idea of beauty. He confesses
his rapturous response to the Acropolis in his book *Anthinéa*
(which was first published in 1901). Once he was so moved
by the exquisite lines and splendor of a column of the Par-
thenon that he embraced it and kissed it. He speaks of this
moment as one of "lyric folly" in which he "revelled with
infinite pleasure." [17] On another occasion he was particularly
moved by the sight of a handsome boy "whom death had
taken at the transitional age between adolescence and manhood. Who has not seen . . . the beautiful faces on which
death had been able to preserve the youth at twenty years?
It has brought them back to the peak of their perfection." [18]
He also praised the statue of the "Lamented Young Man" in
the National Museum in Athens: "Ripe, adolescent, brought
to the supreme moment of his virile springtime—the soul,
as firm as the flesh, gives off emotion without receiving any
in return." [19] Later, during the First World War, Maurras
wrote ecstatic panegyrics to the youths of France who had
died in battle.[20] His aestheticism was rather one-sided, though,
for in his actual dealings with women he resembled the brutish
male current in French bourgeois circles in the early 1900's.

Maurras detested anything that he considered feminine or
effeminate, whether it was Romantic literature or what he
called "sentimental" socialism—Maurras once accused Jean

[16] Roudiez, *op. cit.*, p. 335.
[17] *Anthinéa* (5th edition; Paris: P. Juven, 1926), p. 41.
[18] *Corps glorieux, ou la vertu de la perfection* (Paris: E. Flammarion, 1929), p. 23.
[19] *Ibid.*, p. 20.
[20] *Tombeaux* (Paris: Nouvelle Librairie Nationale, 1921), *passim*.

Jaurès of having a feminine spirit that sought only to stir up the emotions of his working-class audiences.[21] According to Maurras himself, his fear of effeminacy stemmed from an incident in his childhood.[22] It seems that a little girl only two years older than he had asked a group of children to sing a hymn. Although the others obliged, Maurras remained silent. The girl then scolded him and told him that those who sang would grow up to be wise, while those who did not would know nothing. Disturbed by this warning, young Charles ran to his mother, who reassured him that there was no truth in it. Thereafter Maurras avoided all song because song could move him to tears, and he considered tears to be effeminate (though he saw nothing "effeminate" in slobbering over a statue of a beautiful boy).

Despite his occasional moments of lyrical abandon, Maurras consciously tried to be rational and positivistic. He often spoke of the need for the intellect to dominate the emotions.[23] Fearing the consequences of allowing himself to venture into the sea of his passionate yearnings, he took refuge on the sterile promontory of reason. Perhaps Georges Bernanos was right when he said: [24]

Nothing can be understood about Maurras if one judges the man from his writings, for the writings are not the man. It was for himself, for his personal security, that the author of the *Enquête* constructed that vast defensive system of which he was at the same time the master and the prisoner. His doctrine does not explain him at all; it is only a forced effort to justify him and it works indefatigably to close all the breaches by which we could penetrate to his personality and the real truth about him, which is carefully hidden from everyone and, alas, probably forgotten even by himself.

[21] *Enquête sur la monarchie* (Versailles: Bibliothèque des Œuvres Politiques, 1929), p. 501.
[22] *La Musique intérieure*, p. 13.
[23] E.g., *Les Amants de Venise: Georges Sand et Musset* (Paris: E. Flammarion, 1926), p. 288.
[24] *Nous autres français* (Paris: Nouvelle Revue Française, 1939), p. 61.

Maurras had little physical or personal charm to add to the seductions of his intelligence. His body was thin and his complexion swarthy. He had a low brow covered with straight black hair, and a small pointed beard partially concealed his chin. His difficulty in hearing caused him to squint, and this made the expression on his face sad and forbidding. Though usually polite, he was extremely jumpy and he showed a pedantic concern for grammatical forms in ordinary conversation.[25] He had no wit, reproached others who did, and disliked frivolous or imaginative people.[26] The kind of irony he occasionally enjoyed expressed the pathetic rumbling of his internal hate. When he lost his temper, he antagonized everyone around him—so much so that once an exasperated waiter in the Café Flore threw a stack of saucers at his head.[27] But he himself shunned physical violence and channeled most of his aggressive impulses through the written word.

Perhaps the outstanding feature of Maurras' personality was his stubborn determination to be right at all times and to impose his ideas on other people. His collaborator Léon Daudet once said that Maurras was the kind of person who always wins an argument.[28] He had no desire for public office.[29] Instead, he wanted to be a sort of literary pope and political prophet, and among his own followers he succeeded in attaining this position. Every day he received adulatory letters from *bien-pensant* dowagers and petty noblemen as well as requests from obscure poets for his sponsorship. From the earliest years

[25] Louis Dimier, *Vingt ans de l'Action française et d'autres souvenirs* (Paris: Nouvelle Libraire Nationale, 1926), p. 13.

[26] Lazare de Gérin Ricard and Louis Truc, *Histoire de l'Action Française* (Paris: Fournier-Valdès, 1949), p. 88.

[27] Dimier, *op. cit.*, p. 14.

[28] Leon Daudet, *Souvenirs des milieux cittéraires, politiques, artistiques, et medicaux* (Paris: Nouvelle Librairie Nationale, 1926), II, 185; Henri Massis quotes Maurras as saying: "Je me fous de tout, sauf d'avoir finalement raison," in his book *Maurras et notre temps* (2 vols., Paris: La Palatine, 1951), II, 86.

[29] Statement made by Émile Buré in a personal interview.

of the Action Française Maurras had a group of young disciples who faithfully attended his séances at the Café Flore. He provided seemingly airtight arguments for thousands of like-minded Frenchmen until the mid-twentieth century. Seldom has a leader of his type had such a hold on his devotees.

Everything about Maurras—his manners, his tastes, his conversation, and his writings—reflected the environment of small literary reviews and Left-Bank cafés in which he spent his early manhood. He analyzed politics and social problems with the standards and prejudices of literary criticism. Beauty was order, and order was everything, according to him.[30] His exclusive devotion to intellectual pursuits, coupled with his lack of understanding of the needs and interests of the common man, made him unfit for leadership in the French community. Like Plato, he was looking for the ideal ruler who would put his political ideas into practice. Both thinkers were ultimately to learn that there were stronger pressures than philosophy at work on dictators like Dionysios and Pétain.

* * *

In the Paris of 1900 the cafés were not the only gathering places for intellectuals; the salons still harbored their contingent and gave the Action Française its second most famous leader—Léon Daudet. He infused the movement with a touch of wit and Parisian sophistication. His portly figure, beaming, clean-shaven face, and superficially jolly manner seemed slightly out of place among the lean, intense youths who sat at Maurras' feet. But, in spite of these characteristics and the brilliant background from which he came, Daudet was to become as much a part of the Action Française as his scowling colleague from Martigues.

Léon Daudet was born in the capital in 1867, and he grew up in the company of the leading political and literary personalities who visited his famous father, the novelist Alphonse Daudet. When young Léon was chosen as the outstanding

[30] Maurras, *Le Chemin de paradis* (Paris: E. de Boccard, 1921), p. 215.

pupil in that nursery of brilliant minds, the Lycée Louis-le-Grand, Ernest Renan whispered "we shall make something of you" [31] into his ear as he handed him his prize. Léon Gambetta, Paul Déroulède, Victor Hugo, and many other prominent men also took an interest in him.

After receiving his baccalaureate, Daudet enrolled in the medical school at the University of Paris. Although he remained there for seven years, this pampered young dilettante found its organization distasteful and viewed its faculty as a collection of mandarins. He described the student body as "a veritable medical proletariat in which the competition is cruel, plus a number of hard-working students who were fearful and submissive, and whose success or failure hung in a delicate balance." [32] Daudet was unwilling to become this kind of obsequious drudge. He was also squeamish about handling sick people as an intern, and he developed a horror for what he called an excessive use of surgery.[33] Despite the fact that he never practiced medicine, he acquired a superficial knowledge of human maladies as well as an understanding of clinical analysis. These attributes later helped him to expose the weaknesses of people he did not like and to "dissect" his enemies verbally.

By the mid-nineties Daudet began to reject almost everything that he identified with his father's world. He divorced Victor Hugo's granddaughter (who had become his wife in 1891) and married the daughter of a *bien-pensant* physician named Léon Allard. His anticlerical and antimilitarist ideas also changed. Some of the articles he had contributed to the Leftist semiweekly *Germinal* in 1893 bordered on revolutionary socialism.[34] But by the time of the Dreyfus Affair he was already writing exclusively for reactionary newspapers such as the *Gazette de France, Soleil, Gaulois,* and especially the *Libre Parole.* Gradually he broke away from his liberal and repub-

[31] Daudet, *op. cit.,* I, 3.
[32] *Ibid.,* p. 174.
[33] *Ibid.,* p. 207.
[34] *Germinal,* I (January–June 1893), *passim.*

lican friends and began spending most of his time with anti-Dreyfusards like Édouard Drumont, Jules Lemaître, and the habitués of Madame de Loynes's salon. He became a practicing Catholic at the turn of the century and joined Maurras' neoroyalist circle in 1904.[35]

Neither among his father's friends nor his schoolmates had young Léon met any royalists. Alphonse Daudet had been an ardent republican and had felt that only the Republic could bring about the *revanche* he so earnestly desired.[36] In his home Léon had sometimes heard Napoleon III and the imperial court condemned (though Alphonse himself had served as the Duc de Morny's *attaché de cabinet* from 1861 to 1865), but he was unaware of any royalist movement in the 1880's.[37] As for the Jews, he says that he regarded them at first as being "only slightly different from other Frenchmen" until the appearance of Drumont's *La France Juive* in 1886.[38]

During the late eighties and early nineties Daudet—who, unlike Maurras, was extremely sociable—moved about freely in the salons of Parisian society and often came into contact with prominent Jews. In his memoirs he describes those whom he met with bitter satire and ridicule. He insists that they all spoke a mixture of French and German, talked incessantly of money, interest, and bankruptcies, and possessed a repugnant odor.[39] Yet his claim that these social contacts, along with Drumont's book, made him an antisemite is not very convincing. The true cause of his antisemitism is uncertain, though some of his contemporaries suggest that Daudet turned against the Jews and the republican regime out of resentment toward his father, to whom he felt inferior as a writer.

Daudet never tried to organize the disordered mass of his hates, hopes, and hobbies into a systematic doctrine. The Action Française supplied him with the formal theory he needed,

[35] Daudet, *op. cit.*, II, 182.
[36] *Ibid.*, I, 4.
[37] *Ibid.*, p. 20.
[38] *Ibid.*, pp. 352–353.
[39] *Ibid.*, p. 11.

but he did not become a fanatic and he did not lose his appreciation of the comic side of life (though his son's death under mysterious circumstances in the 1920's almost drove him insane). His responses were usually subjective rather than doctrinaire. For example, he found many of the writers with whose political bias he sympathized boring, and he enjoyed Proust, Baudelaire, and Céline, whose influence was unhealthy from the nationalist point of view. He was also free from the narrow Latinism of Maurras and his docile disciples.

Although Daudet shared the antidemocratic attitudes of his colleagues in the Action Française, he was more cosmopolitan than most of them. He traveled all over Western Europe and he was secretly admired by many Frenchmen as a *bon vivant*.[40] His world was that of the salon and the gourmet's dinner. Like an eighteenth-century gentleman, he judged people by their looks, their tastes, their manners, and the kind of table they set. He thoroughly disliked many of the modern conveniences that removed the personal touch from daily living—things like commercial hotels, prepared food sauces, and public transportation.[41] One senses in him a fear of being lost in the crowd and reduced to the common level.

For all his apparent sophistication, Daudet was profoundly ignorant of the twentieth-century world. In none of his writings does he ever show any real understanding of the forces at work in modern society. He explained political and economic developments of which he disapproved as the work of racial or partisan conspiracies and bad leaders. Still, by means of his amusing newspaper articles (in the daily *Action Française*, which was founded in 1908) and his ability to speak effectively before large audiences, he attracted more sympathy to the Action Française than any of its other spokesmen.

* * *

[40] Statement made in a personal interview by Georges Valois, editor-in-chief of the Parisian daily *Libération*.
[41] Daudet, *op. cit.*, II, 86–87.

The other founders of the Action Française—Henri Vaugeois and Maurice Pujo—were café intellectuals like Maurras,
but without his literary talent. These two men first met as
students in the early 1890's and they both joined various extremist movements in the Latin Quarter. At that time anarchism attracted many amateur supporters of its "brave gestures,"
and Pujo circulated a petition demanding clemency for Auguste Vaillant, who had thrown a bomb into the chamber
of deputies.[42] He also dabbled in literature and started an
iconoclastic review called *L'Art et la Vie* with several of his
classmates. Although young Pujo came from a *bien-pensant*
background, he flung himself into the revolutionary atmosphere of the Left Bank. (Later in his life, however, he returned
to the fold of the pious and decorated his apartment with
hackneyed church-art.) After the Dreyfus Affair he wanted
to devote himself to literary criticism, but he claims that
Vaugeois persuaded him to stick to "politics." [43]

Henri Vaugeois was less of a rebel against his family background than Pujo, though he too was searching for fresh out-
lets of expression. Like his father (who was a professor and
dean of the law school at the University of Caën), he went
through the academic program leading to a teaching career.
In the late nineties he became a philosophy instructor in a
college forty miles east of Paris. Meanwhile, his quest for
intellectual certainty had attracted him successively to Spinoza
and Marx.[44] He soon rejected the easygoing liberalism of Voltaire and Anatole France as well as the humanitarian ideals
of the French Revolution. His hostility toward Jews, Freemasons, democrats, and foreigners in France seemed to grow
out of the Dreyfus Affair, but they were also part of a more
fundamental reaction against modern society.

In 1898 Vaugeois and Pujo left the Union for Moral Action

[42] Coudekerque-Lambrecht, *op. cit.*, p. 40.
[43] Statement made by Maurice Pujo in a personal interview.
[44] Henri Vaugeois, *La Fin de l'erreur française* (Paris: Librairie
de l'Action Française, 1928), p. vi.

—a liberal Protestant movement that sided with the Dreyfusards—and founded the first Comité de l'Action Française.
Vaugeois later said that he had done this in order to fight
"against the coming of socialism—with all its darkness—and
the second world reign of the Jews." [45] He knew what he was
against, but he did not yet know what he was for. The revival
of the reactionary cause among the anti-Dreyfusards helped
him to find the answer. So did his dismissal from his teaching
post, as the result of his participation in Déroulède's attempted
coup d'état in February 1899.[46]

Although Vaugeois gave up his academic career, he retained
his pedantic temperament. He was always more of a moralist
than a politician.[47] When he later became the director of the
daily *Action Française*, he clung to this moralistic response
and adapted it to the needs of the new dogma he had accepted.
He may have missed his calling by not becoming a Calvinist
minister. His Norman background—upright, strait-laced, no
"Latin" license—and his training in moral philosophy certainly prepared him for this profession. On the other hand,
his sparkling eyes, sonorous voice, and habit of gesticulation
gave him much personal charm and persuasiveness.[48] He was
the movement's best fund raiser until his death in 1916.

*　*　*

Jacques Bainville was the only leader of the Action Française who made enough money from his books to live com-
fortably. He was born in 1879 at Vincennes, just outside of
Paris, into an upper middle-class and politically conservative
family. Instead of becoming a lawyer like his father, Bainville
left school at the age of nineteen and sought a career as a
free-lance writer. By 1901 he had accepted Maurras' monarchist views and joined his movement,[49] but his main activity

[45] *Ibid.*, p. xii.
[46] Coudekerque-Lambrecht, *op. cit.*, p. 39.
[47] Statement made by Henri Massis in a personal interview.
[48] Daudet, *op. cit.*, II, 182.
[49] *Revue de l'Action Française*, III (1901), 698.

until his death in 1936 was writing popular history. His *Histoire de France* alone went through more than three hundred editions.

Aside from his articles in the periodicals of the Action Française, Bainville wrote for the *Gazette de France* before the First World War and was an editor of the *Revue Universelle* during the interwar period. He and Henri Massis made this review a haven for conservative-nationalist, traditionalist, and reactionary writers. In his later years Bainville looked like a "man of distinction" in an advertisement for a fine brandy. This dapper, clean-shaven little Frenchman had chiseled features and was always fastidious in his dress and manners. His literary style reflected his personality and appearance; it was closely knit, serious, polished, and glib.

The other writers of the Action Française—including Maurras himself—would probably have starved without the income from their movement. They were members of the new academic proletariat, which was growing as a result of expanding facilities for higher education in the late nineteenth century. The plight of these people was worse in underdeveloped countries than in the Western world. But even there university students who had studied the humanities and the law found that there were not enough jobs for all of them on the professional level. Some of these graduates took routine positions at low wages; others swelled the ranks of the café intellectuals. Their discontent bred resentment, which they often rationalized in the form of social criticism.[50]

In France the standard of living of these discontented intellectuals was not much higher than that of the better-paid workers, and their lack of a definite vocation made their economic future precarious. They formed small literary and political cliques, founded ephemeral reviews, and took part in street demonstrations. Most of them became anarchists, revolutionary socialists, or syndicalists, though a few turned to nationalism, provincialism, antisemitism, reaction, and even

[50] Joseph A. Schumpeter, *Capitalism, Socialism, and Democracy* (New York: Harper, 1947), p. 153.

occultism as an outlet. In any case, they were all ready to attack the existing political system as the source of their personal misfortune.

The founders of the Action Française were caught in a web
of circumstances that they aggravated by their own activities.
For there were more intellectuals than contemporary society
required. The real significance of this oversupply was not only
that the intellectual professions were losing their social prestige but also that their activities were beginning to be
viewed with hostility by an increasing number of half-
educated people.[51] Those few intellectuals for whom the Action Française was a means of livelihood and the many others
for whom it was a kind of private cult felt an awareness of this
situation intuitively. But they were mistaken in blaming it
on the political system rather than on modern economic and
social developments.

Although Maurras and his colleagues were ostensibly working for a restoration of the monarchy, what they really wanted
was a world in which they could write their poems and essays
without having to worry about where they would get money
to live. Their sensitive natures revolted against the mercenary
spirit of modern society. In order to earn a living they had
to appeal to the general public. Since they could not satisfy
its tastes, they also expressed their longing for a return to the
Old Regime in their literary criticism. Throughout the twentieth century the men of letters in the Action Française praised
the virtues of classical French literature and condemned most
of what had been written (except by a handful of writers who
shared their pattern of response) since the Revolution.

*   *   *

While the Radicals and Socialists were taking their revenge
on the army and the church between 1900 and 1905, the Action Française remained an unknown clique of café intellec-

[51] Karl Mannheim, *Man and Society in an Age of Reconstruction*
(New York: Harcourt Brace, 1940), p. 100.

tuals in the Latin Quarter of Paris. The publication of their little review was to be their main activity during those years. Under the heading *Une Réforme Parlementaire* one of the regular feature sections contained articles criticizing the parliamentary system and calling for a return to authority. The column *La Vie Nationale* was subdivided into army, navy, and colonies; another, labeled *Action Militaire*, included pedantic studies by reactionary officers. Its editor, Colonel de Villebois-Mareuil, said that "one of the first duties of the Action Française is to emphasize the military tradition of this country." [52] The movement continued to glorify the army throughout the twentieth century.

A gesture that had no apparent relationship to French militarism was the backing the Action Française gave to Lieutenant-Colonel Monteil's committee to aid the Boers in their fight for independence.[53] This action becomes understandable only when it is seen as an effort to exploit anti-British feeling in France, which was especially strong because of the Fashoda crisis. For the Action Française was already seeking new rallying points in its search for support. (It should also be noted that Lieutenant-Colonel Monteil was a royalist and a leading anti-Dreyfusard.) During the early months of 1900 news of the war in the Transvaal appeared regularly in the review, and when Colonel de Villebois-Mareuil was killed in the fighting the editors said that he had died for France.

But militarism and anglophobia had only a limited appeal to other reactionaries, and they did not satisfy the intellectual pretensions of the Action Française leaders. Maurras and Bainville were the only editors of the review who were monarchists before 1901. The others were bound together by their anti-Dreyfusard feelings and a desire for some kind of strong ruler. Beyond that their goals did not differ fundamentally from those of the League of the French Fatherland, and without a definite political doctrine they could not hope to lure

[52] *Revue de l'Action Française,* I (August 1899), 29.
[53] *Ibid.* (November 1899), 473.

people away from it. The Action Française needed an idea that would unite its leaders and appeal to outsiders. Maurras' integral nationalism—nationalism made complete by royalism —was to serve this dual purpose.

There was room for a new monarchist movement. In March 1900 the committee of the Duc d'Orléans lost two of its main champions when André Buffet and the Comte de Lur-Saluces were temporarily exiled for plotting against the Republic during the previous summer. The *Gazette de France,* to which certain families continued to subscribe because of tradition or habit but which they no longer read, was the only propaganda outlet the militant royalists had left. As a means of reviving their hopes, Maurras published a series of articles on monarchism in it during the summer and autumn of 1900.

The success of Maurras' *Enquête sur la Monarchie* as a piece of political journalism soon persuaded the other leaders of the Action Française to accept the monarchist position. This "survey" presented the views of prominent counterrevolutionaries and of nationalist writers like Paul Bourget, Maurice Barrès, Jules Lemaître, and François Coppée. Maurras added comments of his own to these testimonials and tried to show that the doctrine of the traditional royalists was essentially the same as his. The fact that the Duc d'Orléans had publicly expressed his interest in the *Enquête* [54] gained attention in the Parisian press and won favor for Maurras among the supporters of the pretender. When the *Revue de l'Action Française* officially adopted monarchism a year later, it used the *Enquête* to attract their backing.

Charles Maurras was able to remain a permanent fixture of the French political scene for almost fifty years by resisting all efforts to transform his movement into a party or a pressure group. The other leagues all lost their driving force when they tried to change their methods. Such was the case of the League of the French Fatherland after it decided to run

[54] *Enquête sur la monarchie,* pp. 105–106.

candidiates in the 1902 elections. Its first setback was the resignation of its best-known intellectual sponsor, Maurice Barrès. He did the same thing that Maurras would have done if the Action Française had decided to become a nationalist party—he walked out.

The pattern of reactionary behavior in twentieth-century France was set by the relations between Barrès, the Action Française, and the League of the French Fatherland in the early 1900's. Even after Maurras persuaded his associates to embrace the royalist cause, the author of L'Appel au Soldat continued to work with them.[55] Both, in turn, supported Gabriel Syveton, the only candidate on the League of the French Fatherland list who ever got elected. This league's program called for a strong executive to end what it called "political anarchy." It renounced "parliamentarianism" but at the same time it championed universal suffrage. Barrès did not believe that the military dictator he wanted could gain power by electoral means. Like Maurras, he was primarily interested in long-range plans for a political and cultural revival in France.[56] But his brand of nationalism was really closer to that of Mussolini than it was to the Bonapartism of the League of the French Fatherland or the neomonarchism of the Action Française.

Although Syveton seemed to incarnate the whole reactionary cause in 1903, his career—along with that of the League of the French Fatherland—came to a dramatic close two years later. The issue that culminated in Syveton's death originated in 1900, when the Waldeck-Rousseau government decided to weaken the alleged hold of the antisemitic nobility on the army. General Gallifet, the minister of war at that time, had decreed that all generals would henceforth be appointed by his ministry rather than by the existing military commission. His agents then proceeded to investigate suspect officers and to

[55] Maurras, *Au Signe de Flore*, p. 117.
[56] Barrès, *Scènes et doctrines*, p. 101.

note on filing cards (*fiches*) whether or not they went to church regularly, who their friends were, and how they felt about the Republic.

When the existence of these *fiches* became publicly known in 1904, the nationalist press protested and attacked the current minister of war, General André. The chamber of deputies then held a public hearing in November at which General André was made to answer for the policies of his subordinates. After he had finished making his statement, Syveton approached him and struck him. Despite the unparliamentary nature of this act and the fact that General André was an old man, Syveton became a hero for most French reactionaries.

The government decided to prosecute Syveton a few weeks later. In order to defend himself, he called upon the support of the military leaders who had convicted Dreyfus.[57] Then, the night before his trial, he was found dead in his apartment in front of an open gas jet. The police classified his death as a suicide. The liberals charged that Syveton killed himself because of a sordid crisis in his personal life; the reactionaries accused the Dreyfusards of murdering him in fear of what he might say at his trial.

Whatever the truth about Syveton's death may be, the only parliamentary representative of the reactionary nationalists was dead. They gave him a solemn funeral and made a martyr of him. Each year thereafter the Action Française organized a demonstration at his grave on the anniversary of his burial. Its leaders were to accumulate a whole gallery of martyrs, of whom Syveton was the first. Along with the other reactionaries, they viewed the blows he had administered to General André as an attack on the hated Republic and everything it represented. Now Maurras and his fellow café intellectuals continued the fight alone.

[57] Dimier, *op. cit.*, p. 22.

4

❧ ❧ ❧ ❧

Ideas First

Throughout its history the Action Française used ideas as
its main "weapons" and made Charles Maurras its infallible prophet and pope on doctrinal matters. Many of Maurras' ideas were themselves derivative.[1] His "organizing empiricism" stemmed partly from Comte and Sainte-Beuve, his
"positivist" approach to history from Taine, his admiration for
the Old Regime from De Bonald, his federalism and corporatism from Proudhon and La Tour du Pin, his antisemitism
from Drumont, and his nationalism from Barrès. Maurras did
not take over the theories of any of these men completely. He

[1] The sources of Maurras' thought have been analyzed by William
Curt Buthman, *The Rise of Integral Nationalism in France* (New
York: Columbia University Press, 1939); Charlotte Touzalin Muret,
French Royalist Doctrines Since the Revolution (New York: Columbia
University Press, 1933); Alphonse V. Roche, *Les Idées traditionalistes
en France de Rivarol à Charles Maurras* (Urbana, Illinois: The Univer-
sity of Illinois Press, 1937); and Michael Curtis, *Three Against the
Third Republic: Sorel, Barrès, and Maurras* (Princeton, New Jersey:
Princeton University Press, 1959).

drew upon them eclectically to support his own outlook, which was that of an aesthete and literary critic.

Maurras himself once said that his ideas were the by-product of his aesthetic principles: [2]

I battled for ten years for the traditions of French taste, but I entertained no hope of seeing them restored until the day when I conceived the possibility of re-establishing the ensemble of our national traditions.

Hence Maurras the literary critic became Maurras the royalist in order to restore a society congenial to the classical tradition of French literature and faithful to the Greek principles of beauty handed down to France by Rome. He was an aesthete before he was a nationalist and a nationalist before he became a royalist. His nationalism was cultural before it finally became political.

Maurras' social thought must be pieced together from his scores of books and thousands of articles written over a period of sixty-five years, for the method he used to construct it was dialectical. He resolved the apparent paradox of an apostle of authority championing the value of argument by restricting it to theoretical matters while proscribing it from the field of action.[3] Like a true doctrinaire, he separated ends from means and justified all sorts of opportunism regarding the latter. He was ready to achieve his goals *par tous les moyens,* and he used the tactics of logic and politics—both of which he enjoyed aesthetically—in the service of a philosophical ideal.

The best way to present Maurras' ideas is to examine his basic assumptions and prejudices first and then describe his views on politics, society, economics, and the church. He admitted that it was not his philosophy but the fact that he had been born a Frenchman that made him see the monarchy as the "natural" regime for France.[4] Unlike Montesquieu, he

[2] *Gazette de France,* December 12, 1901.
[3] *Mes Idées politiques* (Paris: Fayard, 1937), p. 131.
[4] *Enquête sur la monarchie* (Versailles: Bibliothèque des Œuvres Politiques, 1929), p. 65.

felt that all types of government should be based on authority, order, and hierarchy.[5] The keystone of his doctrine is not monarchism but a strong antidemocratic bias.

Since Maurras insisted that democracy brings equality with it, he spent his life attacking these two values. Like Taine, he assumed that most modern men are little better than their primitive forbears. They may have developed further mentally, but only a few superior intellects escape mediocrity.[6] The ideal of equality is bad, he argued, because it undermines societies and destroys civilizations. He equated civilization with quality and democracy with quantity and equality [7] and said that one had to choose between inequality and death.[8]

To Maurras an egalitarian society meant "a government of numbers," [9] which was incapable of preserving the order that is essential to civilized communities and could lead only to decadence and anarchy. Because he assumed that hierarchy— or stratification—was natural to all types of human organization, Maurras wanted to revive what he called "protective and necessary inequalities" [10] in the form of hereditary privileged classes. (If he had read George Orwell's *Animal Farm*, Maurras might have learned that equality can also be ordered and graded and that some citizens can be "more equal" than others.) Privilege alone guarantees quality—by restraining man's envy and cupidity and by satisfying his desire for harmony, order, and status.[11] Finally, according to Maurras, the whole system can work only if the principle of authority is recognized by all.

[5] *Action Française*, August 20, 1912.
[6] Buthman, *op. cit.*, p. 66.
[7] *Dictionnaire politique et critique* (Paris: Cité Des Livres, 1933), p. 256.
[8] *Enquête*, p. 119.
[9] *La Démocratie religieuse* (Paris: Nouvelle Librairie Nationale, 1921), p. 397.
[10] *Mes Idées politiques*, pp. xv and xvii.
[11] *Ibid.*, p. 339.

Why did these basic assumptions and prejudices lead Maurras to become a monarchist? He did not believe that monarchies exist by virtue of any special divine right. On the contrary, he maintained that all legitimate power is based on "beneficent force" and that those who hold it are justified by the results they achieve.[12] Even so, a king cannot function effectively unless his office is hereditary: "The only rational and sensible form of the authority of one person is that which remains in a single family, from first born to first born, according to a law that excludes competition." [13] Otherwise, a dictator or an elected monarch would do just as well. Maurras saw the elimination of competition for power as the main benefit of hereditary monarchy. By substituting heredity for election he hoped to overcome the "evils" of democracy.[14]

Maurras' political thought is dominated by a conceptual framework that is essentially social: "Monarchy is neither universal, nor eternal; what is eternal and universal is government by families." [15] Man's need to live in common is more "necessary" than the existence of the state or of a particular nationality.[16] In his polemics Maurras often seemed to consider forms of government—especially the monarchy—as ends in themselves. But, like the Greek philosophers, he equated "politics" with the good society in his theoretical writings.

According to Maurras, the group is more important than the individual, and its smooth functioning must take precedence over the rights of man. The rulers in any society must have more privileges and inherited economic security than the ruled,[17] though everyone should have a "place." There should also be as little social mobility as possible in order to avoid

---

[12] De Démos à Cesar (2 vols.; Paris: Éditions du Capitole, 1930), pp. 93 and 149–151.
[13] Mes Idées politiques, p. 275.
[14] Ibid., p. 163.
[15] La Démocratie religieuse, p. 116.
[16] Action Française, July 23, 1916.
[17] Ibid., August 4, 1914, and April 4, 1916.

competition for status, which destroys respect for authority and weakens the established order.[18] Maurras would allow a few talented commoners to rise, but he abhorred the modern mass striving to "get ahead" as well as the danger of some people becoming *déclassés* in a highly competitive economic environment.

It is an open question where and when Maurras saw his ideal society in the past. He could have found it in the Middle Ages, in seventeenth-century France or Spain, or even in the England of 1900. For, though Maurras disliked everything British, he thought that most Englishmen of that period knew their "place" and respected their "betters" to a greater extent than Frenchmen. He seemed to like the period before 1789 in his own country, but he was also attracted to earlier aristocratic or oligarchical republics—like Athens, Rome, Carthage, and Venice—where power was inherited. In fact, he mentioned several of these as examples of his dictum that "the government of families is the eternal good." [19]

Maurras said that the whole of France's history required her people to submit to the authority of the royal family.[20] Only in this way could their country remain a nation—instead of becoming a mere geographical expression, as Gaul had been when the Romans arrived. France could not be ruled by a business elite, like Carthage, a landed gentry, like Rome, or a priestly caste, like India. She was too complex socially and economically for any kind of hereditary government except a monarchy. The Republic was monstrous because it allowed groups with special interests to try to control it, thus leading to the disintegration of the national community. Only a king could resolve the conflicting concerns of its citizens.[21]

In the modern world, where all nations sought to further their own ends and where there was no common political bond

[18] *Revue Hebdomadaire*, December 15, 1923.
[19] *La Démocratie religieuse*, p. 84.
[20] *Mes Idées politiques*, p. 266.
[21] *Enquête*, p. 346.

outside the fatherland, Maurras believed that the nation-state was the best guardian of a community's values.[22] The Roman Empire had once united many fatherlands and provided two centuries of "peaceful coexistence." In the Middle Ages the Catholic Church had also been a kind of supranational political organization, but all semblance of unity had disappeared after the Reformation. Since then the nations of Europe had become political rivals in an unrestrained struggle for power.[23] Therefore, the people who loved France would have to give their first thoughts to her vital interests. The national integrity and safety were supposed to be looked after by the state. But what kind of government did the French state have? Was it able to fulfill this duty?

Having asked himself these questions, Maurras concluded that the Third Republic was incapable of preserving the national interests and safety of France because it was based on the false principles of the Revolution. His passion for order in society made him anti-individualistic; his contempt for the common man made him antidemocratic; his nativism and narrow racism made the ideal of brotherhood repugnant to him. Consequently, his whole point of view was antithetical to the slogans of the revolutionary tradition: *Liberté, Égalité, Fraternité.*

For Maurras religious individualism was embodied in the Reformation, political individualism was the guiding principle of the Revolution, and individualism in art was the essence of Romanticism [24] (so that the Reformation, the Revolution, and the Romantic movement were all bad in his eyes). Individualism was a false ideal for society because it cleared the way for disorder and chaos. Maurras insisted that society did not arise from a contract of wills but from a fact of nature,[25] and he pointed to the Dreyfus Affair as a tragic illustration of the

[22] *Ibid.*, p. 472.
[23] *Ibid.*, p. 412.
[24] *Ibid.*, p. 67.
[25] *Ibid.*, p. 79.

havoc that an appeal to the rights of the individual could wreak. If individualism were a true value, the Dreyfusards would have been justified in disorganizing the army, public opinion, and the defense of the state itself, for the sake of one person.[26] Maurras believed that they were obviously not justified in doing so.

The Revolution, according to Maurras, had diverted the function of the state from that of guardian of the public safety to that of guarantor of the falsely called "natural rights" of the individual. As a result, all the social ties among Frenchmen were relaxed or dissolved, and France was reduced to a condition of atomization in which each person lived isolated from his individual competitors. Like the bulk of Maurras' analysis, this observation overlooks the economic causes of social change. Maurras criticized the revolutionary leaders for their laissez-faire economic policies, their destruction of the church's control over the family and education, and their abolition of class privilege. But he did not see that, in substituting contract for status as the basis of society, the middle classes were trying to use legal means—culminating in the Napoleonic Code—to impose a whole new value-system on the rest of the country. They installed a rational economic order in which precapitalist occupational and administrative groups no longer had a meaningful function.

Maurras resented the efforts of the new regime to destroy these groups and all the secondary institutions that had made French society into a nation. The professional guilds were abolished, and charity, education, and even science—as a result of government control of the universities and the Institut de France—became state services. In addition, the provinces were obliterated, and the privileges of the towns and the communes were subordinated to the central authority.[27] Maurras thought that even the family—the smallest social unit in human society—was being supplanted by the individual. Every

26 *Ibid.*, p. 73.
27 *Ibid.*, p. 83.

natural bond except that of common nationality was corrupted by the false philosophy of individualism. And the Dreyfusards, according to Maurras, were willing to sacrifice the nation itself rather than submit to the condemnation of one man.

In order to restore France to her former greatness, the secondary institutions that the Revolution had destroyed had to be revived and the monarchy put back in power. Sixty-three years ago Maurras said that there were several groups in France campaigning for the restoration of the family, the liberties of the communes, the provinces, and the professional corporations, as well as those that wanted to re-establish a stable principle of political authority.[28] The monarchy, which was traditional, hereditary, antiparliamentary, and decentralizing, could satisfy all their demands. As a matter of fact, only the monarchy could do so. Maurras summarized his view that royalism was the only integral and complete nationalism as follows: [29]

The king incarnates the conservative instinct of the nation. Thus, the king will govern. The assemblies—the real social representation of the nation—will control the government. The country will administer itself, thanks to the free exercise of the rights of association, from which decentralization is born.

As Maurras knew, the reactionaries were not the only nationalists in France at the turn of the century. There were others who wanted to see a dictator in the Elysée Palace and the functions of parliament reduced to a minimum. The remnants of the Boulangist movement led by Déroulède and Barrès had been ready to reform the Republic along nationalist lines without destroying it completely. Maurras himself insisted that a truly nationalist republic was impossible, not only because of the false principles on which this notion was based, but also because such a regime would still be controlled by a bloc of non-French cosmopolites. He called this group the

[28] *Gazette de France*, May 6, 1899.
[29] *Enquête*, p. 171.

"four confederated states": Jews, Freemasons, Protestants, and resident aliens (*métèques*).[30] They ran the French state for their own purposes and would never allow it to change.[31]

Maurras charged that this bloc, which he also referred to as the "Old Republican Party," was against everything that an ordered French society demanded. It opposed a strong army; it pillaged the wealth of the country in order to subsidize democracy; it was anti-Catholic; it fostered the principles of the Revolution.[32] Obviously, the state must be wrested from the hands of the people in this bloc and given back to true French leaders. What Maurras refused to see was that in the twentieth century the "Old Republican Party" included not only Jews, Freemasons, Protestants, and *métèques* but also the majority of the French bourgeoisie. There were many wealthy middle-class Frenchmen who might have wished for a more conservative government and more repressive measures against the increasing threat of socialism, but few of them had any enthusiasm for a return to the Old Regime.

In the crises of the interwar period—especially in 1926, 1934, and 1936—wealthy conservatives who feared a Communist revolution turned to more modern types of extremist movements than the Action Française in order to prevent such a catastrophe. Maurras, too, was sensitive to the Communist danger. Nevertheless, he continued to insist that the hereditary monarchy alone could satisfy the interests of all Frenchmen, for the Republic catered only to the plutocracy. Maurras maintained that this group already had too much power, as was inevitable in a democracy, in which votes and men could be bought.[33] He shared the Socialists' resentment of government by the rich, and he opposed socialism on political rather than economic grounds. The nationalist monarchy, once it had purged this ideology of its egalitarian and cosmopolitan

---

[30] *La Démocratie religieuse,* p. 245.
[31] *Enquête,* p. 535.
[32] *Ibid.,* pp. 535–536.
[33] *Action Française,* August 1, 1921.

aspects, could, according to him, pursue a socialist policy,[34] in the sense of protecting the welfare of all classes and controlling economic competition.

Maurras championed the monarchy because, as a personal government, it would avoid the anonymity and anarchy of the existing regime and would prevent the state from falling into the hands of "Finance." [35] It is interesting that the prophet of counterrevolution should share the same feeling as Marx regarding the control of the bourgeois state by the wealthy capitalists. According to both thinkers, this control had come about as a result of nineteenth-century liberalism, with its emphasis on cutthroat competition. But Maurras was concerned with restoring a quasi-feudal society, not with creating a classless one based on an industrial economy. He said that democracy, in the name of abstract Liberty, suppressed individual liberties and ended in despotism.[36] The Liberty principle uprooted the individual from his family, his province, and his occupation for the benefit of the state.

It was only in these traditional structural contexts, Maurras believed, that the individual person was free to express himself and to feel secure. For this reason, in addition to calling for the rehabilitation of the family and diverse professional organizations, Maurras sought to restore the old provinces as centers of community activity. He wanted to undo the work of the Revolution, which had destroyed them and replaced them with artificial *départements*, which he called "the worst antiphysical mechanisms applied to the body of France." [37] The *département* prevented traditional local life from expressing itself. Hence it must be abolished, and the country's administrative divisions must again be made to conform to geog-

[34] *Gaulois, germains, latins* (Paris: Nouvelle Librairie Nationale, 1926), p. 171.
[35] *Kiel et Tanger*, p. 390.
[36] *La Démocratic religieuse*, p. 295.
[37] *La République et la décentralisation. Un Débat de 1903* (Paris: Nouvelle Librairie Nationale, 1923), p. 87.

raphy and history. The monarchy, Maurras claimed, was traditionally sympathetic to the idea of decentralization. This was certainly not true—even by the time of Richelieu and Louis XIV—but it was one of Maurras' favorite arguments for a restoration.

Maurras and his associates could not achieve their aims by parliamentary means; they knew that they could do so only by force.[38] "The crowd," Maurras wrote, "always follows. It follows energetic minorities, and these minorities make history." [39] He also said: "In the matter of method, doctrine, and the means as well as the end, the country, in its heart, is completely in accord with us." [40] The first of these statements is entirely in agreement with Maurras' temperament and his conception of the role of the elite. The second statement is a typical piece of Maurrassian hedging. There was no basis for claiming that even a sizable minority of the country was remotely sympathetic to the doctrines of the Action Française, much less "completely in accord" with its methods as well as its doctrine. The phrase "in its heart" constitutes the hedging. It implies that if people knew what was good for them they would support the Action Française.

The program of this movement was "to constitute a royalist state of mind and to prepare the *coup de force* for establishing the monarchy." [41] In practice, Maurras resembled Maurice Barrès in his hope of winning a section of the army to his cause—"We cannot help but succeed with the generals." [42] He maintained that he wanted a conservative revolution unified by an idea that was true [43] and that his proposed military coup was to differ from what he called "the mere *pronuncia-*

[38] *Enquête*, p. 418.
[39] *Ibid.*, p. 415.
[40] *Ibid.*, p. 419.
[41] *Si le coup de force est possible*, p. 567; this work appeared as a pamphlet in 1909 and was incorporated into an enlarged edition of the *Enquête* in 1925.
[42] *Ibid.*, p. 576.
[43] *Enquête*, pp. 420–423.

mientos of Spanish and South American generals." [44] Once the propaganda of the Action Française had persuaded enough high-ranking officers to march, that organization, along with the other reactionary groups in the country, would seize control of the government. Existing anti-Masonic and antisemitic forces would have the task of arresting those persons whom Maurras considered subversive. Meanwhile, the Action Française would concentrate its efforts exclusively on gaining control of the ministry of the interior, especially the communications centers. [45]

It is in his descriptions and analyses of different ways to overthrow the government that Maurras most clearly shows that he was somewhere between the traditional plotter of palace revolutions and the modern conspirator trying to set up a totalitarian dictatorship; that is to say, he was between the two types in temperament. The means he proposed and the consequences he contemplated are amazingly close to those of Lenin, Mussolini, and especially Franco.

Maurras always insisted that the fact that the Action Française had a doctrine made it different from other groups that were trying to overthrow the existing regime. The others failed, he maintained, because they had no fixed set of principles. [46] He reviewed the case of Boulanger in 1889 and the events of October 25, 1898, when General Chanoine, the minister of war, declared that Dreyfus was guilty and resigned from the chamber of deputies as an angry crowd rioted outside. Maurras also analyzed the failure of Déroulède and his followers to persuade a royalist general to march on the presidential palace on February 18, 1899. The February riots in 1934 failed too, according to Maurras, because the leagues that tried to destroy parliamentary institutions at that time had no consistent philosophy.

Neither Bonapartism nor fascism appealed to Maurras. He

[44] *Si le coup de force est possible*, p. 548.
[45] *Ibid.*, pp. 569–570.
[46] *Ibid.*, p. 559.

was wary of the man who, "for the moment or the second, was the master of some fraction of the public force on those days of ebullition when there is electricity in the air." [47] Not only did such a person lack any legitimate claim to power, but he and his followers could easily be bought by powerful financial groups, as was the case with Pierre Taittinger's Jeunesses Patriotes and François Coty's Solidarité Française in the 1920's and 1930's. Maurras said: "The elected dictator is the servant of the plutocracy, like Theodore Roosevelt, or the servant of public opinion, like Napoleon III. Our dictator must be the servant only of France, and such a man can only be the king." [48] This point of view, which was at first directed against the ideas of Paul Déroulède and later against the French fascists, clearly distinguishes Maurras from fascist theorists. What he and his disciples wanted was a dictator-King— a man who would resemble a modern dictator in his powers— as opposed to a constitutional monarch—but who, because of his traditional and legitimate claim to authority, would be independent of the plutocracy and the mob.

*

Maurras' formula for a sound social and economic organization was peace among the classes, hierarchy, and corporatism.[49] He blamed the Revolution for having perverted the natural functioning of French society by rejecting these principles. In replacing the authority of the king with popular elections and in trying to enforce legal equality, the democrats opened the door for economic class conflicts. It was because Maurras saw "the false political doctrine of democracy" at the root of contemporary social unrest [50] that he emphasized political change as the only way to restore the harmony of French society.

[47] *Ibid.*, p. 546.
[48] *Action Française*, April 7, 1908.
[49] *Gazette de France*, July 10, 1902.
[50] *Enquête*, p. 417.

This harmony had to be based on a hierarchical social structure in which everyone had certain duties and differentiated rights. The central government was to have no authority over the citizens without giving them an equivalent amount of local freedom. On the other hand, there was to be no liberty without a corresponding amount of responsibility.[51] The nobility was to be reconstituted, but it was to be open to all men with creative ability.[52] It would have a place for commoners like Maurras, so that once the monarchy was restored those intellectuals who were now working "in vain" for the public good would operate more effectively. They would serve the prince by guiding his thought and by enlightening the masses.[53]

This Maurrassian conception of the new nobility combined the old *noblesse de l'épée* (feudal nobility), the *noblesse de la robe* (middle-class magistrates of the king), and the *noblesse de la plume* (the intellectuals). Maurras had an obvious predilection for the latter. Indeed, there was a superficial resemblance between the kind of society he desired and imperial China—where the ruling class had also been composed of intellectuals—or ancient Babylon, Egypt, India, and Persia—where the priesthood, the "bearers of intellectualism," as Max Weber called them, had a strong influence on the rulers of those countries. According to Karl Wittfogel, the "bearers of intellectualism" in most oriental despotisms were part of a state apparatus that Maurras would have considered too "monolithic." He wanted *his* educated elite to be an independent force. Like many modern intellectuals, he believed that their function was to criticize the community in which they lived. But, when no one listened to them, they were tempted to dream of becoming the mandarin class or high priesthood in a utopia of their own making.

Maurras also wanted to rehabilitate the peasants and the working classes by making them property owners. He rec-

[51] *Ibid.*, p. 100.
[52] *Ibid.*, p. 98.
[53] *Ibid.*, p. 208.

ognized the merits of the captains of industry who, since the end of the eighteenth century, had created new riches. His main complaint against these bourgeois "dynasties" was that they had neglected the welfare of the working class [54] and had tried to monopolize all the wealth and political power. Maurras felt that the workers' demands for social justice were often "very human" [55] and essential for the preservation of the French race. He rejected Marxist proposals for satisfying these demands because Marxism was an internationalist ideology, whereas he believed that the nation-state was the natural political unit in the modern world. Instead of encouraging class warfare, he strove to integrate the French workers into the national economic and social structure by giving them some kind of property—that is, by "deproletarizing" them.[56]

According to Maurras, "there is no reason why the laws of peace among the classes should inspire less enthusiasm than the idea of their conflicts." [57] He repeatedly blamed the Third Republic for the poverty of the French working class and said that "there is no relationship between the republican form [of government] and the liberation of the proletariat." [58] The monarchy alone could free the workers because it would destroy one of the evils of the republic, namely, the exploitation of this group of Frenchmen by the class of politicians.

Maurras objected particularly to what he called the manipulation of the workers by the Socialists, for he maintained that the appearance of socialism in France at the turn of the twentieth century was "a political scandal, nothing more!" [59] The growth of Socialist parties may have been understandable in Germany, England, and Belgium but not in France, which was less industrialized than these countries. Socialist politi-

[54] *Action Française*, January 8, 1910.
[55] *Ibid.*, January 28, 1927.
[56] *Ibid.*, January 8, 1910.
[57] *Ibid.*, March 3, 1920.
[58] *Ibid.*, December 16, 1912.
[59] *Enquête*, p. 517.

cians were foreign to her labor movement, and the workers had a right not to be agitated and exploited by them.[60]

Despite their professed concern for the industrial workers, Maurras and his followers favored an agrarian economy, and their first consideration was for rural interests. Maurras tried to relate the two by saying that labor conditions could not be improved unless the lot of the peasants was ameliorated first. This was true, he insisted, because it was poverty in the rural areas that drove people to seek employment in urban industries, and these new competitors aggravated the existing hardships of the city workers. If this exodus from the country-side could be stopped, competition among the workers would cease.[61]

Actually, rural people were not deserting the French country-side for the reasons Maurras assumed. Those who left were mainly the sons and daughters of marginal farmers and arti-sans. They were not so much "pushed" by lack of economic opportunities at home (they would have stayed there had there been nowhere else to go) as they were "pulled" by the prospect of jobs elsewhere. There has been a shortage of labor in the dynamic sections of the French economy throughout most of the twentieth century, and there have been too many French-men engaged in agricultural pursuits, given the national market for their products. Far from neglecting the small farmers, the republican governments helped them to stay in business—albeit at a near subsistence level in many cases—by not making them pay their direct taxes and by putting up high tariffs against foreign competitors.

But Maurras' explanation of the "poverty" in rural France was that the peasants were being dispossessed by tax collectors and moneylenders.[62] He said that they had enjoyed full owner-ship of their land after their ancient communal rights had disappeared and that they now faced the novel situation of

[60] *Ibid.*, p. 57.
[61] *Ibid.*, p. 56.
[62] *Action Française*, July 8, 1908.

owning nothing, either personally, or in common. Here we see how Maurras shared the reactionary prejudice against mobile wealth. He charged that the over-centralized state mulcted the farmer with its heavy tax levies while the possessors of "anonymous and vagabond wealth"—who were mostly Jews—took what he had left in interest on loans and mortgages. The fact that the victim sometimes abandoned his farm altogether was bad for the defense of the fatherland—since the peasants were the backbone of the army—and it hurt the nation's productive capacity.

Reactionaries like Maurras spent much of their time attacking the democratic regime for causing the depressed condition of the masses, but they were really opposed to industrial society itself. Maurras himself recognized the fact that industrialization was the main cause of modern class strife when he spoke of this problem in imperial Germany during the late nineteenth century. As a matter of fact, he often pointed to Bismarck's labor laws as an example of how the social question could be solved under a monarchy. But the Bismarckian solution did not end social unrest in Germany, and Maurras had to look elsewhere in his search for the means of re-establishing class harmony in France. He found this in the Middle Ages. In that period the peasants, who were socially conservative, were the largest group in the country. If this situation could be restored, along with the monarchy, it would have a stabilizing effect on industrial relations and allow their organization along corporatist lines.

Corporatism occupied only a small place in Maurras' social philosophy. La Tour du Pin was its main French spokesman in the early twentieth century, but he was an active member of the Action Française for only a short time. Within the movement Firmin Baconnier expanded Maurras' ideas on this subject. Maurras himself favored the corporation (guild), not only because of the economic prosperity it gave to its members, but also because it integrated them socially.[63] Baconnier

[63] *Ibid.*, June 7, 1920.

added that the craftsman in his guild was a part of a larger economic community, the town, and that he had to serve its needs as well as his own. Indeed, he continued, "the rights of professional artisans are subordinate to the fulfillment of social and national duties." [64]

In modern times the organization that most closely resembled the medieval guild was the *syndicat*—the continental version of the trade-union. The syndicalists, like the Action Française theorists, wanted to reorganize France along occupational—or functional—lines, though, like the Socialists, they believed that there was an inevitable conflict of interests between the capitalist and working classes. Despite his abhorrence of class warfare, Maurras saw in syndicalism the germ of a corporative society.[65] Ultimately, according to him, the *syndicats* would have to include both employers and workers. He himself sought to achieve his goal of social harmony through the restoration of a class hierarchy—in which there was a horizontal solidarity—but he also believed that there was a kind of vertical solidarity between workers and employers in the same industry.[66]

With an apparent blindness to the impersonal, bureaucratic structure and functioning of a modern industrial firm, Maurras asserted that all men connected with the manufacture of a specific product were united by a common bond [67] and that this functional tie should be expressed structurally. Like the medieval craft guilds, the corporations advocated by the Action Française would provide retirement pensions, social services, recreation, and on-the-job training for their members.[68] The employers, in turn, would take an interest in their workers' welfare.

[64] *Le Salut par la corporation* (Paris: Les Œuvres Françaises, 1935), p. 10.
[65] *Mes Idées politiques*, p. 245.
[66] *Ibid.*, p. 221.
[67] *Action Française*, September 6, 1908.
[68] *Revue de l'Action Française*, IV (June 1901), 97–99.

Thus Maurras believed that the corporation would eliminate class conflict. Both the workers and the employers would
identify their interests with the "company," which, according
to corporatist theorists, is a kind of family. This notion has
recently appeared in the public relations bulletins of some
giant American industries—for example, the "Bell Telephone
family." But it is difficult to see the comparison between an
assembly-line worker and a medieval cobbler or between a contemporary business executive (Maurras would have called today's "organization man" a lackey of "Finance") and the
proprietor of a fourteenth-century shop. When Mussolini
tried to introduce corporatist forms into the Italian economy,
the net result was more state control. Maurras wanted to
avoid this as much as the chaos created by economic individualism.[69] He thought he had escaped both evils by accepting corporatism, but he had less to say about economics
than about most other subjects.

*

In order to be complete, Maurras believed that his monarchical, stratified, corporatist utopia needed one more ele-
ment—the Roman Catholic Church. He did not subscribe to
the principles of Christianity, and some of his colleagues
were also either avowed atheists or Catholics in name only.
Nevertheless, he respected the church because he believed that
it had preserved many pagan traditions in its ritual and
arrested the development of the anarchy implied in the Gospel
by the strong social consciousness it had inherited from the
Roman Empire. For him it was an external and visible authority, the embodiment of discipline, hierarchy, and order.[70]
These were the values that Maurras cherished, but they

[69] He agreed with La Tour du Pin, who said: "Le régime corporatif
est la seule manière de ne pas aller du libéralisme au socialisme"
(*Aphorismes de politique sociale* [Paris: Nouvelle Librairie Nationale,
1909], p. 20).
[70] *La Démocratie religieuse*, p. 177.

were not based on divine sanction. Although statements can be found in his writings that seem to indicate a concern for the need to curb human vices, such as selfishness, avarice, cupidity, and hatred, Maurras, like Comte—until his later years, when Comte developed a curious pseudoreligion of his own—felt that society, not God, was the authority regarding morality. In this respect Maurras differed from the traditional reactionary writers. The leader of the Action Française was a positivist —he was concerned with the natural rather than the supernatural order in the world. He openly acknowledged his debt to Comte for helping him to develop his method of social analysis, which he called "organizing empiricism." [71]

A moral philosophy without a religious foundation could have little appeal for practicing Catholics, and pious supporters of the Action Française prayed constantly for Maurras' conversion. But he stubbornly refused to compromise his atheism until he was on his death-bed, even when such a gesture might have saved his movement from the papal ban in 1926. His theory of society had no logical place for a supernatural God or for "sentimental" preaching. Maurras hated Christianity almost as much as Nietzsche did. He once told Louis Dimier: "With your religion you have dirtied the world in a most bizarre way for eighteen hundred years." [72]

Maurras was a clerical only because he was an authoritarian and a traditionalist. During the Vichy period he approved of Pétain's efforts to revive the family unit with the aid of the church. He also liked the emphasis on discipline and obedience to authority instilled in French boys and girls by the Catholic teaching orders. Finally, he shared the feeling, once expressed to him by Jules Lemaître, that the church was a part of France's cultural heritage: [73]

[71] "Trois idées politiques," in *Romantisme et révolution* (Paris: Nouvelle Librairie Nationale, 1925), pp. 261–262.
[72] Louis Dimier, *Vingt ans de l'Action Française et d'autres souvenirs* (Paris: Nouvelle Librairie Nationale, 1926), pp. 29–30.
[73] *Enquête*, p. 366.

Even when our religion will be no more than a memory, a sort of inherited emotional disposition, it will be as Catholics as much as Frenchmen that we shall feel ourselves different—without rancor, moreover—from Englishmen and North Germans.

In reality, Lemaître, Maurras, and the other intellectuals in the Action Française were more interested in political action than in religion. Throughout his life-long campaign for his ideal society Maurras subordinated religious, economic, and social questions to politics. He claimed that his doctrine of integral nationalism encompassed all the problems of France: [74]

That is why, without rejecting any eventual alliance, in adhering in advance to all those unions that are or that will be useful to the triple defense of religion, society, and the fatherland, in accepting them and in desiring them all, we hold to this program—politics first [*politique d'abord*] nationalist politics—the politics of integral nationalism.

Maurras' ideas regarding the church were therefore more closely related to the means of making his political philosophy prevail than to its basic values and goals.

*   *   *

Charles Maurras tried to construct a synthesis of counter-revolutionary doctrines in the form of a barrage of solid arguments and subtle ideas. His social thought expressed a set of reactionary attitudes that would not die in France. These were not only antidemocratic and anti-egalitarian but also anti-étatist. Maurras was the champion of those Frenchmen who felt insecure in a modern, impersonal political and economic structure. His program of federalism—or decentralization—reflected a desire to restore the hierarchical society of the medieval manor and town. He wanted to replace the agents of the central power—which, of course, had been developed by the monarchy beginning in the twelfth century—with municipal councils and regional assemblies in which the local

[74] *La Politique religieuse*, pp. 375–376.

aristocracies would be the controlling authorities.[75] Interpersonal relations would thereby be restored to France's political system.

Such a restoration would work only within a framework of stratification, privilege, and hereditary power. According to Maurras, these features, along with the inviolability of property—especially family property—are essential for an ordered and satisfying social life in France.[76] His conception of the union of property and power is feudal. It leads logically to a caste system in spite of the fact that he wanted to keep his privileged classes open to a few men of talent. (After all, even in the Middle Ages, such people could "rise" in the church.)

Maurras believed that only a society founded on the principles of authority, order, and hierarchy could avoid the ravages of class conflict and civil war. Civilization itself, according to him, was threatened by these evils, which were the inevitable consequences of the French Revolution. But again, one asks, what kind of civilization did Maurras prize most highly? If it were that of ancient Greece, he would have to look to Sparta—a Sparta favorable to the arts, though—for Athens in its heyday was a democracy. The Roman Republic at the time of Cicero also appealed to him, but it was a mere interlude of patrician ascendancy between the social strife under the Gracchi and the despotism of the Caesars. One must conclude, then, that despite his reverence for classical culture and the regime of Louis XIV Maurras championed an idealized version of the Middle Ages.

He wanted to restore a society of small producers who took pride in their craftsmanship and respected the sanctity of the family, of petty noblemen who played a paternal role toward the toiling masses, and of local governments that reflected a diversity of interests. Aside from his professed positivism and his advocacy of extremist tactics, Maurras clung

[75] *Action Française*, November 24, 1922.
[76] *Ibid.*, April 4, 1916.

to the values of the prerevolutionary tradition. The Action Française ideology, shorn of its invective and its casuistry, expresses a nostalgia for a hypothetical golden age. It is not of this world.

5

❖ ❖ ❖ ❖ ❖ ❖ ❖ ❖ ❖ ❖ ❖

Operation Action Française

Although writing was the main activity of Maurras and his cohorts, they did try to spread their ideas by other means as well. Beginning in the early 1900's, they sponsored public lectures in Paris and the provinces and study groups in the cafés of the Latin Quarter. Then, when the League of the French Fatherland disintegrated, they decided to form a similar organization of their own. They announced the foundation of the League of the Action Française in their review on January 15, 1905. This move made Maurras' movement the heir of the nationalists of the 1880's and 1890's and the progenitor of the fascists of the 1930's and 1940's.

With the formation of their own league, the café intellectuals of the Action Française entered the arena of political action. Those with a gift for oratory and organization made frequent trips to the provinces, where they set up branches and persuaded sympathetic reactionary groups to join them.[1] Leaguers were urged to spread the movement's ideas in their

[1] *Revue de l'Action Française,* XVI (January 1905), 86.

families, among their friends, and in their clubs and cafés. They promised to argue with their opponents and to be fearless in affirming their royalist faith and their certitude of a monarchical restoration. In addition, they agreed to answer every call from the pretender or from the Action Française for public demonstrations. One section of the new league began its activities by campaigning among the members of a local clerical group, and others soon followed this example.[2]

Yet the main function of the league throughout its lifetime was to reinforce the attitudes of its own members through the ritual of its periodic gatherings. Fearing the government's hostility toward reactionaries, they held their meetings secretly at first and took a solemn oath not to tell outsiders what was said at them. This kind of secrecy was abandoned within a year, though, and sympathetic nonmembers henceforth were invited to participate in the league's activities.

Meanwhile, the number of students who listened regularly to Maurras and his associates in the cafés of the Left Bank had grown considerably. In December 1905 Lucien Moreau, a wealthy dilettante and friend of Maurras, formed them into a group called the Students of the Action Française. Ordinarily they met twice a month in private rooms rented from restaurants or in small lecture halls. By the autumn of 1911 the Paris sections of the organization had seventy-two registered members, although a dozen of these were doing their military service and another dozen had remained at home for that academic year.[3]

The Institut de l'Action Française was the third organization created by Maurras and Vaugeois in 1905. Their initial purpose was to launch a series of public lectures on their doctrines and their adopted intellectual masters of the nineteenth century.[4] They began in March 1905 by sponsoring the

[2] *Ibid.* (February 1905), pp. 258–259.
[3] Archives Nationales, *Action Française*, F⁷12862, December 9, 1911.
[4] Ade Coudekerque-Lambrecht, *Léon de Montesquiou* (Paris: Nouvelle Librairie Nationale, 1925), p. 35.

geographer and archeologist August Longnon in a talk on Fustel de Coulanges, the medievalist who had proclaimed that France was a Roman and not a Germanic creation. The success of this meeting encouraged the movement's leaders to begin looking for a permanent lecture hall and funds for an institute. They found both in less than a year. The necessary financial support came from Baron Parseval and General Récamier, the leaders of a royalist group called Tradition-Progrès. This money paid the rent for a small auditorium in the Hall of the Learned Societies in the Latin Quarter.[5] Additional funds were garnered from paid admissions (but students were admitted free).

Louis Dimier, a teacher of rhetoric and classical languages in the Catholic Institute of Paris, became the director of the Institut de l'Action Française in March 1906, and chairs were set up for different subjects. The one for Nationalism was named after Maurice Barrès, and the one for the Provinces after Louis XI. Maurras discussed Organizing Empiricism under the self-assumed patronage of Sainte-Beuve. The chair for Positivism—so-called in honor of Auguste Comte—was held by the Comte Léon de Montesquiou-Fezenzac, the movement's first convert from high society. Several bishops [6] showed a favorable interest in the course of the *Syllabus*, in which the errors of modernism were "rectified." Dimier himself spoke on the counterrevolutionary philosophers of the nineteenth century, and a young literary critic named Pierre Lasserre gave periodic lectures aimed against the Romantic movement.

Some of these courses appeared in book form. The small printing firm that published them was subsidized and operated by Jean Rivain, a son-in-law of the Comtesse de Courville. He also brought his small reactionary coterie—the Groupe de

[5] Louis Dimier, *Vingt ans de l'Action Française et d'autres souvenirs* (Paris: Nouvelle Librairie Nationale, 1926), p. 93.
[6] Notable among them was the bishop of Montpellier, Monseignor de Cabrières, who later became a cardinal (*ibid.*, p. 99).

Joseph de Maistre—into the Action Française, and its members participated in the work of the institute.[7]

Like the other organizations of the movement, the institute functioned primarily as a means of reinforcing the members' attitudes, but it also tried to attract Parisian students who, according to the Action Française, were being led astray by the state schools. The lecturers set themselves the task of stamping out the "fallacy of democracy." They also wanted to counteract what they considered the "accumulation of weak lies that obscured the glorious accomplishments of the kings of France."[8] A few nationalist-minded youths came to these lectures to hear the point of view of their professors at the University of Paris refuted, especially in the immediate pre-war years.

French extremist movements like the Action Française often invited a "contradictor" to their public meetings. He delivered his own prepared or improvised attack on what the organization's leaders had said. Then there was an open discussion. The contradictor was not a mere devil's advocate but a real opponent. His function was to challenge the views of the audience, which was then reassured by hearing them publicly defended. The psychological effect of this kind of performance resembled that of a morality play.

*   *   *

Ritual meetings of the faithful were all very comforting, but Maurras and Vaugeois had always dreamed of spreading their message to the public through a newspaper. During the first few years of their movement's existence they had neither

[7] Ibid., p. 103. In 1910 Rivain founded the *Revue Critique des Idées et des Livres*, which included works by literary critics who were not members of the Action Française and which was read by people with diverse political views (Georges Valois, *Basile: Ou La Politique de la calomnie* [Paris: Georges Valois, 1927], p. xii).

[8] Léon Daudet, *Souvenirs des milieux littéraires, politiques, artistiques, et médicaux* (Paris: Nouvelle Librairie Nationale, 1920), II, 226–227.

the clientele, the money, nor the know-how to found one. By 1906, however, they were beginning to attract a larger following (see Chapter 6) and they had made a convert of Léon Daudet, one of France's most skilled journalists. After an unsuccessful attempt to buy Drumont's *Libre Parole*—which was going bankrupt—they accepted Daudet's help in establishing their own daily, the *Action Française*. From the day of its first issue (March 20, 1908), it was his newspaper as much as Maurras'. Not only did his articles gain readers for it, but he also provided the principal source of capital to get it started.

For Madame de Loynes (the ex-patroness of the League of the French Fatherland) had just died and left one hundred thousand francs to Daudet's wife, who gave them to her husband to launch the new publication.[9] In order to find additional funds, the movement's leaders met with the Marquise de MacMahon and her brother-in-law the Comte Eugène de Lur Saluces. Together they decided to make a public appeal in the *Revue de l'Action Française*,[10] and within a few weeks they managed to raise two hundred thousand francs from the review's six thousand subscribers and occasional readers.[11] Thus, with Madame de Loynes's legacy, the daily *Action Française* had a starting capital of three hundred thousand francs.

Daudet became the editor-in-chief, and Henri Vaugeois was given the title of political director. Maurras' name did not appear on the masthead, but he furnished the editorial on the front page every day as well as the review of the Parisian press. Doctor Joseph Maurras, Charles's brother, wrote a daily column on medicine under the pseudonym of Vesalius; Léon Allard, Daudet's father-in-law, was in charge of the section on agriculture, and Daudet's wife, writing under the name of Pampille, was the fashion editor. Frédéric Delebecque, a retired army officer, handled all matters concerning the Drey-

[9] *Ibid.*, p. 194.
[10] *Ibid.*, p. 197.
[11] Statement made by Maurice Pujo in a personal interview.

fus Affair, and Pierre Lasserre contributed articles on literary criticism. The administration of the newspaper was in the hands of Bernard de Vésins,[12] a recruit from clerical circles.

From the beginning the *Action Française* employed almost every type of muckraking, sensationalism, and mudslinging known to the yellow press. Its editors had two sets of needs to satisfy—the need of a partisan league to attract support and the need of a newspaper to keep up its circulation. As Maurice Pujo put it: [13]

> The only means at all efficacious for making oneself heard will be to disturb the false public order, which masks scandal, and to create the opportune news item that will bring this scandal into the broad daylight of the street. This will force the other newspapers to acknowledge it and will make the authorities do something about it.

But, like the other agencies of the movement, the *Action Française* also gave comfort and reassurance to its own followers.

Besides the government itself, the *Action Française* had several stock scapegoats: Jews, foreign residents in France—Maurras called them *métèques*, and this word soon came into general usage—Freemasons, and Dreyfusards. Unfavorable news reports involving Jews appeared in almost every issue. In April 1908, for example, Vaugeois publicized the poisoning of a soldier from tubercular meat furnished to the army by a Jewish packing house. His comment was: "We have decided to eliminate their poison. And they know that for us that poison is themselves, their race, and nothing else, so now they are given notice." [14] A month later the newspaper began its periodic attacks on the foreigners in the Latin Quarter, accusing them of all sorts of subversive activities and demanding their surveillance by the police.

[12] *Action Française*, March 20, 1938; article by Daudet on the occasion of the thirtieth anniversary of the newspaper.
[13] Maurice Pujo, *Les Camelots du Roi* (Paris: E. Flammarion, 1933), p. xvi.
[14] *Action Française*, April 7, 1908.

The Masonic organization had often been condemned by the church for its occult rites and oaths, and the *Action Française* could always attack it when other issues were lacking. One of its tactics was to print sensational articles written by renegade Masons. These exposés bore such titles as "Behind the Locked Doors of Masonry" or "I Was a Mason!" In addition, the newspaper staff published a book giving the names and addresses of thirty thousand Masons in France. This list was supposed to reveal to all true Frenchmen the identity of the conspirators who controlled the country's destiny by hidden means. There was just enough truth in this charge to make it seem plausible.

In its campaigns to keep anti-Dreyfusard feelings alive the *Action Française* combined slanted news reports with public demonstrations and manufactured symbols. The movement had already begun rehashing the Affair in July 1906 when the supreme appellate court overruled the Rennes court-martial and vindicated Captain Dreyfus. A few weeks later he had also been made a Chevalier of the Legion of Honor. From then on the Action Française condemned every effort of the government to honor him and his defenders. Whenever a statue of a former Dreyfusard was being dedicated somewhere, it sent its forces to the scene to heckle the speakers and ridicule the ceremony. In April 1908 its newspaper also sponsored a nationwide subscription campaign to buy a commemorative medal for General Mercier, whom it called "the justiciar of the traitor Dreyfus." [15]

Maurras and his cohorts knew that this kind of agitation would have no significant effect; their avowed purpose was to gain publicity by provoking the state to prosecute them.[16] They challenged it directly by publishing a letter of Major Cuignet (one of the judges at the Rennes court-martial) in which he charged that the supreme appellate court had falsified Article 445 of the legal code when it had exonerated

[15] *Ibid.*, April 15, 1908.
[16] Archives Nationales, *Action Française*, F⁷12862, December 18, 1907.

Dreyfus. The editors of the *Action Française* printed the text of the code and what they called the falsified version side by side—along with Major Cuignet's letter—every day from June 1908 to August 1914. Zealots of the movement also posted clippings of this item all over France. The government was supposed to react to such provocation, but it did nothing. Consequently, the leaders of Action Française decided to send someone to insult the president and judges of the high court itself while it was in session.[17]

* * *

The annals of the Action Française are filled with epic gestures, one of which, at least according to Maurice Pujo,[18] instigated the founding of the Camelots du Roi in November 1908. Pujo was referring to the incident in which Maxime Réal del Sarte, a student at the École des Beaux Arts, interrupted the proceedings of the supreme appellate court by decrying its exoneration of Dreyfus and its alleged falsification of the legal code in his favor. Sarte's gesture (which had been instigated by the leaders of the Action Française) was followed up a few days later when a young royalist named Henry des Lyons and four or five of his companions paraded through the corridors of the Palais de Justice carrying placards denouncing the high court (Pujo was there too). These youths had previously been selling the *Gazette de France* in front of their neighborhood churches. Then, on November 16, they joined some of the student members of the Action Française to form the Camelots du Roi—hawkers of the king.

Although the fashionable members of the royalist committees hoped to keep the Camelots under their control, the leaders of the Action Française integrated them into their movement. By doing so they were able to supervise the boys who were not members of their own student group.[19] Henry

[17] *Ibid.*, September 17, 1908.
[18] Pujo, *op. cit.*, pp. 33–34.
[19] *Ibid.*, p. 208.

des Lyons was made secretary of the Camelots; Maxime Réal del Sarte became its president, and Maurice Pujo coordinated its operations with the needs of the league. The activities of the Camelots gave the Action Française most of its notoriety. Without them it would never have been anything more than a coterie of café intellectuals.

After having gained as much royalist and clerical support as it could get in the years 1905–1908 (see pp. 122–123), the Action Française wanted to attract additional followers among France's conservative patriots; it also had to give the Camelots du Roi something to do besides selling newspapers. The leaders of the only surviving nationalist league decided to serve both purposes by starting a campaign to glorify Joan of Arc as the symbol of French patriotism. Their opportunity came when one of her detractors, Professor Thalamas of the Lycée Condorcet, was scheduled to give a series of eight lectures at the Sorbonne in November 1908.

Thalamas had already become a controversial figure for his "debunking" of Joan and her exploits, and the Action Française was not going to allow him to defame France's most glorious heroine in the halls of her greatest university. A contingent of Camelots and Students of the Action Française broke up Thalamas' first lecture with whistles and catcalls. Thereafter the police and the university authorities tried to control access to the auditorium in order to prevent further disturbances. But some of the Students of the Action Française knew the secret byways of the Sorbonne and managed to get in from the roof. As a crowning act of defiance, they dashed up to the podium and gave the professor a sound thrashing. A few days later Maurice Pujo decided that he would give a course of his own to counteract Thalamas' lies. His Camelots dispossessed a Latin professor from one of the classrooms in the university for him, but the police soon stepped in and stopped his performance.[20] During the next three months the university community was divided into two

[20] Coudekerque-Lambrecht, op. cit., p. 400.

hostile camps, the Thalamists and the reactionary nationalists.[21] This episode was the first of a long series in which the
Action Française used the Camelots to attract nationalist support.

The Camelots usually confined their operations to the Latin
Quarter, but they sometimes ventured into the boulevards of
the Right Bank. On one such occasion a group of them broke
the window of an "English-Jewish" shop because they claimed
that there was a caricature of Joan of Arc displayed in it.[22]
A typical day for the Camelots in the early weeks of 1909 included rallies against Thalamas at the Sorbonne, street fights
with the Thalamists, and demonstrations in front of Dreyfus'
house, accompanied by cries of "Down with the traitor." Pujo,
Sarte, and other leaders of the group were put in jail several
times. Those Camelots who succeeded in escaping arrest went
on to the statues of Joan of Arc in various parts of the city or
to the statue of the city of Strasbourg in the Place de la Concorde. In the evening they frequently assembled in front of
the office of the *Action Française* and cheered its editors.[23]

During the excitement of the Thalamas affair, a number of
youths joined the Camelots mainly because of their desire for
action and rowdyism rather than their devotion to the royalist
cause. Typical of these were twenty young idlers who had belonged to a group called the Action Royaliste du Quartier
Latin. The leaders of the Action Française persuaded them to
join the Camelots and bought them drinks and meals on the
days of their demonstrations.[24] These young rowdies soon
presented a serious problem when it became apparent that
they expected some sort of financial reimbursement for their
"services." In June 1909 there was a "purge" within the ranks
of the Camelots. Pujo claims that the reason for expelling
certain members was that they had frequented ill-famed dance

[21] *Action Française, Temps, Matin,* February 6, 1909.

[22] Pujo, *op. cit.,* p. 141.

[23] *Ibid.,* pp. 147–148.

[24] Archives Nationales, *Action Française,* F⁷12862, December 21, 1908.

halls; but he also admitted that police spies and vagrants had to be weeded out constantly.[25]

After the "purge," the Association of the Camelots du Roi required the absolute devotion of its members to the royalist cause. A Camelot had to be at least eighteen years old and he had to have a steady form of employment. Before he was admitted to membership, an investigation was made of his identity, occupation, family, the political organizations to which he had belonged, and the amount of time he could devote to the movement. He had to promise to sell the *Action Française* each Sunday at a location that would be assigned to him after he had obtained a vendor's license.

Those Camelots who lost their jobs because they were arrested while acting on behalf of the movement were given temporary assistance from a special fund named after Joan of Arc, but they had to find work quickly.[26] When they came to the office of the newspaper to ask the editors to find them employment, Vaugeois and Daudet were never there to receive them. These Camelots then created a disturbance in the corridors of the building in which the movement had its headquarters, shouting that the leaders of the Action Française were "phonies" (*fumistes*).[27] In order to get rid of them, members of the staff took their names and addresses and promised to notify them as soon as jobs were available. One means of seeking positions for them was a special help wanted section in the *Action Française*.

The Camelots, especially the section in Paris, experienced many internal intrigues, scandals, and rivalries for leadership. Members shifted from one royalist organization to another and engaged in the sort of recriminations that are so common among rival extremists. Even a loyal Camelot was disciplined when he became involved in some moral scandal or when he was delinquent in his assigned duties. For the latter offense

[25] Pujo, *op. cit.*, p. 149.
[26] *Revue de l'Action Française*, XXVIII (January 1909), 84.
[27] Archives Nationales, *Action Française*, F⁷12862, April 8, 1909.

he was usually barred for a month from the meetings of the Camelots and from the office of the newspaper. Such punishment was a disgrace and a frustration to a youth who had adjusted himself to the values of the group. When the misconduct was of a moral nature, such as homosexual acts, the culprits were thrown out permanently.[28] A considerable number of Camelots lived by selling the *Action Française* every day in the streets. When they were "off duty," they frequently loitered around the offices of the newspaper—which they substituted for local pool rooms—and were on hand for any kind of dirty work that might be demanded of them.[29]

But the official role of the Camelot was to sell the *Action Française* and royalist tracts. In this way he proved his devotion to the cause. The monotonous and often unpleasant task of hawking newspapers on a Sunday morning was supposed to make him diligent and give him practice in maintaining possession of the street. His other functions were of two kinds: policing the meetings of the Action Française and taking part in the movement's diverse public demonstrations.[30] In 1909 the Camelots had a national organization with sixty-five sections throughout France. The Paris area listed six hundred members, of whom only about one hundred and fifty were active.[31]

Within the structure of the Camelots the Action Française in 1910 created a special group "destined to form the cadres of troops for use in all possible eventualities." [32] It was called the Commissaires of the Action Française, and in some ways it may be considered a precursor of the fascist strong-arm gangs of later years. The Commissaires maintained order at

[28] Archives Nationales, *Camelots du Roi*, F⁷12864, April 25, 1913.
[29] *Ibid.*, January 23, 1911.
[30] *Revue de l'Action Française*, XXXIII (December 1910), 544.
[31] Archives Nationales, *Camelots du Roi*, F⁷12864, November 28, 1909.
[32] Émile Brun, ex-national delegate for the southeast section of the National Federation of the Camelots du Roi; *Révélations sur les organisations de l'Action Française* (Paris: pamphlet, published privately, 1936), p. 3.

meetings in the working-class suburbs of Paris, especially
against attacks and interruptions by Socialists and other enemies. Maxime Réal del Sarte and Marius Plateau (an errand
boy in the Paris Bourse) organized the more muscular members of the movement into "task forces." The Action Française bought a small island in the Seine for them and fitted
it out for use as a training center. There the Commissaires
and the Camelots held "tactical exercises" and athletic contests, and whenever they were called out for demonstrations
they carried lead-filled canes and bludgeons.[33] For high school
students who were not old enough to be Camelots a club
called the Lycéens of the Action Française was formed.

These young rowdies gained notoriety in February 1911
when they tried to stop the presentation of Henri Bernstein's
Après-Moi at the Théâtre Français. In addition to being a
Jew, Bernstein had deserted the army during his period of
military service. The Camelots and Lycéens vowed not to allow their national theater to be desecrated by such an author,
and they interrupted the opening performance of his play by
hooting him until the police threw them out. For the next
few nights they demonstrated outside, though a few of them
managed to get past the guards at the door. Once inside they
harassed the actors by interjecting facetious comments into
their dialogue. Each night the crowd in front of the theater
grew larger and attracted "patriots" who were not connected
with the movement. Bernstein fought duels with Daudet and
other Action Française leaders, but the government finally
persuaded him to withdraw Après-Moi from the boards.

The Bernstein affair ended in a much vaunted victory for
the Camelots du Roi [34] and helped them to become the self-
styled defenders of the reactionary nationalist cause in France.
In addition to posing as the knightly champions of the king,
they tried to "steal the thunder" of the other antisemitic, antidemocratic, and antiforeign organizations. Their chivalric de-

[33] Archives Nationales, *Camelots du Roi*, F⁷12864, March 11, 1912.
[34] *Action Française*, February 11–26, 1911.

fense of Joan of Arc from attack by the secular, bourgeois, and prosaic functionaries of the republican government earned them the secret admiration of many Frenchmen who disliked the existing regime for one reason or another.

*　*　*

Throughout the history of the Action Française its leaders remained a group of professional reactionaries in royalist and nationalist trappings. Maurras, Vaugeois, and Daudet were not genteel *bien-pensants* pining for the good old days under Louis XVI or Charles X. They flaunted their newly acquired devotion to the monarchy and the church like converts to all putative panaceas from Marxism to psychoanalysis. Though they posed as superpatriots, they hated much of the French way of life and were proud of their classification by the Sureté Générale as "subversives." They were "I'd-rather-be-right" and "comes-the-revolution" zealots, intolerant even of like-minded people who did not accept every point in their own narrow ideology. At the same time they were ready to make tactical alliances with all kinds of extremists against their current enemies and former friends.

Whenever possible, the Action Française followed a policy of "favoring the worst" (*politique du pire*). In practice, this meant that its attacks were far more intense against the moderate republicans than against the Left-wing extremists. Although they were poles apart ideologically and temperamentally, the reactionary Right and the revolutionary Left were both out to destroy the bourgeois republic. This common purpose encouraged the Action Française and the Socialists to follow the same propaganda line during the railroad strike of October 1910. Along with Jaurès' *Humanité* and Gustave Hervé's *Guerre Sociale*, the *Action Française* attacked Prime Minister Briand for using troops against the strikers and criticized the bankers and administrators of the railroads—especially the Rothschilds. But such alliances died as quickly as they had come into being.

Innumerable examples could be given of incidents used by Maurras and his associates for attacking the government. They range all the way from the first Moroccan crisis in 1905 to the spectacular theft of the "Mona Lisa" from the Louvre in 1911. On this occasion the *Action Française* began its campaign by blaming the administration of the museum for not having enough guards. It contended that this deplorable situation was the result of Jewish influence, since the museum's director had been a Dreyfusard.[35] Later it tried to discredit the ministry of the interior and its law-enforcement agents for not having caught the thieves.[36] Such chiding of the police for its failure to solve a crime made good journalistic copy and attracted readers who liked to see the government ridiculed.

*

The leaders of the Action Française were happiest in their role as critics, but they felt obliged to live up to the "action" in their name by plotting the overthrow of the hated republican regime. Instead of actually *doing* anything, though, Maurras wrote a book called *Si le Coup de Force Est Possible* with Colonel Larpent and Major Delbecque. Fifteen thousand copies of it were bought within a year of its publication in 1909, and even the *Enquête sur la Monarchie* had not outsold it by 1920.[37] This popularity is understandable, since the *coup de force* was the event for which all members of the movement were planning and hoping. In their book Maurras and his coauthors examined different methods of overthrowing governments and finally decided on a revolt led by a group of generals who had been properly indoctrinated.[38] While

[35] *Ibid.*, August 23, 1911.
[36] *Ibid.*, March 30, 1912.
[37] *Enquête sur la monarchie*, p. 236.
[38] *Si le coup de force est possible*, in the 1929 edition of the *Enquête*, p. 577.

Daudet, Maurras, and Vaugeois worked on the top brass in the army, the members of the league were to help prepare other reactionaries for this event by spreading the movement's propaganda throughout the country.[39]

Many traditional royalists did not want to see France "liberated" by these hotheads. As *bien-pensants* they deplored Maurras' crude brand of antisemitism and the rowdyism of the Camelots. Their objections were the main cause of a temporary rift between the Action Française and the pretender's political bureau in the winter of 1910–1911. Maurras and his friends were furious when this happened and, succumbing to their own propaganda, blamed the Jews for persuading the Duc d'Orléans to rebuke them. They were determined to put him on the throne of his ancestors in spite of himself. Hence the national and regional leaders of their movement circulated rumors that action was being taken to bring about the restoration very soon. This tactic won back the support of some royalists, and it persuaded the pretender not to repudiate his self-appointed champions. But it was clear that he and his followers were unwilling allies of the Action Française.

Although the café intellectuals who ran this movement wanted to preserve their role as free-lance prophets, they needed money to spread their message. Maurras was no Isaiah, whose aristocratic birth and connections at the royal court in Jerusalem had assured him of a hearing among influential people. Like other twentieth-century propagandists, Maurras had to work through the mass media of communication, and these were expensive. Since his daily newspaper did not pay its own way, it had to be subsidized by membership dues from the league, subscription campaigns, collections at annual conventions, and private donations. Wealthy royalists occasionally made contributions ranging from three hundred to ten thou-

---

39 *Ligue de l'Action Française, groupe Picard; "Ce que nous voulons," Conférence faite le 10 mars 1912 par Maurice Dupont* (Amiens: 1912, privately printed pamphlet), p. 17.

sand francs,[40] but these gifts were the movement's most uncertain source of income.

Until 1914 the *Action Française* conducted a continuous fund-raising drive "against Jewish gold." In 1908 it collected almost twenty-six thousand francs, in 1909, thirty-six thousand, in 1910, sixty-nine thousand, in 1911, fifty-six thousand —the rift with the pretender in early 1911 accounts for this decline—and in 1912, ninety-six thousand.[41] The newspaper published lists of names and amounts received regularly, stating that the money raised in this way was used to give subscriptions to the *Action Française* at reduced rates to clubs, cafés, clergymen, students, and workers.[42] The antisemitic country gentry were the main contributors to this fund. They believed that by helping to spread Maurras' doctrines among the common people they were creating sympathy for royalism and hostility against the parvenu Jewish capitalists who were allegedly running the Republic.

These petty contributions supported only a fraction of the movement's needs, and it was constantly having financial difficulties. It got money from Madame Lebaudy by preserving the memory of her late friend Gabriel Syveton in annual celebrations.[43] Another means of augmenting its revenue was to collect funds for a gold medal to be given to some hero of the reactionary cause. In the autumn of 1910, for example, its leaders had a Camelot named Lucien Lacour strike Briand in the face and then claimed that by doing this he had struck a blow against the Republic. The medal for which Maurras' followers were sending in their francs was not purchased for more than a year, and it cost only a fraction of the sum raised.[44]

[40] Archives Nationales, *Action Française*, F⁷12862, August 13, 1913.
[41] *Action Française*, March 21, 1913.
[42] *Ibid.*
[43] *Ibid.*, December 20, 1908, and December 9, 1909.
[44] Archives Nationales, *Action Française*, F⁷12862, January 6, 1912. According to these police records, the directors of the newspaper spent one hundred and sixty thousand francs in 1911. Most of this money had been used to pay the expenses of moving to a new office.

In May 1914 Maurras appealed directly to his readers for help,[45] but it was Vaugeois who finally raised the needed funds privately.[46]

* * *

Besides the league and the Camelots du Roi, the Action Française had two female auxiliary organizations: the Dames de l'Action Française and the Jeunes Filles Royalistes. The former was founded by the Marquise de MacMahon at the time of the church inventories in 1906. Most of its members had been associated with the royalist committees of the Comte de Chambord and the Comte de Paris, and nearly all of them were members of the aristocracy. Their chief role was *bienfaisance*—"doing good" for the needy. The Action Française encouraged them to combine their charity meetings with lectures on royalism. They also raised funds for the dissemination of the movement's ideas by increasing membership fees and by organizing artistic evenings at which they asked for contributions.[47] Finally, like the members of the league, they tried to convert their acquaintances to Maurras' doctrines.

The Jeunes Filles Royalistes became a subsidiary of the Dames de l'Action Française soon after it was founded. Antoinette de Montlivault had organized its first section by uniting some pious girls in the Loire region who called themselves the Noëlistes.[48] In 1908 there were twenty-five sections of the Jeunes Filles Royalistes in France and by 1910 there were seventy-two, with a total of thirty-six hundred members.[49] These girls took part in their mothers' charity affairs, afternoon lectures, and artistic evenings. They were "boosters"

[45] *Action Française*, May 14, 1914.
[46] Maurras, *Tombeaux*, p. 157.
[47] *Dames de l'Action Française* (Paris, 1911, pamphlet), p. 4.
[48] Statement by Louis Gonnet (secretary to Maurras before 1914 and administrative director of the Action Française during the Vichy period) in a personal interview.
[49] *Revue de l'Action Française*, XXXIII (December 1910), 498.

rather than active propagandists, though they occasionally distributed leaflets.

These ladies' auxiliaries participated in the national congresses of the league, the first of which was held at the Hall of the Learned Societies in Paris in December 1907. More than a hundred persons attended, including delegates from the provinces.[50] First Mademoiselle de Montlivault spoke about the activities of her royalist girls. Following her report, the Comtesse de Larègle described the work of the Dames Royalistes, an organization that was directly associated with the royalist committees of the pretender and that should not be confused with the Dames de l'Action Française. The progress being made in organizing sections in the provinces was also discussed. Then a delegate from the Finistère in Brittany told of the campaign of the Action Française in that area and claimed that the antiroyalist forces and the local clergy were united in hindering the distribution of its propaganda.

The representative from the section in Roubaix, an industrial town in northern France, told the convention that his group was neither academic nor aristocratic but proletarian. He seemed to be implying that most of the other sections were largely academic or aristocratic and that his own was therefore different. This man lamented the absence of people in the liberal professions who might have given vigorous leadership to his section. He went on to explain how its members spread the ideas of the Action Française by passing out leaflets containing statements of the pretender to the workers at the factory gates. They also sold their local royalist weekly, the *Reveil Français*, at all public meetings of Catholic welfare and charity groups and at gatherings in honor of the archbishop or prominent officials.[51]

Provincial sections of the league were supposed to respond spontaneously to their own problems and were theoretically bound only by the general principles of the Action Française.

[50] *Ibid.*, XXXI (December 1909), 476.
[51] *Ibid.*, XXVIII (January 1908), 43.

Actually, the leaders in Paris wanted to control the whole royalist movement in France. A government security agent gives the following eyewitness account of the national convention of the league in 1910: [52]

The congress was not a congress in the sense of being essentially a conference of delegates for the purpose of settling issues and debating on important questions. At the congress of the Action Française, the members come from the provinces to receive instructions set up in advance. . . . They are expected to approve them without discussion. . . . All the reports had been reserved . . . for the members of the directing committee of the Action Française in Paris or for its most loyal lieutenants in the provinces. All these reports were submitted in advance to Maurras for his approval.

It would be false to say that the congress discussed anything or that it approved anything. Its delegates were told "what we have done is good, that is what you must think." They said yes, and that is all.

This shows the will of the Action Française to apply the principle of authority and centralization.

The whole congress was directed toward the following goal: to dazzle the people who came from the provinces, to persuade them of the vitality of the Action Française and of the great results that its power had achieved—to gain their support, to give them confidence, and to stimulate their fanatical devotion to the headquarters in Paris. This goal was attained by and large.

This police spy goes on to discuss the composition of the congress:

Of the provincial delegates, about half (around thirty) consisted of very young men, incapable of any serious influence or of achieving any important local successes. Among the other half of the provincial delegates about two-thirds were serious people between thirty and forty-five. About ten of them were reserve officers in the army. The remaining third of the second half were old men, too far gone for the cause to have any influence.

A total of three hundred people probably attended the congress, but of that number, at least two hundred and twenty were Parisians, many of whom just stopped in for one session. I did not

[52] Archives Nationales, *Action Française*, F⁷12862, December 6, 1910.

see many of the same faces at the different sessions. Without any bluffing, the total number of people who came from the provinces expressly for the congress was not more than sixty.

Here is my general impression of the congress. There is no doubt that it was a success. It constituted a step forward for the Action Française . . . and reflected important gains made by the movement in the country since the previous year. The enthusiasm of the delegates was greatly increased and bordered on religious mysticism. This enthusiasm is taking more and more as its object the personality of Maurras and his lieutenants, and less and less the royalist idea.

The prejudices of this man, who was probably about thirty-five or forty years old, are evident in his account, and some of the conclusions he draws from his observations are unwarranted. Nevertheless, it may be assumed that the observations themselves are trustworthy. They indicate that the Action Française made exaggerated claims regarding the composition of the movement and the number of provincial delegates who attended the national convention. The agent's remark about the importance of Maurras to the movement's pattern of response is especially significant.

*　*　*

Before the formation of the League of the Action Française in 1905 the leaders in Paris had to rely on local royalist committees and on their own speakers who went on lecture tours to spread their ideas in the provinces. They had almost no control over the organizations through which they worked and they had to depend on the voluntary cooperation of these groups for the success of their own undertakings. The usual procedure was to work with a member of an existing royalist association or weekly newspaper. For example, Marie de Roux organized a series of lectures in Poitiers in 1904 and invited members of the Action Française from Paris to speak to the local supporters of the pretender.[53] Marie de Roux lived in the Poitiers area and had many friends there. He had adopted the

[53] *Revue de l'Action Française*, XV (October 1904), 89.

ideas of the Action Française after contact with acquaintances in Paris who were already active sympathizers. When the league was finally organized, he became one of its regional leaders in western France.

In the eastern part of the country Hubert Bailly, the editor of the *Reveil de la Haute-Saône*, had been pleading the royalist cause at Besançon. He founded the *Brigade de Fer*, which he called the "weekly organ of integral nationalism in Franche-Comté," in 1904. In it he published some of the propaganda tracts of the Action Française and actively supported their ideas. When a section of the Camelots du Roi was formed in Franche-Comté in 1909, its members sold the *Brigade de Fer* and the *Action Française* every Sunday.[54]

Among the most important provincial newspapers that worked with the *Action Française* were the *Soleil du Midi* in Marseilles, the *Nouvelliste de Bordeaux*, and the *Éclair* in Montpellier. These publications had a small but steady following many years before the Action Française founded its own daily, and they often reprinted speeches made by the editors of the *Revue de l'Action Française*. Some of the local noblemen in western France also tried to establish study circles in which royalist ideas inspired by the Action Française would be aired. One such group, called the Action Royaliste Populaire, was organized in Nantes within the framework of the already existing Association of the Chouans of Brittany.[55]

In their relations with the provincial royalist press Maurras and Daudet had the advantages of journalistic talent and prestige. Most of these local publications were traditionalist in tone and exceedingly dull in content. Their subscribers did not need to be converted to monarchism by pseudoscientific arguments, and their publishers made little effort to win new followers. By 1909, however, the Action Française had gained

[54] *Une Campagne royaliste en Franche-Comté; compte-rendu des travaux de la fédération régionale des Camelots du Roi du Doubs et de la Haute Saône* (Besançon, 1911, privately printed pamphlet), p. 1.
[55] *Revue de l'Action Française*, XV (October 1904), 91.

control of several of them, including the *Vérité Politique* in Chambéry, the *Mémorial des Pyrénées* in southwestern France, the *Espérance du Peuple* in Nantes, the *Nord Royaliste* in Rouen, and the *Midi Royaliste* in Marseille.[56] It was also able to place "canned" editorials and articles in other periodicals of this type from time to time.

A number of provincial royalist groups never joined the League of the Action Française but attached themselves to it as affiliates. This form of association was chosen by the Jeunesse Royaliste Lorraine and the Comité Havrais d'Études Historiques.[57] The league itself had more than two hundred sections and subsections in 1912,[58] a figure that was not surpassed until after the First World War and does not include the Camelots du Roi.

*

In order to show how the Action Française functioned outside of Paris, several of its local sections are discussed in some detail in the following pages. The first example is a group of Camelots du Roi in Franche-Comté.[59] In May 1909 students in Besançon organized a royalist youth club called the Avant-Garde Royaliste de Franche-Comté. A few months later they joined the National Federation of the Camelots du Roi. In addition to selling the *Action Française*, they sold two locally owned royalist weeklies, distributed leaflets, and put up posters in public places. Their headquarters had a window at the street level, which was used for displaying books, notices, news items, and photographs. Caricatures of prominent government officials—especially Briand—scenes from the life of Joan of

---

[56] *Action Française*, September 23, 1911.
[57] *Revue de l'Action Française*, XVI (March 1905), 368, and XVII (June 1905), 168.
[58] *Ibid.*, XXXVII (December 1912), 23.
[59] *Une Campagne royaliste en Franche-Comté*; this account was written by René Parmentier, the president of the group; all information concerning this campaign comes from this source.

Arc, and a bust of the Orleanist pretender were permanent items in the display. The headquarters also served as a small library and lecture room. Usually the speakers were local leaders of the Camelots, although occasionally Action Française personnel from Paris came to inspire the group.

A study circle was also set up in Besançon. Examples of the topics it discussed were "The Dreyfus Affair," "Nietszche and his Morality," "The Crimes of the Third Republic," and "Freemasonry and the Army." These provincial discussion groups were even more pseudointellectual in character than those in the capital. The subjects treated and the limited nature of the reading material used indicate the unscientific and partisan attitude of the people who participated in them. Although the Action Française had its share of symbols and public demonstrations, its members, especially those in the provinces, utilized the study circle as a means of communion with the rationalized prejudices of Maurras that held them together.

Besides the group in Besançon with its fifty members, there was a branch of twenty-five Camelots in nearby Vesoul and another hundred in six subsections of the Regional Federation in Franche-Comté. Thus in this fairly populous and decidedly clerical province of eastern France there were about two hundred Camelots du Roi.

René Parmentier, the guiding spirit and president of the Federation of the Camelots du Roi in this region, was a student at the University of Besançon and a member of a local chapter of the Jeunesse Catholique (see p. 159). Its sponsor, Abbé Marmier, reprimanded Parmentier for his royalist activities and threatened to exclude him from the group if he did not renounce them. Parmentier then criticized the abbé and the Jeunesse Catholique for playing partisan politics on the side of the conservative republicans. The incident created a minor scandal in bien-pensant circles in Besançon and was a typical example of the friction that existed between the Action Française and rival Catholic organizations. Parmentier and his friends finally resigned from the Jeunesse Catholique and declared that by working for the return of the monarchy they were doing more than it was to reestablish the faith of their fathers.

In Franche-Comté the demonstrations of the Camelots followed the usual pattern: celebration of the anniversary of Joan of Arc, hissing "radical" politicians and republican dignitaries who passed through Besançon, and interruption of "antipatriotic" gatherings. The leaders of the local Camelots were sometimes arrested for their activities but they were usually released on probation. In December 1910 the group was invited by the Archbishop of Besançon to a Mass given at the end of a diocesan congress. It was even allowed to bring its special flag along. Such a situation—in which the lower clergy disapproved of the Camelots and the prelates favored them—was not uncommon in other parts of the country.

In central France a section of the League of the Action Française was founded at Chalons-sur-Saône in the spring of 1910.[60] The Marquise de MacMahon and Bernard de Vésins came from Paris to speak before it in February 1911. A few months later the group invited Dom Besse, a Benedictine monk who wrote for the *Action Française*, to give a series of lectures along with two law professors from the Catholic University in Lyon. Members of the regional committee of the Duc d'Orléans listened to these speakers and some of them soon became active in the league.

By the end of 1912 the local branch of the Action Française had enough support to sponsor lectures in the suburbs of Chalons. Their titles included "The Democratic Republic against the Fatherland," "The Monarchy of Public Safety," "The Monarchy and Syndicalism," "The Professional Vote or Representation by Interest Groups," and "Jewish-German Espionage and Government Complicity." Most of the out-

[60] *Une Campagne de l'Action Française en chalonnais,* 1912–1913 (Chalons-sur-Saône, 1913, privately printed pamphlet). The information in the next two paragraphs comes from this report.

siders in the audience did not join the movement, but the league was able to win enough followers to organize subsections in two neighboring towns. In Chalons itself leaguers posted notices on the walls of buildings and held meetings once a month. (A contradictor was invited, of course.) Their headquarters had a public reading room and a librarian.

Chalons also had a section of Camelots, who met each Friday evening to study royalist doctrines. The fact that they were completely under the control of the league's very respectable leaders [61] can be partially explained by the absence of a large student body in Chalons. At Besançon, which had a state university and a Catholic college, the Camelots were the animating force of the Action Française.

In the Champagne area Vitry, Reims, and four other towns had branches of the league and the Camelots.[62] The head of the section in Reims was the mayor of the commune; in Vitry it was a local nobleman named Roger de Felcourt. On one gala occasion a speaker from Paris attracted six hundred people, who met in a barn to hear him. They were almost all clericals, and a Mass was performed for their benefit before the meeting. As elsewhere, the Camelots in Reims posted bills and got arrested for shouting "Vive le Roi" while selling their newspapers. The older leaguers became indignant over the fact that these boys were handcuffed and treated like ordinary felons. From their point of view the hawkers of the king were honest Frenchmen, and the republican authorities were the real criminals.

* * *

[61] The section's first president was Charles Morin, a local lawyer who had just come back from Brussels, where he had received encouragement from the pretender. The vice-president was Commandant des Brosses, a retired army major. The affiliated Dames Royalistes were led by the Comtesse d'Étampes, with Madame des Brosses as vice-president; Mademoiselle de Mazenod was the head of the Jeunes Filles Royalistes.

[62] *Ligue de l'Action Française, section champenoise* (Reims, 1912, privately printed pamphlet). All information on the Action Française in the Champagne area comes from this report.

In general, the provincial structure of the Action Française comprised two main types—lecture societies catering to the older *bien-pensants* and youth groups specializing in public demonstrations and the distribution of royalist newspapers and leaflets. Their activities resembled those of the movement in the capital, but the local sections worked more closely with royalists and clericals who were not directly associated with the league. The ladies, too, tried to combine their allegiance to Maurras and the king with their social and charitable functions.

The social composition of the movement in the provinces was more homogeneous than it was in the capital. There were fewer intellectuals among the league's officers and fewer lower middle-class youths in the Camelots. As might be expected, the provincial members of the Action Française were more conservative and conventional in their attitudes and behavior than their Parisian colleagues. They were usually monarchists by tradition and extremely pious. Maurras and Vaugeois therefore saw to it that the more "respectable" leaders of the league —especially aristocrats and priests—were kept in the limelight at national conventions and sent out as visiting speakers to local sections.

6

❦ ❦ ❦ ❦ ❦ ❦ ❦ ❦ ❦

A Movement of Déclassés

The sections of French society that supplied the Action Française with the bulk of its members had previously provided the core of the anti-Dreyfusard camp. A number of politicians had opposed or defended Dreyfus mainly as a means of furthering their own careers,[1] and certain obscure writers and ambitious wives had tried to "crash" high society by joining the nationalist leagues to which the Parisian aristocracy belonged.[2] But, aside from this minority of opportunists and

[1] Georges Clemenceau, a militant patriot, made a political "comeback" after his "disgrace" in the early nineties by becoming one of Dreyfus' staunchest champions. On the other hand, the internationalist revolutionary socialist Jules Guesde said that Dreyfus was merely a rich Jew and therefore unworthy of working-class support.

[2] Actually these people were not accepted socially by the *bien-pensants* with whom they sought to identify themselves. Commenting on a visit to her sister-in-law, the Duchesse de Guérmantes said: "Je suis allée chez Marie-Aynard avant-hier. C'était charmant autrefois. Maintenant on y trouve toutes les personnes qu'on a passé sa vie à éviter, sous prétexte qu'elles sont contre Dreyfus, et d'autres dont on n'a pas idée

social climbers, most of the anti-Dreyfusards were sincerely reactionary.

Their social status can be partially determined from the lists of contributors published by the *Libre Parole* in its fund-raising campaign for Colonel Henry's widow between mid-December 1898 and mid-January 1899. Of the seven thousand or so who stated their rank or occupation, about twenty-five hundred were military men and their wives. The other major categories were nobility (about five hundred), clergy (three hundred), people in the legal, medical, academic, and other liberal professions (more than six hundred), students and ex-students (almost five hundred), men of letters and journalists (almost two hundred), artists (about one hundred), and politicians (more than one hundred). One hundred traveling salesmen and fifty pharmacists complete the list. Except for the last two groups (the traveling salesmen may have been anti-semites as a result of their unpleasant contacts with Jewish buyers), it is restricted to the oldest prestige-laden groups in France.

There is no scientific way of identifying the eight thousand contributors who preferred to remain anonymous, but certain inferences can be made about them. According to the 1896 census, the largest categories of the French population were farmers, white-collar employees, shopkeepers, craftsmen, and industrial workers. If people from these social groups had sent in donations, why would they have been less willing to mention their occupation or rank than noblemen, army officers, priests, and lawyers? One hundred traveling salesmen did so. Why should an equal number of small merchants have held this information back if they too had supported the *Libre Parole's* campaign? Though this kind of speculation is far from conclusive, it does suggest that the people who gave their *état civil* were a fairly representative cross section of all the militant anti-Dreyfusards.

---

qui c'est" (Marcel Proust, *À La Recherche du temps perdu* [15 vols.; Paris: Gallimard, 1919–1927], Vol. VII: *Le Côté de Guermantes*, pp. 80–81).

The majority of those contributors who did not identify themselves accompanied their offerings with expressions of hatred toward the Jews, Protestants, free-thinkers, and republicans and called for their collective massacre. They also vented their rage on prominent Dreyfusards, on the intellectuals in general, and on the judges who had ordered a review of Dreyfus' trial. An abbé gave five francs "for a rug made out of a kike's skin that I can put beside my bed and step on in the morning and evening." Other country priests used similarly abusive language. One army officer offered fifty francs "in anticipation of the order to test the new cannons and explosives on the hundred thousand Jews who are poisoning the country." Another wanted "to hang the head [*sic*] of the Jews in front of a butcher shop, to make drums out of their skins, to stick pins in them until they croak."

Not all of these anti-Dreyfusards were royalists, but they all resented the way in which French culture was changing. Despite the fact that these changes were primarily economic, technological, and social, many people continued to view them in political terms. Forms of government had become identified with ways of life in their thinking since 1789. Each regime since the Revolution did seem to have a certain style,[3] which was visible in the public behavior of government leaders and in the design of clothes, furniture, and architecture. But many reactionaries also felt the effects of industrialization, modifications in the social structure, the decline of religion, and the development of new artistic forms. The monarchy was merely a symbol of better days for them. What they really hated was the *petit-bourgeois* mass democracy that had been announced in the 1790's and that seemed to be setting the tone of French life by the turn of the twentieth century.

As the self-styled heir of the anti-Dreyfusard cause, the Action Française was especially attractive to people who feared that they were losing their former social status and prestige.

[3] E.g., the egalitarian pose of the Jacobins, the ostentation and fanfare of the two Napoleons, the umbrella-carrying, bourgeois respectability of Louis Philippe.

Their reactionary outlook was "a symptom of dissociation between culturally prescribed aspirations and socially structured avenues for realizing these aspirations." [4] By the end of the nineteenth century France was not the only country in which the provincial gentry found it increasingly difficult to "lord it over" the common folk, put off creditors, and live in comfortable idleness. Anton Chekhov's *The Cherry Orchard* and Lillian Hellman's *The Little Foxes* describe the similar plight of these "noblemen" in Russia and the American South. Priests, monks, and nuns also saw their traditional immunities and privileges threatened in an age of growing indifference toward religion. Many intellectuals felt isolated from the general public (even before they tried to win it back by committing what Julian Benda was later to call "treason") and dependent upon the state for an inadequate supply of honors and jobs. Finally, the army officers offered the most dramatic example of a French social group suffering a setback —though only a temporary one—in the early 1900's.

When the Action Française was founded, European society retained many of its traditional features. The members of each class were still identifiable by their style of life—manners, taste, dress, speech, living quarters—and by the amount of prestige generally accorded to them. They preserved their exclusiveness by restricting access to their homes and families to people in their own peer-groups. Though wealth was beginning to replace birth as a symbol of status, it was not in itself a criterion of a person's acceptability as a guest or a marriage partner. Social classes remained distinguishable by their capacity to resist penetration from the social system as a whole and by the fact that their economic function was only one of numerous functions they served.

The members of a given class can conflict with each other on the basis of occupation, age, ethnic origin, religion, politics, and roles as producers and consumers. Classes interact re-

[4] Robert K. Merton, *Social Theory and Social Structure* (Glencoe, Illinois: The Free Press, 1949), p. 128.

ciprocally with all social groups,[5] but in the France of 1900 few people allowed such conflicts to separate them completely from the class into which they had been born. Neither the military (as in Germany) nor the intelligentsia (as in Russia) constituted a separate stratum in the French class system. Even the peasants could be included in its middle and lower categories.

At the turn of the century most Frenchmen still viewed the nobility as the highest class. The forty thousand families that claimed to belong to it had lost their legal privileges, but they had managed to keep much of their traditional prestige. As in the past, the governments of the Third Republic seemed to prefer men with titles to commoners when choosing ambassadors and generals. Much of the lower and middle gentry lived in genteel poverty (though a young nobleman could sometimes "regild the family escutcheon" by marrying the daughter of a French or an American millionaire), but the upper ranks were usually rich. Noblemen still owned much of the land in the country, and people like the Duc de Choiseul and the Marquis de Nicolaï had large incomes from their blocks of apartment buildings in the capital.[6]

Another sign of the nobility's prestige was the fact that rich

[5] A sports team, a conjugal family, a political party, a labor union, a monastic order, an association of lawyers, and a national minority are all social groups. These vary according to the number of functions they serve, size, degree of permanence, amount of time spent in them by their members, degree of dispersion (geographical proximity of members and frequency of contacts), mode of participation (voluntary, forced, unconscious), "openness" or exclusiveness, degree of formal and informal organization, kinds of functions, conciliatory or divisive orientation, degree of impenetrability from the total social system, degree of compatibility with other social groups, modes of control over members, the manner in which decisions are made (authoritarian, democratic), and degree of internal unity. (Georges Gurvitch, *La Vocation actuelle de la sociologie* [Paris: Presses Universitaires de France, 1950], p. 292 f.)

[6] Jules d'Auriac, *La Nationalité française* (Paris: E. Flammarion, 1913), p. 268.

bourgeois continued to seek entry into its ranks through marriage or through the purchase of real or fictitious titles. The descendants of the great families and country gentry of the Old Regime looked down on these upstarts as they had done since the time of Molière's *Le Bourgeois Gentilhomme*. In the nineteenth century they were also careful to distinguish themselves from those people whose noble status had been granted by the greatest parvenu of all—Napoleon Bonaparte. The Comte de Saint-Victor might run a factory and his wife might never be invited to tea by the Princesse de Broglie, but their names appeared in *Tout Paris* (France's social register) and they too tried to "live nobly."

By the end of the nineteenth century virtually all Frenchmen who were not noble and who did not work with their hands defined themselves as "bourgeois." First, there were the old patrician families, many of which were of prerevolutionary or revolutionary origin. They often owned large estates or lived on the interest from their investments. A second group, sometimes, but not usually, intermingled with the first, comprised the financial and industrial plutocracy. These "bourgeois dynasties" furnished most of the country's cabinet ministers, high magistrates, and top civil servants.[7] Professional men and businessmen and farmers who had other people working for them constituted what might be called the middle class proper. Below them was the lower middle class, which had grown considerably during the last third of the century as a result of France's economic expansion and which consisted increasingly of working people on their way up and bourgeois on their way down. It included small shopkeepers, self-employed farmers, specialized government functionaries, skilled commercial employees, and school teachers. Almost all of these grand- and petit-bourgeois Frenchmen opposed any threat to their property or status from the revolutionary proletariat. Yet some of them still considered themselves Leftists

[7] Emmanuel Beau de Loménie, *Les Responsabilités des dynasties bourgeoises* (3 vols.; Paris: Denoël, 1943–1954), *passim*.

politically—a habit inherited from the time when their for-
bears had had to fight for these two "rights."

Wage earners—whether they worked in factories, mines,
fields, or services—were separated from their "betters" by all
sorts of distinctions. It was difficult for the child of an industrial worker or farm laborer to rise socially by means of wealth,
marriage, or education. The middle and upper classes mingled
in trains, theaters, restaurants, and schools but they kept the
masses out. Noblemen, industrialists, and lawyers could send
their children to liberal-arts colleges, but most young Frenchmen left school at the age of twelve and pursued the occupations of their parents. Some farm girls went into domestic
service in the cities, but this was an example of "horizontal"
rather than "vertical" mobility.

Although French clergymen came from diverse social and
economic backgrounds, they usually identified themselves with
the church's interests and shared a common pattern of response. It can be maintained that members of the clergy never
lose completely the attitudes of the class into which they are
born and that they express these attitudes in time of crisis. In
1789, for example, most of the higher prelates had opposed
reforms, although many of the poorer priests had favored
them. But when the revolutionary government threatened
the Catholic religion itself, the majority of men and women
in holy orders turned against it. Despite the traditional differences between ultramontanes and Gallicans, both groups
had condemned the Italian seizure of Rome in 1870 and had
wanted their country to do something about it. The *ralliement*
in the 1890's had reconciled many clergymen to the Republic,
but they again became hostile to it when it threatened their
property, educational privileges, and immunity from military
service in the early 1900's.

* * *

Increasingly strained relations between church and state
during the so-called Dreyfusard revolution provided the Ac-

tion Française with its first significant group of recruits. At first the only outsiders who had paid any attention to the movement had been students in the Latin Quarter, writers like Maurice Barrès and Jules Lemaître, and a few die-hard royalists. Pope Leo XIII's encyclicals had restrained many Catholics from supporting the pretender, but his successor was less friendly to the liberal republic. Pius X's first act in 1903 was to declare that no bishop could henceforth be chosen unless the Holy See was consulted first. This announcement led Maurras to hope that the new pope might be persuaded to encourage a hostile attitude toward the republican regime among the faithful and thus provided new backers for his movement.[8]

The anticlerical laws associated with Émile Combes had already irritated many Catholics and had made Leo XIII apprehensive. Before 1905 France's clergy controlled no parties or committees engaging in political action, nor did it use Catholic welfare organizations for this purpose.[9] Even so, the government was limiting its educational activities, dissolving its monastic orders, and finally, threatening to seize its property. The visit of President Loubet to the King of Italy in April 1904 brought a particularly strong protest from Pius X. He reaffirmed the charge that the pope was a prisoner in Rome, and demanded that the heads of Catholic states refuse to recognize this city as the Italian capital. In response to this declaration, the French government broke off its relations with the Vatican, and in November Combes presented to the chamber of deputies a project for a law that would bring about the complete separation of church and state. It went into effect in December 1905, under the ministry of Aristide Briand.

A month later the government began to take an inventory of all church-held property in order to recover what belonged

[8] Louis Dimier, Vingt ans de l'Action Française et d'autres souvenirs (Paris: Nouvelle Librairie Nationale, 1926), p. 57.
[9] Archives Nationales, Parti royaliste, F⁷12861, November 28, 1905.

to the state. This measure provoked widespread hostility against the current regime in Catholic circles. There were dramatic scenes in front of the churches, where priests and army officers resisted the policemen who tried to force their way inside. Members of the Action Française made themselves conspicuous in these disturbances, and several of them, including Lieutenant-Colonel Boisfleury and the Comte Léon de Montesquiou-Fézenzac, lost their commissions in the army as punishment for their unseemly behavior. Within two months, however, Clemenceau (the new minister of the interior) abandoned the inventories. He said that he was not prepared to risk civil war "for a few candlesticks," especially on the eve of the national elections.

Clemenceau succeeded in liquidating the anticlerical policy of his predecessors, but the Action Française benefitted from the permanent resentment this had caused within the clergy. Beginning in 1905, a considerable number of priests and monks were joining Maurras' new league and disseminating its propaganda.[10] One seminary student was attracted to it because he too viewed "the false principles of the Revolution as the basic cause of political anarchy and religious persecution."[11] A priest in the Languedoc told the editors of the *Revue de l'Action Française* that he wanted to enter the battle for the traditional monarchy because his "sacerdotal dignity and his pride as a Frenchman revolted against the yoke of the monstrous Judeo-Masonic Republic."[12] Some members of the disbanded teaching orders became particularly useful propagandists for the movement's ideas. The best example was the group of Assumptionists that continued to write for the Catholic daily *La Croix* (which had a circulation of one hundred and forty thousand in 1914).[13]

[10] Archives Nationales, *Action Française*, F⁷12862, May 15, 1906.
[11] Letter published in the *Revue de l'Action Française*, XVII (June 1905), 394.
[12] *Ibid.*, XXII (August 1906), 230.
[13] Archives Nationales, *Dossiers des journaux*, F⁷12844, 1917.

In addition to clergymen and laymen close to the church, a number of royalist aristocrats joined the Action Française in 1905. Notable among them were the Marquise de Mac-Mahon—a niece of the famous Marshal and a sponsor of several Catholic welfare groups—and the Marquis de La Tour du Pin—the well-known corporatist philosopher. In that same year the Duc d'Orléans had reopened his headquarters in Paris, appointed the Duc de La Rochefoucault-Doudeauville as his chief representative in France,[14] and increased his subsidies to the *Soleil, Gaulois,* and *Libre Parole.*[15] Local noblemen began setting up royalist committees in almost every department in the country, and some of them also joined the League of the Action Française.

The league sought financial backing as well as recruits from the aristocratic champions of the pretender, but it soon found itself in competition with a rival called the Avant-Garde Royaliste. This group had about fifty members and was under the leadership of Firmin Baconnier, Vincent le Méro, and some of the staff writers on the *Libre Parole.*[16] In 1907 it changed its name to the Accord Social and began spreading its propaganda in the Catholic labor unions. Some royalist noblemen belonged to both organizations, but by the end of 1908 they were giving more money to the Accord Social than to the Action Française.[17]

In 1909 and 1910 the Action Française faced increasing hostility from the leaders of the Accord Social, the central committee of the Duc d'Orléans, and Arthur Meyer's *Gaulois.* Finally, Baconnier and the Comte de Larègle of the Accord Social, along with other royalist leaders, persuaded the pretender to disavow the Action Française in late November 1910.[18] His decision to do so split his supporters into two hos-

---

[14] Archives Nationales, *Parti royaliste,* F⁷12861, November 28, 1905.
[15] *Ibid., Action Française,* F⁷12862, January 18, 1909.
[16] *Revue de l'Action Française,* XVI (February 1905), 255.
[17] Archives Nationales, *Action Française,* F⁷12862, December 21, 1908.
[18] *Ibid.,* November 30, 1910.

tile factions and forced the local leaders of his organization to make a choice. Some of them resigned from their positions and openly backed the Action Française; others renounced it.[19]

For more than a month, beginning on December 20, 1910, the *Action Française* published the letters of eight hundred and eleven subscribers who expressed their continuing support of the movement.[20] One hundred and fifty-one of these were written by people who claimed to be noble and of whom ninety-six owned at least one château in the provinces. Only fifty-three of the one hundred and fifty-one names can be found in any of six different biographical dictionaries of the French nobility. Of those whose titles dated back to the Old Regime four were definitely identified with the *haute noblesse,* nine with the *noblesse moyenne,* and seventeen with the *petite*

[19] Letters published in the *Action Française,* December 20, 1910 and following issues.

[20] The following sources were checked to identify these names: *Annuaire Chaix des Sociétés par Actions et Compagnies* (Paris, 1911); *Annuaire de la Haute-Loire* (Le Puy, 1911); *Annuaire de la Ville de Rouen* (Rouen, 1911); *Annuaire du Département de la Marne* (Chalons-sur-Marne, 1911); *Annuaire des Landes* (Mont-de-Marsan, 1911); *Annuaire des Basses-Pyrénnées* (Bayonne, 1911); *Annuaire de l'Allier* (Moulins, 1911); *Annuaire Spéciale de l'État-Major Général de l'Armée* (Paris, 1904); *Annuaire des Propriétaires et des Propriétés de Paris* (Paris, 1910); *Annuaire de la Boulangerie, de la Minoterie, Meunerie et de la Construction de Pétrins Mécaniques des Syndicats du Midi* (Marseille, 1911); *Didot-Bottin, Annuaire du Commerce,* Vol. I: *Départements* (Paris, 1911); *Annuaire des Châteaux* (Paris, 1909–1910); *Tout-Paris: Annuaire de la Société Parisienne* (Paris, 1911); *Annuaire de la Noblesse de France* (Paris, 1911); *Almanach Royal, Impérial et National* (Paris, 1911); La Chénaye-Desbois, *Dictionnaire de la Noblesse* (Paris: La Veuve Duchesne, 1770–1786); A. Révérend, *Armorial du Premier Empire* (Paris: Au Bureau de l'Annuaire de la Noblesse, 1894–97); *Rex, Annuaire Généalogique de la Noblesse Française* (Paris, 1912); Jean de Bonnefon, *La Noblesse de France et les Anoblis de la République* (Paris: La Société d'Editions Mansi et Cie., 1910); Henri Cousin, *Des Noms de Noblesse et des titres nobiliares, spécialement depuis la Révolution* (Dijon: Imprimerie Barbier-Marilier, 1905); Charles Grandmaison, *Dictionnaire Héraldique* (Paris: J. P. Migne, ed., 1852).

noblesse. Seven names belonged to people whose families were ennobled after 1789, and one was illegitimately assumed. Sixteen more names appeared in the lists of the *ancienne noblesse,* but the persons who signed them could not be precisely identified. The important fact is that among eight hundred names on a typical pre-1914 list of Action Française supporters about fifteen per cent were aristocrats and at least two thirds of them had authentic titles.

When one examines the two hundred odd sections of the League of the Action Française in the immediate prewar years one finds that in more than half the presiding officers used noble titles [21] of which more than three fourths were authentic. In addition, many nobles whose names did not appear in the publications of the Action Française in 1910–1911 had backed it previously and were to return to it again after the reconciliation between the leaders of the movement and the pretender in May 1911.[22] Even in the "royalist workers' groups" (see Chapter 8) the leaders usually came from the local gentry.[23]

Among the former Legitimists who rallied to the Orleanist pretender and who supported the Action Française were the Barons de La Charette, Parseval, and La Barre de Nanteuil.[24] The Marquis de Baudry d'Asson, an old Vendéan, also served the movement until he was killed in the First World War.[25] When Léon Daudet left the *Libre Parole* in 1907 to found the *Action Française* he brought with him the major portion

[21] *Almanach de l'Action Française* (Paris: Nouvelle Librairie Nationale, 1910), p. 147.
[22] *Action Française,* May 19, 1911.
[23] E.g., the Comte Henri de Larègle was head of such a group in Paris (*Revue de l'Action Française,* XVIII [August 1905], 287), while Count Robert de Mathan led a similar one in Rouen (*ibid.,* XXVIII [January 1908], 43).
[24] Maurras, *Au Signe de Flore* (Paris: Collection Hier, 1931), p. 286.
[25] Maurras, *Tombeaux* (Paris: Nouvelle Librairie Nationale, 1921), p. 62.

of Drumont's aristocratic clientele.[26] The Marquis de Chene-vières, the Marquis de La Bourdonnaye, and several other wealthy aristocrats each gave the Action Française gifts of ten thousand francs in 1913.[27] Another generous donor was the Comtesse de Courville [28] (whose husband was director of the famous munitions works at Le Creusot). She was also head of the Dames Royalistes and the chief backer of the Nouvelle Librairie Nationale, the publishing house of the Action Française.

Although Maurras' movement had the periodic backing and cooperation of some of the near-great and parvenu nobles, none of the really great names of France can be definitely associated with it. In the early twentieth century most members of the high aristocracy lived in their own little world, read the *Gaulois*, and did not engage in politics. Those who might have been attracted to the Action Française for ideological reasons shied away from it when it tried to "flirt" with the syndicalists in 1912 (see p. 189 ff.) and when the pope was about to condemn it on the eve of the war. Their behavior shows that it was never considered quite respectable by the bulk of the nobility (and the clergy) and that the support it received from them was often provisional.

*

Between 1910 and 1926 the average membership of the Action Française varied between thirty and forty thousand: of these, about fifteen per cent were petty noblemen and about ten per cent were priests and monks; almost fifty per cent belonged to the upper middle and middle classes—especially lawyers,[29] writers,[30] army and navy officers, professors, and doc-

---

[26] Raphaël Viau, *Vingt ans d'antisémitisme, 1889–1909* (Paris: E. Fasquelle, 1910), p. 338.
[27] Archives Nationales, *Action Française*, F⁷12862, August 13, 1913.
[28] *Ibid.*, March 22, 1915.
[29] Lawyers headed sections of the League of the Action Française in

tors. Socially the movement appealed mainly to the *déclassé*
nobility and a section of the *bien-pensant* bourgeoisie. An example of its efforts to cultivate this source of recruits—as well
as expressing its own virulent antisemitism—was a satirical
revue put on by the Camelots du Roi and their lady-friends
in 1911. It was called *Dégonflons l'Youtre* ("Let's Take the
Kikes Down a Peg"). The advertisements for this show [31]
said that evening dress was *de rigueur* for spectators. Thus,
despite its half-hearted efforts to gain mass support through
its newspapers and its street demonstrations, the Action
Française reserved its social activities (the aforementioned
performance was like salon entertainment) for a self-consciously elegant elite.

The Action Française had virtually no appeal for bourgeois
or working-class Frenchmen engaged in the production or
distribution of goods. Wealthy *rentiers* and employers favored
a conservative republic based on order and voted for the legal
Right-wing parties, and the bulk of the well-to-do merchants
and farmers were loyal republicans. Marxist and syndicalist
activities caused some alarm among these "capitalists," but
Maurras got little backing from them. Even "workers" who
opposed the existing economic system saw no salvation in
his reactionary ideas. In all of the published lists of Action
Française members over a period of forty years there was

---

the department of Hautes-Pyrénées, in Poitiers, and in Lyon (*Action
Française*, December 24, 1911).

[30] Among the eight hundred names on the lists of supporters published
by the *Action Française* in the winter of 1910–1911 at least thirty
belonged to men of letters. They included Philippe Guéneau de Mussy
(who translated *Le Saint sacrifice de la messe*, a book written by a
foreign Jesuit), Jules Guillebert (*Lilas et muguets*, a novel, and
Poésies dédiées à François Coppée), Guy de Bremond d'Ars (editor
of the *Revue Catholique et Royaliste*), Robert Valléry-Radot (about
twenty works of literary criticism and fiction), René Bazin (a prolific
writer and a member of the French Academy), and Charles Boudon
(*Les Roses de feu: quatre sonnets païens*).

[31] *Action Française*, December 14, 1911.

only a handful of wage earners in industry, mining, transportation, or any of the public services (police and fire depart-
ments, sanitation, communication). The occasional domestic
servant or farm laborer who joined the movement was usually
imitating his employer or his priest.

About twenty-five to thirty per cent of the Action Française membership represented the lower middle class, which,
by the early 1900's was the largest single segment of the
French population. Industrialization was just beginning to
threaten the social and economic status of some of these
people and to create anxiety and frustration among them as
a consequence. But the appeal of the Action Française was
limited mainly to the few who believed that it was the revolutionary ideal of mass democracy, not the economic system,
that prevented them from preserving their traditional values.

In general, small farmers wanted neither reaction nor
revolution. The Third Republic satisfied them, and they had
no desire to support a reactionary movement that favored
those authoritarian institutions from which their ancestors
had freed themselves. Small property holding usually created
an atmosphere of political democracy; its social effects were
more complex, though most peasant proprietors tended to
oppose extremist movements of all kinds.[32] Still, the Action
Française received occasional letters from such people—mainly
in the peripheral provinces—expressing their approval of its
activities.[33] Those who naïvely supported Maurras' movement
because it praised the good old days and condemned the
democratic regime were usually clericals and traditional royalists.

One of the few times that the Action Française made a
direct bid for support from small shopkeepers was in early
1913, when it was engaged in a campaign against the Maggi

[32] André Siegfried, *Tableau politique de la France de l'ouest* (Paris:
Plon, 1913), p. 373.
[33] E.g., *Revue de l'Action Française*, V (October 1901), 587–588;
Action Française, January 15, 1911.

company (see p. 144) and other large distributors of dairy products and grain. Léon Daudet denounced these companies at a public meeting of Paris grocers,[34] but though his oratory could bring applause from these people by attacking their competitors it could not win them over to Maurras' movement. The few self-employed merchants who did support it lived in the Vendée, eastern Brittany, and the economically backward areas of the Southwest. These *petit-bourgeois* malcontents did not take an active part in the Action Française. They were usually cranks who read its newspaper, sent in small contributions, and wrote long letters to the editors.

Other recruits from the lower middle class included school teachers, librarians, noncommissioned officers, and traveling salesmen,[35] but the largest contingent was made up of white-collar workers in Paris. Many of them had recently come to the city from the provinces,[36] where they were used to personal and traditional kinds of relationships. They felt disoriented by the cosmopolitan, impersonal features of urban society and disturbed by the precariousness of their social status. The following letter to the *Action Française* expresses one government worker's reactionary response:

Because I am a functionary of the Republic I am reduced to concealing my name, under the risk of bringing down upon my head the Judeo-Masonic thunderbolts of the government spies who are the heads of my department. I have been an assiduous reader of the Action Française for a long time, and today more than ever I realize that it is the only force capable of wiping out the evil from which we are suffering, the only force capable of returning to good

[34] Archives Nationales, *Action Française*, F⁷12862, April 14, 1913.
[35] Letters and lists of subscribers to fund-raising drives in the *Action Française*, December 23, 1910 to February 7, 1911, and May 1 to June 12, 1914.
[36] According to the 1896, 1901, and 1911 censuses more than fifty per cent of the Frenchmen living in Paris were born outside the metropolitan area (Louis Chevalier, *La Formation de la population parisienne au XIXe siècle* [Paris: Presses Universitaires de France, 1950], p. 46), and white-collar workers formed the largest proportion of these "immigrants" (*ibid.*, p. 80).

Frenchmen their France of former times. Being a convinced Catholic and a disabused Bonapartist I. . . .[37]

Similar letters from other civil servants expressed their feeling that they were being kept in inferior positions because of their royalist or clerical sympathies and their hope that the Action Française would rid them of their oppressors.[38] Clerks in stores and offices usually said that it was the Jews who were "persecuting" them.[39]

Before the First World War the majority of the Camelots du Roi in Paris were also commercial employees. Maurice Pujo says that many of them had been raised in Catholic orphan asylums.[40] When the Parisian Camelots demonstrated against President Fallières on July 14, 1911, fifty of them were arrested, and their names, ages, and civil status were reported in the press.[41] Twenty-four were clerks, six were students, five were artisans, one was a professor, and another was a journalist; at least four were on the payroll of the *Action Française*. Most of them varied in age from sixteen to twenty-four; three were twenty-eight or twenty-nine, and the journalist was forty-three. Seven youths who did not give their occupations were what the French call *fils de famille*—for example, the son of a retired army colonel, two sons of a noblewoman, and the son of a prominent lawyer.

Evidence from police records confirms the fact that most of the Camelots in the capital before 1914 were employees in stores and offices, *fils de famille*, artisans, and students.[42] In Paris the collegiate members of the Camelots were mainly from vocational or technical schools rather than the Sorbonne.[43] Young men studying liberal arts or the law belonged

[37] *Action Française*, December 24, 1910.
[38] Letters to the editor, *ibid.*, April 29, 1908, and December 31, 1910.
[39] *Ibid.*, December 24, 1910.
[40] Statement made in a personal interview.
[41] *Le Journal*, July 15, 1911.
[42] Archives Nationales, *Camelots du Roi*, F⁷12864, November 16, 1909.
[43] *Ibid.*, April 7, 1910.

to the separate student organization of the Action Française and did not often mingle with the Parisian Camelots. In the provinces, on the other hand, the two groups had an overlapping membership.

*   *   *

The First World War did not disrupt the social structure of France as much as that of defeated nations like Russia and Germany, but it did hasten the breakdown of some barriers. As the country became increasingly industrialized, social status was bound to be determined more by wealth than by birth. The war stimulated the expansion of heavy industry, increased the number of white-collar employees, and produced a group of new-rich profiteers. In the postwar period economic factors intensified the polarization of French society. This tendency, in turn, was expressed politically by the efforts of bankers and industrialists to control the agencies of decision making and mass communication and by the growth of the Communist Party. The majority of Frenchmen continued to behave according to their traditional class norms, although many of them became more conscious of their roles in specific occupational groups.

As in prewar days, the members of the Action Française were mainly people who performed various kinds of services or who were economically marginal. Those who were self-employed did not usually feel a common bond with others in the same occupation. They were more individualistic and, at the same time, more class conscious than their compatriots in the modern sections of the economy. The *Action Française* had few subscribers and little financial support from Frenchmen engaged in industry, agriculture—the decline in support from farmers and other rural people is especially noteworthy, for it was proportionately greater than the numerical decline of this segment of the population [44]—or large-scale commerce.

[44] Forty-four per cent (8,830,000) of the economically active population (20,720,000) was engaged in agricultural pursuits in 1906. Thirty

Most of its readers were professional men—especially from the clergy, the army and navy, law, medicine, and engineering —pious old ladies, students, white-collar employees, and petty country noblemen.[45]

In addition to the writers on the staff of the *Action Française*, others who were not directly affiliated with the movement were sympathetic to it. For example, at the 1926 trial of Maurras for one of his many threats against republican politicians, Fortunat Strowski, Jérome Thâraud, Henri Massis, and Jacques Maritain came to his defense.[46] Georges Bernanos was also a "fellow traveler" until the early thirties,[47] along with Henri Bordeaux, Albert Thibaudet, and the historians Joseph Calmette and the Duc de La Force. Military leaders like Marshals Pétain and Franchet d'Espérey and General Weygand and even Raymond Poincaré himself paid tribute to Maurras at various times during the interwar period.

The biggest change in the social composition of the Action Française occurred after it was condemned by the Vatican in December 1926 (see p. 169 ff.). Aside from the clergy itself, the movement lost support from thousands of Catholic students, intellectuals, and *bien-pensant* dowagers. In order to make up for these losses, it began recruiting in the state universities and among the conservative middle classes in the provinces. As a result, the lists of names published in the *Action Française* during the 1930's differed somewhat from

---

years later this group represented thirty-five per cent (7,140,000) of approximately the same total (Jean Daric, "La Structure économique et sociale de la population française," *Les Cahiers français*, No. 10 [October 1956], p. 3). Those rare farmers who still supported the Action Française in 1936 were mostly *colons* in North Africa.

[45] E.g., letters in the *Action Française*, April 3, 12, 28, October 16, 1923, January 6, February 5, 19, 30, March 27, 31, May 15, August 25, September 18, November 26, 1924, April 19, May 13, June 24, 1925, January 10, and November 18, 1926.

[46] Gérin Ricard, *op. cit.*, p. 235.

[47] Georges Bernanos, *Scandale de la vérité* (Paris: Nouvelle Revue Française, 1939), p. 33.

those of the prewar era. They lacked color, glamour, and fame. There were no duchesses, no cardinals, no members of the French Academy, and few generals. Because of the papal condemnation, such people no longer supported the movement publicly, though many of them still shared its outlook privately.[48]

Financial contributions to the newspaper in the 1930's came mostly from white-collar employees, petty officials (including many in the military services), small merchants (especially purveyors of books and church art), students, pensioners, and a few doctors and lawyers. Those from factory owners or workers were negligible. In addition to the absence of clergymen, there was a decline in the number and rank of nobles who sent money to Maurras and his colleagues.[49]

One new group that seemed to favor the movement consisted of a growing number of colonists in the overseas empire, especially in North Africa. These people were mostly government and military functionaries and property owners.[50] Although some of them had always been reactionaries, others acquired this pattern of response through their paternalistic and authoritarian role vis-à-vis the "natives" or as a result of their belief that Moslem demands for independence were linked with liberalism and communism. Their hostility to the Popular Front regime was comparable to that of the most extreme reactionaries at home.

Most Frenchmen who remember the 1930's say that the social background of the Camelots du Roi was also more "bourgeois" than it had been before the war.[51] Disavowed by

[48] A notable exception was Georges Claude, an eminent chemist and member of the Académie des Sciences. He gave considerable sums of money to support the movement's newspaper in the 1930's and continued to do so until 1941.

[49] E.g., letters in the Action Française, October 25, December 28, 31, 1935, and January 1, 1936.

[50] Ibid.

[51] The observations in this paragraph are based on my own interviews with Maurice Pujo and with other former members of the Action

the pope in 1926 and by the pretender in 1937, the Action Française no longer gave the impression of being primarily a clerical and royalist movement. After its failure to overthrow the regime in February 1934 (see p. 209 ff.), some of its long-time followers deserted it for the more dynamic national-ist and fascist leagues. In the provinces it gained new recruits among middle-class people who considered themselves too "respectable" to join the outright fascists. But in the capital the Camelots were as boisterous as their more plebeian for-bears of prewar days, and the movement's daily newspaper staff attracted hotheaded young intellectuals like Robert Brasillach, Dominique Sordet, and Lucien Rebatet, some of whom were to embrace the Nazis a few years later.

Thus, aside from the loss of some clericals, the movement's membership did not change much during the interwar years. It still consisted mainly of people who did not fit into the twentieth-century economic structure and modern society in general. Most of them were either reactionaries by tradition or came from those classes and occupational groups that were losing status and prestige. Consciously or unconsciously they were *déclassés*.

Française. I have also borrowed from Samuel M. Osgood, "The Action Française between the Wars" (a paper presented at the annual meet-ing of the Society of French Historical Studies, University of Rochester, April 9, 1960), which cites police files of the 1930's.

7

❦ ❦ ❦ ❦ ❦ ❦ ❦ ❦ ❦ ❦ ❦

Patriots and the Great War

The Action Française never appealed to the majority of Frenchmen, but it won many new admirers among conservative patriots in the years immediately preceding World War I. Nationalist movements all over Europe were having their heyday during the diplomatic crises leading up to the general conflict. Some French newspapers exaggerated international incidents in order to increase their circulation; others did so in return for payment from special interest groups, including foreign powers. Whatever its underlying purpose may have been, this saber-rattling journalism aroused public opinion and interfered with official policy making. Old-style secret diplomacy was seriously hampered by such pressure—some historians even claim that it was the masses that pushed their governments into war in 1914. Although it may be argued that large metropolitan dailies reflect public opinion rather than mold it, the *Action Française* and much of the notoriously venal Parisian press used the tense atmosphere of the times as a means of propagating their special points of view.

Maurras' thesis was that the Republic could never provide a strong foreign policy that would safeguard the national security. Like Bainville, he said that even a mediocre king knew how to preserve his patrimony better than the most able republican minister. For the publicists of the Action Française the realities of the European balance of power had scarcely changed since the Middle Ages, when Germany had been a constant menace, England coveted France's shores, and Rome was the arbiter. Mere republicans could not be expected to remember such age-old conflicts and eternal national enemies. They were too busy trying to stay in office and they could easily be "bought" (as if royalist ministers had never been "bought"!).

According to Maurras, Bismarck had led France's leaders astray in the 1880's by convincing them that Indochina and Tunisia would be easy to take and could become a source of great riches.[1] Bismarck had indeed encouraged Gambetta and Ferry to embark on a program of colonial expansion with the hope of making the French forget the lost provinces. Even so, these two ministers—and Hanotaux after them—sincerely believed that their country would strengthen rather than dissipate its resources by becoming a major colonial power. They may also have thought that they had profited from the mistakes of the Bourbons, who had lost France's vast possessions in North America and India in the eighteenth century by fighting ruinous wars on the European continent.

But Maurras was inconsistent in his views on imperialism. He condemned it in Tunisia and Indochina, claiming that by tying her forces down there France had lost what he called the "French territories" of Egypt and Syria.[2] At the same time, he approved of her Moroccan adventure, even though it too diverted military units from the Continent, where they might have been needed more, for the dramatic visit of the Kaiser to

[1] *Kiel et Tanger* (1895–1905) (Paris: Nouvelle Librairie Nationale, 1916), p. 10.
[2] *Ibid.*, p. 11.

Tangiers on March 31, 1905, caused a crisis in Franco-German relations. It is generally agreed that foreign minister Delcassé had not consulted Germany concerning French penetration in Morocco and that he urged his government not to participate in the 1906 Algeciras conference, at which Germany demanded an open-door policy in that weak but economically attractive North African kingdom. Most of the patriotic indignation in France resulted from the fact that the Rouvier government bowed to Germany's demands, forced Delcassé to resign, and agreed to attend the conference. Nevertheless, the Action Française later tried to discredit Delcassé's firm stand against the Germans and called him England's lackey.[3]

The appearance of the German gunboat Panther at Agadir on July 1, 1911, precipitated a new Franco-German crisis over Morocco. This time France won a diplomatic victory because of the backing of her English friends. The event brought Poincaré into power six months later and helped the cause of the aggressive nationalists. Bainville then wrote a series of articles in the Action Française entitled "Le Coup d'Agadir," in which he tried to show that the republican government, which had thought it had pacified the Germans by ceding them a bit of territory in the Congo, had only whetted their appetite for more.

Another example will illustrate further the unrealistic line the Action Française was forced to take in its effort to prove that all republican foreign policy was bad. Maurras maintained that in 1898 France could have blocked British domination of Africa (and the projected Cape-to-Cairo railroad) by joining her East and West African colonies. If she had done this, he said, the question of Egypt, India, and the Mediterranean, "and all the other seas over which the flag of his Gracious Majesty ruled uncontested until recently [1763!] would have been reopened." [4] But by risking war with England at Fashoda

[3] Action Française, July 3, 1911.
[4] Kiel et Tanger, p. 40.

France would have weakened herself vis-à-vis Germany and lost an indispensable ally.

In addition to his unrelenting criticism of republican foreign policy, Maurras contended that the monarchical states of Europe were hesitant to deal with the changing ministries of the Third Republic. This point had some validity, but Great Britain, though a monarchy, was just as unreliable. On the other hand, Czarist Russia stuck to her alliance with republican France despite the strong personal ties between Nicholas II and William II.

France could not have hoped to face Germany without Russian and British support, yet Maurras rarely missed an opportunity to create suspicion concerning Great Britain's motives. He charged that the English made France a mere tool of their own policy, that they needed her army to fight Germany on the Continent but that they did not necessarily need a French victory. According to him, they wanted France to carry on a war of attrition that would prevent the German army from reaching the Channel.[5]

Maurras expressed the reactionary nationalist view that France should only have allies she could dominate. Although he recognized the fact that several great empires had arisen whose size and power overshadowed those of France, he said that she did not have to suffer the fate of ancient Greece. Maurras' blueprint for the foreign policy of a strong middle-sized nation—which he said his country would be with a king —called for independent maneuvering between the competing empires. If France could organize a *bloc* of medium- and small-sized nations, she could pursue her own interests despite her reduced power.[6] This suggestion was remarkably prophetic of recent French efforts to lead a union of six western European states as a "Third Force" between the United States and the Soviet Union. But in 1914 France could never have regained

[5] *Ibid.*, p. 189.
[6] *Ibid.*, pp. 203–206.

Alsace-Lorraine without waging war against the new German
Empire and she could not have been victorious in such a
struggle without the aid of Great Britain, Russia, and the
United States.

* * *

Increasing international tension after 1911 created a political
climate favorable to a vigorously nationalistic foreign policy
in France. This change was dramatized by the fall of the
Caillaux ministry in January 1912 [7] and the appointment of
Raymond Poincaré, a Lorrainer and an ardent patriot, as
premier. Poincaré soon became the leader of a campaign to
strengthen the country's defenses and to encourage patriotic
sentiments among the people. As concern over the German
menace grew, many Frenchmen seemed to share the chauvinistic response of the Action Française. But it was authoritarian
conservatives like Poincaré, Barthou, and Millerand—rather
than die-hard doctrinaires like Barrès and Maurras—who were
mainly responsible for orienting parliament and the Parisian
press toward the new nationalism of the immediate prewar
years. They were the ones who held office and had a real voice
in policy making.[8]

As one means of stimulating nationalist feeling Prime
Minister Poincaré decided to sanction the procession sponsored annually by the Action Française to the statue of Joan
of Arc in the Places des Pyramides on the second Sunday in
May. Previous governments had instructed the police to break
up these demonstrations, but now the cult of the national
heroine had official recognition. The celebration in May 1912
was attended by many patriots who were in no way connected
with the Action Française. Even confirmed enemies of the
movement, like the Catholic poet Charles Péguy, were devoted

[7] Joseph Caillaux, *Devant l'histoire, mes prisons* (Paris: Aux Éditions
de la Sirene, 1920), p. 17.
[8] Eugen Weber, *The Nationalist Revival in France, 1905–1914*
(Berkeley, California: University of California Press, 1959), p. 159.

to the Maid of Orleans. By promoting her glory, the Action Française gained sympathy from thousands of patriotic and pious Frenchmen.

The resurgence of French patriotism and the growth of intellectual movements glorifying action also revived the cult of the army.[9] Ernest Psichari typified the new militaristic spirit among some of the university students. He was a grandson of Ernest Renan and had grown up in the atmosphere of Dreyfusard salons in the early 1900's. When he went to the Sorbonne, he became attracted to the Action Française and changed from an elegant aesthete to a worshipper of force. In 1912 he published a book called *L'Appel des Armes*, in which he contrasted the grandeur of the military way of life with the "decadent" bourgeois culture of his age. Like Péguy, Psichari was to die early in the war. Each of these poet-patriots expressed in his own way the desire of many young Frenchmen to dedicate themselves to the military revival and moral purification of the Fatherland.

All sections of the population were regaining confidence in the army by 1912. Poincaré's war minister, the ex-Socialist Alexandre Millerand, "advertised" this new trend in public opinion by sponsoring numerous torchlight parades.[10] Antimilitarism was still strong in Leftist intellectual circles, but militarism was beginning to penetrate the working class. In fact, the war office was receiving requests for parades in industrial suburbs in which, a few years earlier, an officer appearing in uniform would have been insulted by the local residents.[11]

Capitalizing on this growing militarist feeling, the Action Française became an avid supporter of a "preparedness" pro-

[9] See Agathon (Henri Massis and Alfred Tardé), *Les Jeunes gens d'aujourd'hui* (Paris: Plon-Nourrit, 1913) and Jacques Chastenet, *La France de M. Fallières* (Paris: Fayard, 1949) on anti-intellectualism and the cult of action among French youths in the immediate prewar years.

[10] Denis W. Brogan, *France under the Republic* (New York: Harper, 1940), p. 447.

[11] Girardet, *op. cit.*, p. 246.

gram. "We must envisage war, and if we must fight one day, we must fight well," said one speaker at a rally sponsored by the movement as early as 1910.[12] The Moroccan crisis in 1911 and the Balkan and Italo-Turkish wars in 1912 and 1913 made many Frenchmen aware of the danger of a general conflict. Everyone knew that France had less man power than Germany and that more troops would be necessary in order to face her on equal terms. Jean Jaurès, the leader of the reformist wing of the Socialist Party, wanted to provide them by organizing a national militia, but the government and the generals thought otherwise. They proposed an increase in the period of universal military training from two to three years as a means of raising the size of the standing army. Along with the other nationalists, the Action Française backed this proposal when it was being debated in the chamber of deputies. Finally Prime Minister Louis Barthou (Poincaré was now president of the republic) pushed the new law through both houses of parliament in August 1913.

In its campaigns against internationalists and pacifists the *Action Française* directed its main editorial attacks against the Socialists and soon evoked a response from them. Marcel Sembat wrote a book called *Faites un Roi, Si Non, Faites la Paix* in which he argued that war would bring a return of the monarchy or some form of dictatorship and that Frenchmen who wanted to preserve the Republic should try to keep the peace. Maurras and other reactionary nationalists were making the republican system the scapegoat for every diplomatic defeat and accusing it of neglecting France's military preparedness. It seemed to follow logically—even to the Socialists—that such a regime could never wage a successful war. For Sembat, too, admitted that a government that was incapable of operating the few nationalized industries satisfactorily could never succeed in mobilizing the whole country.[13]

Moderate Leftists also feared that the Republic might not

[12] *Action Française*, September 30, 1910.
[13] *Faites un roi, si non, faites la paix* (Paris: Figuière, 1913), p. 13.

survive a major war. Looking back twenty-five years later, the eminent political commentator Albert Bayet said [14] that all liberals believed that it would have been overthrown if France had been defeated and that if victorious she would have fallen into the hands of the general who had recovered Alsace-Lorraine. The young men of the great universities seemed to be choosing between Maurras and Marx on the eve of 1914. Events were certainly favoring the Action Française at that time, and Maurras "was secure in a position held by no one since Joseph de Maistre as the great 'master of the counterrevolution.'" [15] In a book called *France Herself Again* an exiled French cleric expressed the feelings of many *bienpensants* when he said that the Action Française was "perhaps more resolute than Christian . . . yet the nationalism of these overheated people, helped as it was by an excellent criticism of much in our democracy that was bad, was not wasted." [16]

The Camelots and students of the movement engaged in frequent street battles with Left-wing and pacifist groups, especially those led by the anarchist Miguel Vigo (called Almereyda) in his newspaper the *Bonnet Rouge*.[17] For the first time in their brief careers these youths were on the side of the police in chasing pacifists and anarchists off the streets and in breaking up antipatriotic meetings. The Action Française also continued to bait Jean Jaurès, who was threatening the government with a general strike in case of war in the spring of 1914. (When Jules Guesde, the leader of the revolutionary wing of Jaurès' party, replied that such a strike would be a treasonable act against "the most socialist nation in Europe," Maurras praised him for his "patriotism.")[18] Then, on the eve of the war, a young waiter named Raoul Villain

[14] Statement made in a personal interview.
[15] Denis W. Brogan, *French Personalities and Problems* (New York: A. Knopf, 1947), p. 120.
[16] Ernest Dimnet, *France Herself Again* (London: G. P. Putnam's Sons, 1914), pp. 245–246.
[17] Daudet, *Souvenirs*, II, 267–268.
[18] *Action Française*, July 18, 1914.

killed Jaurès in a Paris restaurant. Although it was never proved that Maurras and his associates had anything to do with this crime, their violent accusations against the Socialist leader helped to create an atmosphere favorable to political assassination.

Along with its clamor for a strong army, the *Action Française* devoted itself to ferreting out "German-Jewish spies" in France. Daudet published a series of his own "investigations" concerning the problem of espionage entitled "L'Avant-Guerre." Almost every day the newspaper printed "revelations" concerning the activities of suspicious Germans in France and of Frenchmen who had allegedly "sold out" to the Fatherland's archenemy. He specifically accused the Maggi Dairy Corporation of being a hotbed of spies, and in January 1913 he stumbled on some letters that seemed to confirm his charges.[19] Actually, this company was an international cartel. Its main office was in Switzerland, and its board of directors there was Swiss. In France its administrators were Swiss and Frenchmen. But the Maggi Corporation operated on a large scale in Germany as well, and there was probably a great deal of German capital behind the whole organization.

By July 1913 the *Action Française* had been so successful in rousing a section of public opinion against the spy danger that the Maggi Corporation sued it for libel. When a Paris tribunal ordered an investigation of the charges made by Daudet,[20] he was obliged to admit that the documents he had published in January had been forged. This revelation caused his newspaper to lose prestige in journalistic circles,[21] even though several members of the Maggi Corporation were found guilty of espionage.

Despite this temporary setback, the Action Française tried to take the lead in every kind of patriotic and anti-German demonstration in the immediate prewar period. Such was the

[19] *Ibid.*, January 5, 1913.
[20] *Ibid.*, July 23, 1913.
[21] Archives Nationales, *Action Française*, F⁷12862, January 11, 1913.

case when the body of Paul Déroulède was brought back to Paris for burial on February 2, 1914. Two hundred thousand Parisians followed his bier from the Gare de Lyon to the church of Saint Augustin, acclaiming the patriot who had saved the spirit of *revanche*. The religious ceremony at the church was followed by speeches in which old friends like Maurice Barrès hailed him as the "Man of the Nation." The League of the Action Française was there in force,[22] but it seems fairly certain that the crowd was responding to the idea of *revanche* more than to the ex-chief of the League of Patriots or to the extreme nationalist groups that were present. Among them, the Action Française was not even calling the tune; it was only part of the chorus.

A few weeks later eight thousand students paraded in front of the statue representing the city of Strasbourg in the Place de la Concorde. They came in units representing different schools and placed wreaths at the foot of the statue in homage to the lost provinces.[23] A large percentage of these students were affiliated with the Action Française, but there were many others from patriotic and Catholic organizations of different political tendencies. Yet, the movement's leaders tried to take credit for organizing this demonstration as well as the annual procession in honor of Joan of Arc in May, which was also attended by thousands of patriotic Frenchmen.

* * *

From the outbreak of the First World War until the Paris Peace Conference the Action Française abandoned much of its habitual behavior—especially its attacks against the existing regime—and supported the republican ministers in their efforts to defeat Germany. Two days after the beginning of hostilities Maurras apologized for the usual column on the Dreyfus Affair in the August 3 issue of the *Action Française*. He said that henceforth it would not reappear because such memories

[22] *Action Française*, February 4, 1913.
[23] *Ibid.*, March 2, 1913.

should no longer be kept alive in the face of the common enemy.[24] The government was what it was, he said on August 6, but it had charge of France's destiny and any criticism of its actions would imperil the national defense. Undoubtedly the wartime press censorship held the editors of the newspaper in check, but their determination to support the *Union Sacrée* was sincere.

To many Frenchmen the First World War was the "great war," the "real war," whereas the conflict that broke out in 1939 was somehow "phony" and meaningless. This response was especially typical of conservative nationalists, though by no means restricted to them. The nation as a whole answered enthusiastically the call to arms in 1914. Its bellicose mood was expressed by both soldiers and civilians and in the chauvinistic songs of the Parisian cabaret singers. Almost everyone was confident that France would win the war within a few weeks, recover the lost provinces, and regain her dominant position in Europe.

As the war dragged on, this initial confidence and enthusiasm gradually waned, but the Action Française continued to support the various ministries in spite of their awkward handling of military reverses.[25] By the spring of 1917, after the failure of the Nivelle offensive, national morale had fallen especially low. Although the restive labor movement did not get out of control, there were actual mutinies at the front. General Pétain, already renowned as the Victor of Verdun, finally put a stop to them in the summer of that year. Even so, the Ribot and Painlevé governments showed considerable weakness in dealing with the problems created by the military setback in April, the Russian Revolution, and enemy efforts to demoralize the country by diplomatic means and propaganda.

Meanwhile, the Action Française was busy manufacturing

[24] *Ibid.*, August 4, 1914.
[25] For example, Maurras condoned Briand's official explanation regarding the massacre of a contingent of French sailors in Athens during the disastrous Gallipoli campaign (*ibid.*, December 3, 1916).

its own propaganda to fan the ebbing flames of French patriotism. Jacques Bainville said that "German barbarism could
be disarmed and the claws of the beast clipped" only by completely dismembering the Second Reich.[26] He encouraged
hatred of both Germans and Russians by charging that the
Bolshevik Revolution was a German plot to destroy the Eastern Front.[27] Maurras was less effective as a popular polemicist
but he echoed Bainville's views.

In the twentieth century the most chauvinistic rabble
rousers become respectable during wartime. Their flag-waving,
enemy-baiting, and traitor-hunting tactics are accepted by
many people who ordinarily frown on such behavior. During
the First World War even eminent scholars were producing
uncritical polemics for mass consumption. Maurras, Bainville,
and Daudet were therefore in good company when they wrote
about the savagery of the "Huns," the glories of the French
army, and the danger from enemy agents.

Léon Daudet continued his prewar practice of unmasking
spies and traitors. The main target of his attacks in 1917 was
the anarchist sheet *Bonnet Rouge*. Its editor *was* a German
agent, and its defeatist line aggravated the crisis of French
morale. The Action Française was not alone in pointing out
the danger, for in July Maurice Barrès questioned minister of
the interior Malvy about the *Bonnet Rouge* in the chamber of
deputies, while Clemenceau raised the same question in the
senate. The police finally arrested Almereyda on August 7, and
he committed suicide in his cell a week later. Malvy resigned
on August 30, but the government still did nothing about the
charges of traitors in its midst.

On the first of October Paul Painlevé, the new premier,
received Daudet and Maurras in order to hear their accusations
against Malvy. Daudet had written a letter to President Poin-

---

[26] *Histoire de deux peuples. La France et l'empire allemand* (Paris:
Nouvelle Librairie Nationale, 1915), p. 50.
[27] *Comment est née la révolution russe* (Paris: Nouvelle Librairie
Nationale, 1917), *passim*.

caré the day before, in which he had accused the former minister of subsidizing the *Bonnet Rouge*. In the interest of national security the *Action Française* did not publish this letter.[28] Malvy found out about it anyway and demanded that his accusers be punished. A few weeks later Painlevé sent police agents to search the offices of the newspaper and the homes of Daudet, Maurras, Maxime Réal del Sarte, Marius Plateau, and Louis Dimier. The official statement regarding the results of this investigation of an alleged royalist plot said that considerable arms and subversive documents had been seized, though there was little evidence that such a plot existed.[29] The Action Française called the incident the *Complot des Panoplies* because the police had found several war trophies in the home of Marius Plateau.

The day after this series of raids Maurras and Daudet were put under house arrest, and a judicial inquiry into their activities was scheduled. Maurras took the incident calmly and warned his friends not to do anything rash.[30] At that time the government's attempt to divert public attention from Malvy by persecuting the Action Française gave the movement a momentary upsurge of popularity. The circulation of the *Action Française*, which had averaged twenty thousand before 1914 and had been thirty-six thousand in October 1915, reached one hundred and fifty-six thousand during the *Complot des Panoplies*.[31] Finally, on November 6, the judge who conducted the hearing concerning Maurras' and Daudet's alleged subversion declared that there was insufficient evidence to prosecute them.[32]

After Clemenceau became premier in mid-November 1917, Daudet urged him to arrest Malvy and Joseph Caillaux, the

[28] Robert Havard de la Montagne, *Histoire de l'Action Française* (Paris: Amiot-Dumont, 1950), p. 86.

[29] François Goguel, *Les Partis politiques sous la IIIe République* (Paris: Éditions du Seuil, 1946), p. 160.

[30] *Action Française*, October 29, 1917.

[31] Archives Nationales, *Dossiers de journaux*, F⁷12844, 1917.

[32] Havard de la Montagne, *op. cit.*, p. 88.

minister of finance, for their defeatist activities. It is difficult to determine the exact role of the Action Française in bringing about their conviction and in paving the way for the Clemenceau dictatorship. In any case, Maurras claimed that the republican government henceforth adopted his brand of patriotism. He said that "ministers and high personages borrowed from us even to the point of using our vocabulary." [33] Clemenceau certainly had other sources of information besides Daudet regarding subversives, though he did listen to the Action Française leaders on occasion. He was not their "man," and they were later to criticize him for not having obtained a sterner peace treaty. But he satisfied their desire for strong leadership during the war, and as long as he remained in office they virtually ceased to behave like royalists.

* * *

In 1918 France was on the winning side, but she had not won the war single-handed. Although the *poilus* had stopped the Kaiser's armies at the Marne in September 1914, they could not have held out indefinitely without Allied support. In fact, since 1870 the French had been unable to challenge German power alone. Clemenceau understood this before the Armistice and throughout the Paris Peace Conference. Intransigent nationalists, on the other hand, were free to demand the bulk of the spoils without regard for the interests and goals of the other victor states.

Maurras later condemned Clemenceau for not having given Marshal Foch specific instructions regarding the terms to be imposed upon the defeated Central Powers.[34] But Foch was the Supreme Commander of all the Allied Forces, not merely a French officer responsible only to his own government. He could not order Generals Pétain, Castelnau, and Franchet d'Espérey to destroy the German army in the Rhineland and

[33] *Quand les français ne s'aiment pas* (Paris: Nouvelle Librairie Nationale, 1926), p. 352.
[34] *Le Procès de Charles Maurras*, p. 67.

to occupy Berlin and Vienna while the Americans and the British were pressing for an armistice with the Provisional Government of the German Republic. The *Action Française* shared in the general enthusiasm of the French people on November 11 but cautioned that the Armistice might prevent the victory from being fully exploited.[35] Like the other reactionary nationalists, Maurras, Daudet, and Bainville were already prepared to have France "go it alone," an attitude they were to cling to for the next twenty-five years.

It was unrealistic of the Action Française and other reactionaries to believe that their country could dominate Europe alone. They were still thinking of the days when Richelieu had made French influence predominant in Europe and his immediate successors had dismembered Germany at the Peace of Westphalia. Clemenceau was supposed to repeat this feat two hundred and seventy years later, despite the fact that the power alignment and the political psychology of Central European leaders had changed radically since the seventeenth century. At that time the people of this area had been divided by religious and dynastic conflicts and had been virtually unmoved by feelings of patriotism. In 1919 there were few Germans who would have been content to be citizens of a resurrected Baden, Hesse, or Lower Saxony. Still, the efforts of General Mangin and other French commanders to sponsor separatist movements in Germany caused considerable alarm, especially to the British foreign office. In supporting these efforts, the Action Française expressed in an extreme form the widespread lack of understanding among many twentieth-century French nationalists for any nationalism other than their own.

During the negotiations at the Peace Conference the *Action Française* demanded a "French Peace" and became especially critical—as far as the press censorship would allow—of Wilson and Lloyd George whenever they refused to cater to France's interests. When the Treaty of Versailles was formally signed on June 28, 1919, the *Action Française* condemned it as a

[35] Havard de la Montagne, *op. cit.*, p. 92.

Wilsonian compromise and charged that the proposed Anglo-American Treaty of Guarantee was an obvious but inadequate ruse to compensate for the "loss" of the Rhine frontier.[36] Jacques Bainville said that the peace settlement was too weak in its severity and too severe in its weakness,[37] and Maurras was to blame it later for what he called the decline of French power in the 1920's.[38] Just as Hitler attacked the German Republic for accepting the Treaty of Versailles, so Maurras blamed the French Republic for sponsoring it. Thus the treaty became another symbol for French reactionaries of the inability of a democratic government to safeguard the national interest.

The French press and political parties abandoned the wartime *Union Sacrée* during the period of the Paris Peace Conference and resumed their traditional ideological controversies with the same old clichés. But after the Armistice the "classic" differences between the politicians of the non-Marxist Left and the moderate Right became increasingly blurred in practice. For, in addition to upsetting the lives of millions of individuals, destroying three ancient empires, and ending the European balance of power, the war had made possible the growth of revolutionary Bolshevism. Here, indeed, was a new bogeyman, not only for reactionaries and conservatives, but also for a number of Radicals. (Even before the Versailles settlement was signed the Left wings of the French Socialist Party and trade-union confederation were beginning to negotiate with Moscow.) Other factors that contributed to a renewal of prewar conservative nationalism were the prestige of the victorious army and a widespread suspicion that French national security was not being fully provided for in the peace treaties.

In France, as in many other countries, there was a kind of

[36] *Action Française*, June 29, 1919.
[37] *Les Conséquences politiques de la paix* (Paris: Nouvelle Librairie Nationale, 1920), *passim*.
[38] *Le Mauvais traité: de la victoire à Locarno—chronique d'une décadence* (Paris: Éditions du Capitole, 1928), *passim*.

mass abandonment of internationalist views and a withdrawal into familiar political and social group activities. The French labor movement, for example, reasserted its independence of action in a series of strikes in 1919–1920 which, because of some Communist attempts to use them for political ends, frightened the bourgeoisie. A large section of the French population wanted a government that would prevent an internal upheaval and preserve order in the country. Therefore, when a national election was scheduled for November 1919, the political parties organized their campaigns mainly around domestic issues.

The Alliance Démocratique, a conservative parliamentary group, proposed an electoral list consisting of all anticollectivist republican parties. Politicians from the Fédération Républicaine and the Action Libérale, as well as numerous anti-Dreyfusard nationalists like Maurice Barrès, Paul de Cassagnac, and the Duc d'Audiffret-Pasquier, joined it to form the Bloc National. This conservative coalition, the broadest of its type since 1885, was organized as a common front against liberalism and Bolshevism, which seemed to be represented by the Radicals and the Socialists, respectively (though these two parties were themselves divided at the time of the election). Alexandre Millerand, himself a renegade Socialist, was the nominal leader of the Bloc. Its original program was avowedly republican, but it envisioned basic constitutional changes in favor of political decentralization, provincial assemblies, and representation of professional groups.

Some of these ideas were close to the program of the Action Française, but this movement had no influence in the Bloc National.[39] Instead, it proposed its own list of candidates under the label of the Union Nationale.[40] Léon Daudet was the only one elected from this list.[41] He ran as an independent repub-

[39] Though it claimed to have originated the idea of the *Bloc* (Havard de la Montagne, *op. cit.*, p. 95).
[40] *Action Française*, October 22, 1919.
[41] *Ibid.*, November 17, 1919.

lican in the Seine (Paris) constituency of the chamber of deputies. This was the first time that the Action Française had presented its own candidates, though before the war it had supported royalist office seekers who were not connected with it directly. The most plausible explanation of this apparent deviation from the movement's traditional hostility to parliamentary institutions is that it hoped to use the tactic—ironically it was also a standard Communist tactic—of "boring from within." In his four years of office Daudet was the chamber's loudest heckler and filibusterer.

The apparent rebirth of the "classical" Right and the election of many practicing Catholics and army officers to the Bleu Horizon chamber (so-called because of the many uniforms in it) seemed to portend a revival of the conservative values of Thiers and MacMahon, sanctified by the sacrifice of the men who had died at the front. Some *bien-pensants* hoped that the unbelievers who had fought alongside priests in the trenches would rejoin the ranks of the faithful. They also believed that they could eliminate class antagonisms by preserving the wartime *Union Sacrée*.[42] When these illusions were shattered, they blamed pernicious foreign influences for the revival of socialistic, anticlerical, and pacifist attitudes among the masses. They refused to see that a continuing hatred of the "Boche" was not a sufficient basis for a new *Ordre Moral*.

Although a sizable minority of the new deputies shared the basic outlook of the Action Française, they were unable to change the course of French history—except to help delay a reconciliation with the Weimar Republic for a few years. At least thirty of these men were royalists and reactionaries who had never taken part in national politics. They sat with Daudet on the Extreme Right and called themselves "independents."[43] But the Radicals recovered their 1919 electoral losses

[42] Paul Sérant, *Où va la droite?* (Paris: Plon, 1958), p. 59.
[43] Xavier Vallat, *Le Nez de Cléopatre: Souvenirs d'un homme de droite (1919–1944)* (Paris: Éditions "Les Quatre Fils Aymon," 1957), p. 49.

in the chamber by gaining seats in the senate in the 1920 and 1921 elections, and the reactionaries were too weak and inexperienced to prevent Prime Minister Millerand from including a Radical senator, Theodore Steeg, in his cabinet. By January 1921 Millerand moved on to the Elysée Palace, and Briand became the head of a Center coalition government that was supported by many Radicals and Independent Socialists.[44] The Third Republic was back to normal, and the Action Française reverted to its policy of die-hard opposition.

[44] Since the early 1900's the candidates of these "Leftist" parties opposed the so-called Moderates at election time and then formed governments with them once they were installed in parliament. As Eugen Weber aptly says, their platforms were "designed to run on, not stand on." ("New Wine In Old Bottles: Les Familles spirituelles de la France," *French Historical Studies*, Vol. I, No. 2 [1959], 223.)

8

❧ ❧ ❧ ❧ ❧ ❧

Catholic Rivals

Together with its auxilaries, the League of the Action Française quickly resumed its operations and regrouped its
forces after the First World War.[1] Its leaders estimated that
it had fifty thousand members [2] and two hundred thousand
supporters in the 1920's,[3] though these figures seem somewhat
exaggerated. The provincial sections of the movement functioned according to their habitual pattern, while in Paris the
Camelots du Roi and the Students of the Action Française
again took up their protest demonstrations and street brawls.
As in prewar days, their annual celebration of Joan of Arc's
birthday was supposed to convince Parisians that the national
heroine belonged to the Old France and that the Republic was
hostile to her champions. The following description of this
event on May 10, 1920, is based on eyewitness accounts.

[1] The national administration of the league was subdivided into ten
zones in the early 1920's (*Action Française*, March 31, 1924).
[2] *Ibid.*, January 14, 1927.
[3] Gérin Ricard, *op. cit.*, p. 165.

In anticipation of the usual disturbances, the police roped off the streets and squares where the Camelots and other Action Française members usually gathered. The officers on duty in the Place des Pyramides let a few people at a time pass through their lines to place wreaths at the foot of the gilded statue of the Maid of Orleans. Eventually several hundred demonstrators, including many priests, who had assembled in this way, began shouting: "Vive Maurras! Vive Daudet! Vive le Roi! Vive la France! Vive l'Armée!" (the sequence of these cries candidly illustrated the movement's priority of values).

When the police tried to break up the demonstration at this point, Maurras and Daudet arrived in the square, surrounded by the elite guards who brandished lead-filled canes. As the cheering increased, a young policeman told a burly priest wearing his war decorations on his cassock to be quiet. The priest pointed to his medals and answered: "I should shut up? I put in four years at Verdun. Were you in the war? No? Then who are you to tell me to shut up?" This priest's response was typical of those people who thought of themselves as the "true Frenchmen" because of their Catholicism and their patriotism. Maurras, Daudet, and the priests retired from the scene when the actual fighting started between the Action Française militants and the police. Each side hated the other with equal passion, and they both suffered minor casualties. Finally the crowd was dispersed, and a handful of Camelots was arrested.

These demonstrations were repeated in the following years, and they gave many Parisians the impression that the Action Française was active and noisy. They appealed especially to those onlookers who shared the dislike of the well-dressed Camelots for "cops." But street brawls between the Camelots and the police were simply a momentary form of excitement for curious strollers and did little to spread the movement's view of the world. Maurras and his followers were at a loss for real issues during the period when the Bloc National was in power, for most of the conservative nationalists were satisfied with this government, especially between January 1922 and

May 1924, when Poincaré was prime minister. It was the victory of the Cartel des Gauches in the May 1924 elections that provided new Rightist allies for the Action Française.

Though the issue of clericalism was no longer related to France's national problems in 1924, the Left- and Right-wing parties revived it when Premier Édouard Herriot tried to impose the 1905 laic laws in the Alsace. Maurras said that these two provinces would ask the League of Nations for autonomy if Herriot persisted in his plan.[4] Between late 1924 and late 1925 his movement used its habitual tactics—newspaper attacks, mass meetings, and protest demonstrations—and it was ultimately joined by several *bien-pensant* groups. Together they finally forced Herriot to back down. The role of the Action Française in this campaign won it new favor in French clerical circles for a short time, but they abandoned the movement almost completely when the pope condemned it in December 1926. In order to understand this papal condemnation, it is necessary to review the relations of the Action Française with the Vatican and the various Catholic movements in France since the early 1900's.

* * *

When Pius X ascended the papal throne in 1903, his reputation as an archconservative prompted Maurras to send Louis Dimier to find out if he would give some encouragement to the *bien-pensants* in their opposition to the Republic. Before leaving on this mission, Dimier visited Paul Bézine, a spokesman for the Duc d'Orleans, and told him that he hoped to persuade the new pope to make a pronouncement that would leave French Catholics free to work for a return of the monarchy.[5] Bézine offered to pay his expenses, and Dimier departed for Rome. There he had a quarter-hour private audience with Pius X, who said that it was no sin not to rally to the republican regime and that it was no concern of the papacy

4 *Action Française*, May 13, 20, 1924.
5 Dimier, *op. cit.*, p. 57.

whether Frenchmen were Orleanists, Bonapartists, or republicans.[6] The reactionary press in Paris played up this interview,
and the official Vatican newspaper, the *Osservatore Romano*,
interpreted it as indicating that the papal position regarding
the policy of *ralliement* had changed considerably.[7]

The Holy See intensified its support of the French clericals
after the separation of church and state in France in 1905.
Even the Action Française seemed to enjoy its favor temporarily, although the bulk of the Catholics never gave this movement any real backing. Aside from the Fédération Républicaine
and the Union des Droites, the Right-wing party that attracted
the largest number was the Action Libérale, which had been
organized in 1899 by a Lyon lawyer named Jacques Piou.

This veteran leader of the *ralliement* wanted to create a
large and durable structure, not an ephemeral one like the
League of the French Fatherland.[8] With this goal in mind, he
emphasized social work as much as possible in his movement
by sponsoring welfare programs, working men's associations,
and youth groups and in several places organized unemployment funds, mutual insurance societies against livestock mor-
tality, and farm credit agencies. By 1905 Piou's organization
had eleven hundred committees in France. He hoped that
people who became interested in it because of its service activities would support its candidates for public office, even
though they did not agree entirely with its political and religious ideas.[9]

From the time it was founded the Action Libérale attracted
former royalists, Bonapartists, clericals, and nationalists—
thereby invading the recruiting ground of the Action Française
—and campaigned vigorously for its electoral candidates
throughout the country. In 1905 Monseignor Ferrata, the
papal nuncio in Paris, urged that all conservative Catholics
engage in *la bonne politique* by backing these men.[10] But in

[6] *Ibid.*, p. 60.   [7] *Ibid.*, p. 61.
[8] Archives Nationales, *Action Libérale*, Sureté Générale, F⁷12719.
August 5, 1905.   [9] *Ibid.*   [10] *Ibid.*, August 5, 1905.

that same year some of Maurras' followers tried to bribe a group of Parisian workers not to vote for Georges Thiébaud (a nationalist writer who had frequently criticized the Action Française).[11] When the Action Libérale was badly defeated in the national elections a year later, they were actually able to attract some of its former supporters who felt that parliamentary means alone were insufficient to defend the church against the anticlerical measures of the Republic.[12] In 1913 they again pursued their policy of "favoring the worst" when they attacked Henri Bazire, who was running on the Action Libérale ticket in the department of Vendée. This tactic helped his anticlerical opponent to win.[13]

Nevertheless, the Action Libérale was well supported, especially by the Catholic middle classes in the provinces. In 1914 it had a dues-paying membership of two hundred and fifty thousand and a voting strength of three quarters of a million.[14] Its young people's auxiliary, the Jeunesse Catholique (which had been founded by Albert de Mun in the 1890's under the name Association Catholique de la Jeunesse Française), was nominally independent but actually under the direction of high-ranking clergymen. The younger prelates were more active in lay organizations than their predecessors had been. They preferred the Jeunesse Catholique to the youth groups of the Action Française because their leaders always wanted to give orders and their orthodoxy was dubious.

Most partisans of the Action Libérale opposed the Action

11 *Ibid., Parti royaliste*, F⁷12861, November 16, 1905.
12 *Revue de l'Action Française*, XXII (July 1906), 167; letters from former members of the Action Libérale.
13 *Ibid., Action Française*, F⁷12862, November 4, 1913.
14 Parker Thomas Moon, *The Labor Problem and the Social Catholic Movement in France* (New York: Macmillan, 1921), p. xi. Unfortunately, I received William Bosworth's *Catholicism and Crisis in Modern France* (Princeton, New Jersey: Princeton University Press, 1962) too late to incorporate its findings on the Action Libérale and other Catholic groups in this chapter.

Française for having abandoned republicanism for monarchism (in many cases they had done just the opposite), although some of the royalists in Piou's movement backed both groups intermittently. Each one attacked the other publicly, but the Catholic Right in France was less concerned with political leagues than with the restoration of the power and prestige of the church under a sympathetic government. A number of these people—churchmen and laymen alike—gave their private blessing to the clerical campaigns of the Action Française without accepting the dogma of Maurras or his particular brand of royalism.

The so-called Liberal Catholics, who were a shade less conservative than the Action Libérale, were all opposed to the Action Française because of its antidemocratic bias.[15] Their main spokesmen were the Comte d'Haussonville and the editors of such newspapers as the Corréspondant, the Figaro, and the Libre Parole (after 1908). Most of the leaders of Catholic orphanages, labor unions, and mutual-aid societies also felt that Maurras' movement was harming the cause of Catholicism more than it was helping it.[16]

But the Action Française had many friends in Catholic circles. Among them were the leaders of the National Association of Catholic Lawyers and the Revue Catholique des Institutions et du Droit as well as some of the disciples of Monseignor Freppel, one of the founders of the Social Catholic movement. The law school of the University of Paris was another stronghold of Action Française sympathizers. Still, the movement was always in danger of losing prominent followers as a result of its extremist activities. After the crisis with the royalist pretender in 1911, Senator de Lamarzelle turned against it,[17] and when it began dealing with the syndicalists (see p. 189 ff.) La Tour du Pin also withdrew his support. Un-

[15] Figaro, November 29, 1905.
[16] Archives Nationales, Action Française, F⁷12862, March 21, 1912.
[17] Ibid.

til then the presence of this respected social philosopher in its ranks had prevented many religious periodicals, clergymen, and members of Catholic welfare boards from publicly criticizing it. Afterward they felt free to do so.

*

Despite opposition from rival clerical groups in France, Maurras and his followers received the qualified approval of the Vatican when it was preoccupied with the question of "modernism" during the decade preceding the First World War. At that time certain ecclesiastics in the Catholic countries of Europe were trying to renovate the theological defenses of the church as a means of "coordinating" its traditions with the intellectual and social climate of the time. Pius X was wary of such opportunism. Where would these "modernists" stop in their efforts to reform Catholicism "by human methods," he asked himself. Until his death in 1914 he denounced the "modernist" movement in a series of pronouncements and encyclicals (especially *Pascendi* in September 1907) and meted out severe punishment to its leaders.[18]

Maurras, Vaugeois, and Daudet did not attempt to pass judgment on "modernism," but the *bien-pensants* in their movement were certainly hostile to it. In condemning the ideals of democracy, egalitarianism, and freedom of thought, Maurras' political doctrine was analogous to Pius X's position with respect to religion. Moreover, the Action Française had a friend in Monseignor Benigni, a highly placed bishop, whose agent M. Belin wrote articles for its periodicals under the pseudonym of Aventino. Benigni himself was attached to the general secretariat of the Vatican, where he organized an "antimodernist league" and published a periodical called the *Corrispondenza di Roma*, in which he attacked "modernist" ideas. He also ran an "information bureau"—the *Sodalitum*

[18] Ferruccio de Carli, *Pio X e il suo tempo* (Florence: A. Salmi, 1951), *passim*.

Pianum—with agents and informers who aided him in denouncing suspects in all of the principal Catholic states.[19] Benigni had considerable influence on Pius X until only a year before the latter's death.

Some of the Liberal Catholics charged that the Action Française had gained Benigni's support by paying him.[20] In any case, he openly approved of Maurras' movement and encouraged the pope in his hostile pronouncements against the French government. By provoking republican reprisals these pronouncements intensified the religious struggle in France, and the neoroyalists exploited it for their own political goals. The papal secretary of state himself, Cardinal Merry del Val, sanctioned Benigni's activities and was sympathetic to the Action Française for several years.[21]

Another temporary bond between the Action Française and the Vatican was their common opposition to the Sillon. This movement, which had been founded in the 1890's, represented a Left-wing Christian-Democratic tendency that has periodically incurred the displeasure of the Holy See. Its leaders, in turn, hated the Action Française for its reactionary outlook and for the blasphemies published by those of its writers—especially Maurras—who were atheists.[22] They regarded these men as liars and sectarians who, under the pretext of defending the church, were actually weakening it by undermining the faith of its followers. The Sillon condemned both capitalist and Marxist materialism as well as the evils of "statism." It favored political democracy, a more equitable distribution of wealth, and the participation of labor in policy making in private enterprises.

According to its founder, Marc Sangnier, the only way to

[19] Nicholas Fontaine, *Saint-Siège*, "*Action Française*," *et* "*Catholiques intégraux*" (Paris: J. Gamber, 1928), p. 142.
[20] Archives Nationales, *Action Française*, F⁷12862, March 21, 1912.
[21] *Ibid.*
[22] L. Laberthonnière, *Autour de l'Action Française* (Paris: Bloud, 1911), p. 5.

make such a program succeed was to launch a spiritual revolution, and he used the fortune he had inherited from his grandfather for this purpose. With his help, the Sillon founded a newspaper and organized branches in all parts of France. Its lectures were well attended, and members of the lower and higher clergy supported them. The superiors of some theological schools taught the principles of the Sillon to their faculty members and students, and a number of priests proclaimed them from their pulpits. There was much competition—especially in the seminaries—between the partisans of the Action Française and the Sillon.[23]

When Pius X finally became convinced that the Sillon was propagating certain "modernist" errors and ordered it dissolved in 1910, its leaders blamed Maurras and his followers for this action. They were out for revenge and they joined other Catholic enemies of the Action Française in deluging churches, monasteries, and welfare organizations with leaflets attacking it. Their most effective argument against it was the anti-Christian bias of some of its writers. They specifically denounced Maurras' *Anthinéa* for its paganism and asked the papal authorities to list it in the Index of Forbidden Books.

The Action Française was certainly as open to criticism from a doctrinal point of view as the Sillon, yet, although the theologians condemned it, the pope suspended sentence. He appreciated its fight against democracy and laicism and he was willing to forgive some of the shortcomings of its leaders. In December 1913 Maurras sent a delegation that included Colonel de Boisfleury and Louis Dimier to the Vatican to plead his case.[24] At the same time he published a book called *L'Action Française et la Religion Catholique,* in which he tried to justify himself and prove his loyalty to the church. Dimier found a champion in Cardinal Billot, a Jesuit professor at the

[23] Letter from an abbé in a provincial seminary, cited in the *Revue de l'Action Française,* XXI (May 1906), 233.
[24] Archives Nationales, *Action Française,* F⁷12862, December 4, 1913.

Roman College and a favorite of Pius X. Billot was an ardent champion of Integral Catholicism and an admirer of Maurras. He pointed out to His Holiness that by denouncing the Action Française he would help the Christian Democrats and weaken the only political movement that denounced the Revolution in its entirety.[25] By means of these arguments Billot and Camille Bellaigue (another friend of the Action Française in the Vatican) temporarily persuaded the pope not to put Maurras' *Anthinéa* on the Index.[26]

Although the Action Française still had a few sympathizers in Rome in 1914, the influence of Benigni, its staunchest advocate, was beginning to wane as early as 1912. Merry del Val had gradually decided that Benigni was going too far in his violent denunciations of various prelates and welfare organizations. One of the crucial factors that brought about his semi-disgrace was his unreasonable attacks on the Archbishop of Cologne and the Christian trade-unions in Germany and Belgium. When his *Corrispondenza di Roma* ceased to appear in 1913, the Action Française lost an important ally at the Holy See.[27] Cardinals Billot and Pio de Lancogna were the only friends it had left there after that.

*

In France itself the Action Française tried to reach the episcopate, the priests, members of the religious orders, and pious laymen through the activities of Abbé Georges Pascal, an apostolic missionary, Dom Besse, a Benedictine monk, Louis Dimier, and Bernard de Vésins. Abbé Pascal seems to have specialized in the direct relations between the Action Française and Rome, while Dom Besse wrote articles for the periodicals of the movement and gave lectures on religion in the principal cities of the country. Under the pretext of attacking "modernism" and liberalism, Dom Besse preached the

[25] Fontaine, *op. cit.*, p. 101.
[26] Dimier, *op. cit.*, p. 219.
[27] Archives Nationales, *Action Française*, F⁷12862, February 28, 1913.

doctrines of Maurras. Dimier and Vésins avoided religious questions and concentrated on politics in their articles and lectures. They tried especially to play on the discontent that the anticlerical policies of the government provoked among French Catholics.

Another active protagonist of the Action Française was Abbé Emmanuel Barbier, a former Jesuit, who edited a review called *La Critique du Libéralisme*. In his writings Barbier denounced as "modernists" or liberals all clergymen who were not in sympathy with the ideas of the Action Française. He antagonized certain bishops who knew that he was influential in Rome, and his diatribes often inspired pontifical reprimands against those whom he accused of being too liberal. But when the bishop of Nice, Monseignor Chapon, was considering condemning Barbier, the latter appealed to Rome and was vindicated.[28]

In addition to prelates, many prominent Catholic laymen, including Albert de Mun, Jacques Piou, Étienne Lamy, and Denys Cochin, were victimized by Barbier's witch hunt against so-called modernists. Finally, in a letter written in October 1914 to Cardinal Ferrata, the new papal secretary of state, Monseignor Mignot, archbishop of Albi, expressed the hope that this campaign would cease now that Pius X was dead. He said that French Catholics, especially simple people, were being tyrannized by the "integrist" journalists.[29]

Although a section of the French episcopate was hostile to the Action Française by the eve of the First World War, Cardinal de Cabrières, archbishop of Montpellier, Monseignor Marty, bishop of Montauban, and other princes of the church were still sympathetic to it. Cardinal Andrieu, bishop of Bordeaux, had favored the movement for a long time but turned against it just before the war. His case is interesting, since it was he who was finally to instigate the papal condemnation of the movement in 1926. In 1909, however, he was

28 *Ibid.*
29 Cited in Fontaine, *op. cit.*, pp. 122–124.

arraigned by the Tribunal Correctionnel of Bordeaux for provocation to disobedience in a public speech in which he had praised the Camelots du Roi. The day after he was forced to pay a six-hundred-franc fine he told his Camelot friends that "everything bad that happens nowadays is a consequence of the principles of 1789." [30] He supported the Action Française until the beginning of 1913, when his attitude changed and he no longer wanted to hear its name. By 1914 he was already trying to persuade the pope to condemn it.

Those bishops who were not openly hostile to the Action Française were taking a more reserved position with respect to it in the immediate prewar years. The crisis with the pretender in 1911, Valois' and Daudet's dealings with the syndicalists, and the fact that one of Maurras' books was almost put on the Index, had alienated many Catholics and had released certain churchmen from the obligation to be silent about the movement for fear of losing the support of their rich patrons.[31] Among the movement's most active enemies were Monseignor Mignot, the archbishop of Albi, Cardinal Amette, the archbishop of Paris, Monseignor Eyssantier, the bishop of La Rochelle, and Monsiegnor Chapon, the bishop of Nice. According to them, it was dangerous for the faith to have the Action Française under the intellectual direction of atheists. They felt that by associating neomonarchism with the church the Action Française was discrediting the Catholic cause and compromising its religious interests.[32]

Besides a growing number of bishops, many members of the religious orders in France also disliked the Action Française by 1914. The Dominicans, Franciscans, and Jesuits who wrote about the movement in their various periodicals almost invariably agreed with the contention of its eccelsiastical ene-

[30] Archives Nationales, *Action Française*, F⁷12862, February 28, 1913.
[31] André Lugan, *La Fin d'une mystification, l'Action Française, son histoire, sa doctrine, sa politique* (Paris: Valois, 1928), p. 17.
[32] Archives Nationales, *Action Française*, F⁷12862, March 21, 1912.

mies that it was dangerous to the faith.[33] In Rome, too, the Jesuits—with the exception of Cardinal Billot—were turning against the Action Française. On the other hand, it was always assured of the valuable and devoted support of the Assumptionists in France. It will be recalled that this order had been dissolved in 1900 and that those of its members who continued to write for *La Croix* and for some of the Catholic provincial weeklies were eager partisans of the Action Française.[34]

In addition to this outside clerical support in newspapers and periodicals, the Action Française had bought Veuillot's *Univers* and was publishing it each week. Its circulation, which was twelve thousand in 1910, declined steadily afterward, and was less than two thirds of that figure by 1912.[35] Still, the Action Française continued to reach a number of *bien-pensant* readers through its friends in the Catholic press.

Although most of the priests in the larger towns were hostile to its ideas and its behavior, the Action Française retained the friendship of the ultrareactionary country priests and abbés—in many cases the same ones who had sent their contributions to the subscription for Colonel Henry's widow in 1898. These die-hard clerics were living in another age. In their remote rural parishes and schools they remained aloof from new spiritual movements like the Sillon, which had been so popular among their urban colleagues. For them the Action Française was a link with the past.

* * *

The Action Française was not officially banned until late 1926, but in January 1914 the Congregation of the Index had unanimously condemned seven books by Maurras as well as the *Revue de l'Action Française* (which disappeared anyway

[33] *Ibid.*
[34] *Ibid.*, October 16, 1912.
[35] *Ibid.*, *Dossiers des Journaux*, F⁷12844, 1917.

in August 1914). Pope Pius X was still sympathetic to the movement because of its "antimodernism" and decided not to publish this decree. After his death in late 1914 his successor, Benedict XV, also postponed its publication for the duration of the war because of the political passions it might stir up among Catholics in the belligerent nations. Then, in the immediate postwar years the condemnation would have been inopportune for conservative French Catholics, since they, like the Action Française, supported the Bloc National in re-establishing diplomatic relations with the Holy See for the first time since 1904. It would also have been badly timed in 1924, when the anticlerical policies of the Cartel demanded unity among the various Catholic groups in France.

Only after the fall of Herriot's government in April 1925 was the atmosphere in the country favorable to a papal ban on the Action Française. By then the Catholic Action organizations had checked Herriot's efforts to extend the laic laws to the Alsace. A month later they forced his successor, Paul Painlevé, to reopen the French embassy at the Vatican. (Briand had opened this embassy in 1921, but Herriot had closed it three years later.)

In France itself the bad feelings between the Action Française and its Catholic rivals grew more intense in late 1925. Six members of the Association Catholique de la Jeunesse Française, including Georges Bidault and René Pleven, were especially active in attacking it.[36] Daudet was also having trouble with the powerful Catholic daily *L'Ouest-Éclair* over a pamphlet by one of its editors, the Abbé Trochu, which condemned his pornographic novel *L'Entremetteuse*.[37] Meanwhile, Pope Pius XI's attention was called by Cardinal Mercier to the movement's pernicious influence on young people in a survey published in Liége under the title *Charles Maurras,*

[36] Adrien Dansette, *Histoire religieuse de la France contemporaine* (2 vols.; Paris: Flammarion, 1948–1951), II: *Sous la IIIe République*, 582.
[37] *Action Française*, February 5, 1924, August 8, 1925.

Maître de la Jeunesse Catholique? Réponse de l'Opinion Catholique.

Maurras wrote a long article called "Nationalisme et Catholicisme," in the *Action Française* for October 5, 1925, answering these charges against him. At that time Pius XI was particularly irritated by Maurras' intransigent nationalism, for he favored the Locarno spirit and Briand's pacifism. The general change in the times finally made the condemnation of the Action Française propitious by early 1926, though it was difficult to condemn the movement on purely doctrinal grounds. Its main ideas were political rather than religious, but the pope felt that its naturalistic conception of man and society reflected itself in the amoral behavior of its leaders. His own words were: "More than its theses, its pattern of response is pernicious." [38]

In August 1926 the pope suggested that Cardinal Andrieu, archbishop of Bordeaux, bring the whole question into the open. This prelate, who was a staunch "integrist" and a former admirer of Maurras, wrote an article condemning his movement in the church weekly *L'Aquitaine* of August 27, 1926. The situation was badly handled in that the attack on the Action Française was not based on any current action or policy of its leaders. The Catholics in the movement responded defensively in a long open letter to Cardinal Andrieu, in which they tried to convince him that the charges against the Action Française were unjustified and that they were part of a Briandist and police plot.[39] A week later the *Action Française* published a direct appeal to the pope, which was signed by the Catholic students, Camelots, and Commissaires of the Action Française.[40] There was little editorializing on papal policy in the newspaper for the next month, but many contributions to its fund-raising drives were accompanied by increasingly aggressive replies to Andrieu's condemnation.

[38] Cited in Dansette, *op. cit.*, p. 569.
[39] *Action Française*, September 3 and 9, 1926.
[40] *Ibid.*, September 13, 1926.

Laymen and prelates who were sympathetic to the movement tried to prevent an open break with Rome. In mid-September, for example, Jacques Maritain published a pamphlet entitled "Une Opinion sur Charles Maurras et le Devoir des Catholiques." He proposed the creation of Catholic clubs led by priests within the Action Française in order to prevent the neglect of spiritual values. Maurras was ready to grant concessions of this sort, and a few weeks later Maritain wrote a letter to the pope justifying the movement. He received no answer.[41] Several high churchmen, including Cardinal Maurin, archbishop of Lyon, and Cardinal Charost, archbishop of Rennes, also tried to effect some sort of compromise.[42] Maurras seemed anxious to aid their endeavors and even agreed to put his book *Anthinéa* on his own "Index." [43]

None of these efforts worked, and in November and early December Pius XI became more and more antagonistic. At the thirteenth congress of the League of the Action Française Admiral Schwerer, the presiding officer, said that he would submit to the pope in religious matters but would take his political orders only from the Action Française.[44] He went on to say that no one in the world had the right or the power to place his religious faith in opposition to his "patriotism" and that he would stand by the movement if it was persecuted further. This threat to disobey the imminent papal ban expressed the feelings of thousands of Catholics in the movement. They were soon to be put to the test, for on November 30 the Vatican circulated a letter to its nuncios saying that it could not accept the solution of having chaplains within the various organizations of the Action Française.[45]

By mid-December the *Osservatore Romano* was making it

---

[41] Dansette, *op. cit.*, p. 586.
[42] E.g., a letter of Cardinal Maurin—originally printed in *La Semaine religieuse de Lyon*—cited in the *Action Française*, October 17, 1926.
[43] *Ibid.*, November 16, 1926.
[44] *Ibid.*, November 26, 1926.
[45] Dansette, *op. cit.*, p. 587.

clearer each day that the Vatican was ready to publish its open condemnation of the Action Française. Maurras wrote an article in his newspaper on December 15 entitled "Rome et la France," in which he accused "pro-German simoniacs" of persuading the pope "to offend the conscience of Frenchmen in their faith and in their honor." Pius XI's answer to this gibe came like a thunderbolt. In his consistorial talk five days later he said "in no case will Catholics be allowed to belong to enterprises of any sort having to do with that school that places party interests above religion . . . to support, encourage, or read the newspapers of these men who, in their writings, are alien to our dogma and our morality." [46] Even though the Action Française was not named, this was a papal ban of the most rigorous kind. It told French Catholics to break completely with the league and the newspaper of the movement.

The response of Maurras and his cohorts was as defiant as the pope's condemnation was unequivocal. On December 24 the *Action Française* published its famous article "Non Possumus," in which it refused to accept the condemnation and accused the Vatican of playing politics. But Catholics cannot say *non possumus* to the pope. In his decree of December 29 he cited the names of Maurras' seven books that had been placed on the Index in January 1914. The addition of the movement's daily newspaper to this list was the final blow.

On May 8, 1927, the Apostolic *Penitenciary* defined the punishment for those Frenchmen who disobeyed the ban. Laymen would be deprived of the right to confession and the sacraments, seminary students would be dismissed from school, and people in holy orders could be stripped of their titles. Though this last measure was rarely applied, it was used against Cardinal Billot, who was reduced to the rank of a simple priest and forced to live in a monastery near Rome.

The papal condemnation of the Action Française was more

[46] *Osservatore Romano*, December 21, 1926.

than an event in its own history; it caused great interest and concern among all French clericals. Liberal and conservative Catholic newspapers such as *La Jeune République, Le Petit Démocrate,* and *L'Ouest-Éclair* had been hostile to the movement, but they had remained silent until its official condemnation. *La Croix* had published an attack on Maurras on October 6, 1926, and then avoided comment on the issue until late December. Francisque Gay's Christian Democratic *La Vie Catholique* had tried to be objective at first, but by mid-October it was printing polemics against the Action Française.

Once the condemnation was final, the leaders of the movement attacked the *Osservatore Romano* itself, calling it the "Diffamatore Romano" and "The German newspaper in Rome." [47] In early 1927 the *Action Française* reproduced letters from people who remained loyal to the movement in a daily column called "La Fidelité Française," but it lost many of its followers (as well as its most prominent clerical leader, Bernard de Vésins). As usual, Maurras and Daudet sought vengeance by rehashing past events and kicking old scapegoats. They charged that Cardinal Andrieu and the pope had been duped by the Christian Democrats, the police, Briand and his "henchmen," and the papal nuncio in Paris, Cardinal Ceretti.[48]

Pius XI was no dupe, though. He was a man of his time, while the leaders of the Action Française were living in another era. By 1926 the general atmosphere in Europe was favorable to peace and democracy, and after Poincaré stabilized the value of the franc the prevailing economic prosperity made most Frenchmen content with the *status quo.* Clericalism and monarchism had become lost causes in France. The pope saw the futility of the "integrist," "antimodernist" position expressed in the *Syllabus of Errors* of 1864. He also felt that the Action Française pattern of response was a vestige from the remote past and had no meaning except to

[47] *Action Française,* December 26, 1926, January 14, 1927.
[48] *Ibid.,* January 5, 1927.

a minority of die-hards. Pius XI favored the Christian Democrats as the group whose behavior and goals were best suited
to furthering Catholic interests in a modern industrial society.
By condemning the Action Française he removed a source of
strife among Catholics of differing political views and made
it possible for them to work in an atmosphere of calm, if not
cooperation.

No open disobedience to the papal ban was possible for
those members of the Action Française who wanted to remain
good Catholics. A few scattered priests continued to give the
sacraments to pious Frenchmen who remained in the movement, but the church gradually filled parish vacancies with
men who favored the condemnation. The doctrinal controversy continued for a couple of years,[49] though for most laymen the choice was clear: the pope or Maurras. Some Catholic
supporters of the Action Française openly refused to submit
to the Vatican decree and either forsook the sacraments of
the church or took them from those priests who would still
administer them.[50] Many others practiced literal submission,
broke their public connections with the movement, and can-
celed their subscriptions to its publications.

But the people in this second group experienced no real
change of heart. Besides, several newspapers in Paris and the
provinces provided them with the ideological and emotional
diet they needed.[51] They did not risk losing absolution by
reading *Candide* (which was edited by Jacques Bainville and
featured articles by Léon Daudet), *Gringoire* (a sensationalist
fascist weekly specializing in vile character assassination), and

[49] Jacques Maritain, after breaking with the Action Française, wrote
Pourquoi Rome a parlé in 1927. In reply to this, Maurice Pujo wrote
a series of articles in the *Action Française* in early 1929 entitled
"*Comment Rome est trompée.*" Finally, Maritain and five priests
wrote *Clairvoyance de Rome* in the summer of 1929.
[50] Adrien Dansette, "L'Eglise et l'Action Française," *Esprit*, XIX
(October 1951), 457.
[51] Yves Simon, *The Road to Vichy 1918–1938* (New York: Sheed
and Ward, 1942), p. 64.

Je Suis Partout (which was ultimately subsidized by the Nazis). There were also the "pious" local dailies—the self-styled defenders of religion against liberalism and socialism—which followed a line close to that of the *Action Française*.

Though the movement never completely recovered the favor it had had in Catholic circles, the church's opposition to communism and socialism, as well as its support—with individual exceptions, of course—of General Franco, made it increasingly susceptible to a reconciliation with the Action Française in the late 1930's. This change developed slowly, for the ban of 1926 was still in effect. The first sign of a softening of the church's attitude came when Cardinal Verdier, archbishop of Paris, permitted religious funerals for Action Française leaguers and Camelots who had died in the riots of February 6, 1934. But this was simply a merciful exception, not a new pattern. When Jacques Bainville died two years later, for example, the same cardinal strictly forbade the sacrament of extreme unction to him. Canon Richard, an Action Française supporter, gave Bainville absolution anyway and was reprimanded by his ecclesiastical superiors for this act of disobedience. In reply to this reprimand, Canon Richard defied Cardinal Verdier and the pope to punish him, since his "conscience" was clear. He compared himself to Antigone, who had also disobeyed the authorities and given her brother a religious burial.[52]

There were touching attempts by friends of the Action Française to restore it to papal favor in the late 1930's. In January 1937 Maurras wrote sweet letters to the ailing Pius XI, but there was no meeting of minds between them. Then in November 1938 a group of French Carmelite sisters finally persuaded the pope to accept a letter signed by all the Action Française leaders.[53] Pius XI died three months later, and the new pontiff, Pius XII, finally lifted the ban on the *Action Française* (though not on some of Maurras' and Daudet's

[52] *Action Française*, February 23, 1936.
[53] *Ibid.*, November 21, 1938.

books) in July 1939. Henceforth, it was no longer a sin to read this newspaper. Cardinal Verdier himself probably influenced the Vatican to revise its position vis-à-vis the Action Française.[54]

*　*　*

It is difficult to determine the extent to which some people are moved by religious feeling or clericalism. The intensity of these two attitudes varies in response to external events, and the implementation of one may conflict with the realization of the other. On the eve of the Second World War a significant number of conservative Catholics still objected to the harm the Action Française was doing to the faith, although they could not help admiring its die-hard opposition to laicism and the principles of 1789. The phrase "the two Frances" has undoubtedly been overworked in explaining modern French history—certainly its validity is questionable for the period since 1914. Nevertheless, the *bien-pensants* did not lose their identity and they were even to experience a brief revival of power under the Vichy regime. Maurras and his movement always had rivals for their support, but they were never (even during the years of the papal ban against them) without sympathizers among those Frenchmen who viewed the church as a bulwark of reaction.[55]

[54] Dansette, *Histoire religieuse*, II, 610.
[55] According to the archbishop of Aix, eleven of the seventeen French cardinals and archbishops were still friendly toward the Action Française during the 1930's (Dansette, "L'Eglise et l'Action Française," *loc. cit.*, p. 448). Even when the movement encouraged persecution of the Jews under the Vichy regime, Cardinal Baudrillart supported it enthusiastically.

9

✤　✤　✤　✤

Labor Lost

One of the most frustrating problems of the Extreme Right in twentieth-century France has been that of winning the country's wage earners away from the Socialists, the trade-unions, and the advocates of the welfare state. Since these groups all seemed to threaten the existing economic structure, Social Catholics and conservative employers worked independently or as allies to counteract their influence. The leaders of the Action Française were the only reactionaries who were ostensibly not concerned with preserving capitalism—especially before 1914. They wanted to use the workers against it, not to destroy class distinctions but to oust the plutocracy from power and restore a precapitalist society.

According to the Action Française, French society should be hierarchical, with a "place" for all social groups, but since the mid-nineteenth century warfare between the classes had made the realization of this ideal increasingly remote. The June Days of 1848 and the bloody repression of the Paris Commune in 1871 were long remembered by victors and vanquished alike. Not only did they alienate the workers from the rest of the population, but they also delayed the solution of the labor question through government protection and an effective trade-union movement.

In the big cities different social groups had become increasingly isolated from one another by the mid-nineteenth century. Until then one could still find them living on separate floors of the same building—with the rich at the street level and the poor in the garrets. But industrialization (and the spectacular renovation of Paris by Baron Haussmann) brought a change in the housing pattern that created whole districts in which one particular class set the standards. In the new factory-suburbs of Paris there were people who rarely saw the Champs Elysées and whose daily speech was far different from that of the aristocrats in the Faubourg Saint-Germain or the intellectuals of the Latin Quarter. The workers developed their own forms of pronunciation and syntax and borrowed many words from the *argot* of the underworld. They became increasingly conscious of being mistreated, despised, and segregated. Perhaps this was why they felt a special need for their own language, especially as the public schools tried to teach them the official language of a society that made no place for them.

French employers were aware of the smoldering hatred of the proletariat, and in the 1860's a few of them had tried to sponsor welfare programs in their factories and mines in order to alleviate the poverty of their workers as well as to keep them from moving around too much. These men believed that the virtue to which they attributed their own success—thrift—had to be instilled in their employees if their lot was to be improved. With this purpose in mind, they set up schemes for credit unions, profit sharing, and home ownership. Although such efforts were modest and met with scant success, they were tried again and again well into the twentieth century. But the people they were supposed to help found it difficult to distinguish between the idea of protection and

the desire for domination on the part of their employers. This
distrust was further irritated by the refusal of the industrialists
to allow them to organize their own unions or even to discuss
such a possibility with them.

Catholic welfare groups appeared soon after the employer-
sponsored programs and were somewhat more successful.[1]
The most noteworthy of these was the Œuvre des Cercles
Catholiques d'Ouvriers, which was founded in 1871 by Albert
de Mun and René de La Tour du Pin. These two men, both
descendants of the old nobility, had become close friends in
a German prison camp during the Franco-Prussian war and
had discovered that they had similar ideas regarding the re-
generation of France through the church.[2] Far from favoring
independent action on the part of the workers, they wanted
to unite them in Christian guilds with their employers and
to place them under the guidance of directing committees
recruited from the upper classes. In the late nineteenth century the Œuvre served as the center for the Social Catholic
movement and for the clerical opponents of nineteenth-century liberalism and trade-unionism.

At first both La Tour du Pin and De Mun advocated a
counterrevolution that would restore the monarchy and the
church to their former positions of power, but De Mun modi-
fied his views after the Boulangist fiasco, and the *ralliement*
convinced him to accept the Third Republic. While continuing to attack the principle of *laissez-faire* capitalism, he used
his influence as a deputy in parliament to support laws favoring the working class. Then, when it became apparent in the
1890's that the Œuvre was not attracting many Catholic
workers because of its emphasis on upper-class leadership, De
Mun created a new organization, the Association Catholique

[1] Jean Montreuil, *Histoire du mouvement ouvrier en France* (Paris:
Aubier, 1946), p. 235.
[2] Albert de Mun, *Ma Vocation sociale: souvenirs de la fondation de
l'Œuvre des Cercles Catholiques d'Ouvriers* (1871–1875) (Paris:
P. Lethielleux, 1909), p. vii.

de la Jeunesse Française, which became a part of the Action Libérale after 1905.

Unlike his friend De Mun, La Tour du Pin did not abandon his royalism, and in 1905 he became associated with the Action Française. He felt that only the Christian monarchy could establish the corporate regime he envisioned. His solution to the problem of labor-management relations was reactionary to the utmost degree, since he wanted to revive the medieval corporations—which had functioned in a restricted, handicraft economy, where master and apprentice had worked side by side—and impose them on an expanding industrial system with an impersonal contract as the only bond between employer and employee. La Tour du Pin's connection with the Action Française makes it apparent that his motive in seeking to influence the labor movement was counterrevolutionary.

The majority of French Catholics who were interested in the problems of the workers were sincere in their humanitarianism and in their conviction that only through the church could the socialist alternative be averted. De Mun and many others adopted the program of Pope Leo XIII as expressed in his famous encyclical *Rerum Novarum* (1891). The principal new idea of this document was that the state should regulate working conditions in the interests of the laboring classes.[3] In addition, the church had to take up again its rightful role as a social force, and all good Catholics had to practice Christian charity by giving their time and money to organizations designed to promote the welfare of the wage earner.[4]

Undoubtedly Leo XIII was worried about the appeal of socialism to the urban masses of Europe and concerned by their almost complete indifference to the religion of their fathers. In France they "seemed to see God behind the employers, the police, and the judges—all arrayed against the

[3] *The Condition of Labor* (*Rerum Novarum*) in *Five Great Encyclicals* (New York: The Paulist Press, 1943), p. 18.
[4] *Ibid.*, p. 26.

hungry strikers. Could this God be the good Lord? And if he were not good, could he even be true?" [5] The pope believed that if Catholicism were to regain its hold on the workers it could no longer remain indifferent to their sufferings. A year after the dissolution of the Sillon the Christian Democrats founded the Jeune République in order to carry on the work outlined in *Rerum Novarum*, but before 1914 it was Social Catholics who were favored by Rome.

Until the First World War the majority of French workers expected no improvement in wages or working conditions from these "do-gooders," from a government that was controlled by the "capitalists," or from their unenterprising, antiunion employers. Social discrimination antagonized them as much as economic injustice, and they saw little chance of avoiding either one through collective bargaining or personal advancement in the social and industrial hierarchy. They viewed themselves as a minority group, segregated from the rest of the nation. Scorning the outside leadership of Socialist politicians, the militant workers sought to better their lot through purely occupational organizations.

The French trade-union movement originated in the late nineteenth century, and at first the various wings of the Socialist Party tried to dominate it. Both the orthodox and revisionist Marxists championed the rights of the working man, but their factional disputes interfered with the functioning of the unions and caused many labor leaders to doubt the efficacy of political pressure and collective bargaining. Some of them adopted the syndicalist approach, which called for a general strike, the abolition of the bourgeois state, and the establishment of a functional economic system. This program partially disrupted the socialists and spread to many countries. It defied the "intellectuals" and politicians and thrived on the hope

[5] Edmond Pognon, "Sociologie de l'athéisme contemporaine," *Témoignages, cahiers de la pierre-qui-vire*, No. 28 (January 1951), p. 15.

of social emancipation, an impatience for deliverance, and a genuinely revolutionary spirit.[6]

As the number of strikes increased at the turn of the century, some of the more practical-minded labor leaders founded local federations of trades, called *bourses du travail*, which served as employment agencies, workers' clubs, and educational centers. By 1902 these bourses were also performing the functions of central trade-unions, and they merged with the C.G.T. (Confédération Générale du Travail). Most of the prewar C.G.T. members were skilled workers in small and middle-sized shops.[7] They preserved the preindustrial craftsman's resistance to discipline and authority, thus hampering their national federation in dealing with employers on an industry-wide basis. Indeed, they distrusted their own union bureaucrats almost as much as those in the government.

In 1906 the C.G.T. declared its independence from all political movements in its Charter of Amiens, but revolutionary syndicalism—though often contradicted in practice—was its official doctrine. Many workers who subscribed to the principles of the general strike and antimilitarism were expressing their *ouvrierisme* without committing themselves to specific actions. They preached class solidarity while refusing to pay sufficient dues to make their unions financially independent and quarreling among themselves over discipline and tactics. The reformists believed in the possibility of dealing with the employers and the government, but they were divided on the issue of working with the Socialist Party. Meanwhile, the "bourgeois" section of the nation took the revolutionary de-

---

[6] Lewis Lorwin, *Syndicalism in France* (New York: Longmans, Green and Co., 1914), p. 205.
[7] Val Lorwin, *The French Labor Movement* (Cambridge, Mass.: Harvard University Press, 1954), p. 41. "The C.G.T. itself was a minority of all organized French workers, who, according to government figures, numbered 1,026,000 in 1914. . . . The organized were a fraction of the six million industrial workers in France." *Ibid.*, p. 43.

clarations of the C.G.T. militants at their face value and opposed the granting of any concessions to labor.

* * *

Beginning in the 1890's the welfare organizations of the
Social Catholics and a number of industrialists tried to provide an alternative to the solution of the labor problem
through class conflict by creating "independent," or "yellow"
unions.[8] Almost from the outset their real purpose was to
prevent strikes. The leader of the "independent" trade-union
movement was a renegade Socialist named Pierre Biétry. By
1902 he made the exaggerated claim that it had three hundred
and seventeen affiliates with two hundred thousand members,
and at its first national congress in that same year he outlined
its ostensible aim as follows: (1) collective property—workers
buy stock in the company in which they are employed and
become little capitalists—as opposed to "collectivist" property; (2) decentralization, as opposed to the statism of the
"Reds"; (3) intelligent patriotism, as opposed to internation-
alism; (4) a strong army in place of the antimilitarism of the
"Reds"; (5) complete liberty of conscience; (6) an entente
cordiale between worker and employer; (7) the right to strike
("legitimate" strikes only. This professed aim was stated for
tactical purposes. Actually, Biétry's followers invariably acted
as strike-breakers.); (8) an eight-hour working day.[9]

Although the "independent" trade-union movement claimed
to be nonpolitical, its antistrike policy soon led it to devote
most of its activities to combating the syndicalist and Socialist
unions. Shortly after its first national congress, it began calling itself the National Socialist Party (Parti Socialiste

[8] August Pawlowski, Les Syndicats jaunes (Paris: Alcan, 1911), p. 9.
This name came from the yellow paper which the members of the
Montceau-les-Mines company union pasted over its windows after
strikers had smashed all the panes (Georges Weill, Histoire du
mouvement social en France [Paris: Alcan, 1924], p. 425, n. 1).
[9] Pierre Biétry, Les Jaunes de France et la question ouvrière (Paris:
Paclot, 1907), p. 112.

Nationale) [10] and tried to win workers away from the Socialists and syndicalists. In 1906 Biétry said: "We are antisocialists before all else." [11] Since this was the avowed purpose of his followers, the reactionary forces in the country tried to use them for their own ends.

In 1899—the first year of its existence—the *Revue de l'Action Française* stated its position regarding labor in connection with a strike at the Schneider-Creusot munitions plant. (It will be recalled that the wife of the director of this factory later gave considerable sums of money to the Action Française.) The author of this commentary, Jules Caplain-Cortambert, warned the strikers that a prolonged walkout would have a bad effect on French armament production and help Germany. He also argued that the workers were dependent on French capital and that by striking they were destroying that capital of which they might someday hope to possess a small amount.[12] All this—the appeal to patriotism, the promise of a share in the wealth of the company, and the admonition not to strike—was remarkably similar to Biétry's program. In fact, the first "independent" union in the country was organized to prevent further strikes at the Schneider-Creusot works.

The Action Française was not the only reactionary movement in sympathy with nonstriking workers. *La Croix* and the *Gaulois* opened a subscription campaign in the winter of 1901 for the members of the "yellow union" of a northern mining town who were "reduced to misery by strikers who prevented them from working." [13] Biétry and his associates soon found that they were being offered moral and financial backing by these newspapers as well as by the editors of the *Libre Parole*, the leaders of a Catholic businessmen's asso-

[10] Pawlowski, *op. cit.*, p. 35.
[11] *Ibid.*, p. 42.
[12] I (October 1899), 380.
[13] Archives Nationales, *Dossiers de journaux*, F⁷12844, *La Croix*, February 15, 1901.

ciation called the Cercle Catholique du Luxembourg, and a royalist organization known as the Entente Nationale.[14]

As the "yellow unions" became more and more involved with reactionary political movements, their "independence" was restricted, and the scope of the activities they hoped to engage in shrank. Biétry was obligated to his benefactors and did not hesitate to express his appreciation publicly. On many occasions he met with Catholics, royalists, and antisemites and accepted their suggestions regarding policy. Gaston Méry and Léon Daudet, both on the staff of the *Libre Parole* in 1905, tried to give the movement an antisemitic bias. Biétry himself was happy to follow their line, but some of his original followers deserted him when he did so.[15] They felt that his organization was deviating from its corporatist goals and becoming the tool of the enemies of organized labor.

For Biétry used his "scabs" to fight trade-unions and to stir up trouble whenever he was paid to do so. By 1908 he was receiving financial support from the royalist readers of the *Soleil*, the Action Libérale, and other clerical organizations.[16] These people considered him a man well placed to embarrass the government when it tried to interfere in labor disputes and to assume legal responsibility in case of violence. He gave himself credit when the situation was calm and collected from the employers' committees. If there was unrest, he was remunerated from the treasuries of the royalist leagues, which hoped that he would attract working-class backing for the Duc d'Orléans.

Although Maurras himself showed little interest in labor problems, Daudet, Vaugeois, and other prominent people in the Action Française tried to gain sympathy and support from the working class. First of all, they believed that their movement would not be able to carry out a successful *coup de force* if the workers were to defend the Republic. In the second

[14] *Ibid.*, *Mouvement antisémitique*, F⁷12459, May 11, 1905.
[15] *Ibid.*
[16] *Ibid.*, *Action Française*, F⁷12862, February 4, 1908.

place, they felt that a period of economic disturbances—especially strikes and riots, in which royalist agents played a prominent role—might constitute a favorable occasion for such a coup. Finally, one of the surest means the Action Française had for persuading wealthy reactionaries to back its activities financially was to give the impression that it had a substantial following among the toiling masses.[17]

Hence in the spring of 1906 its leaders had decided at a secret meeting to offer Biétry their patronage,[18] and the Marquise de MacMahon saw to it that he was given money from time to time.[19] Within two years, however, the Action Française turned against him. It felt that he was a bluffer who was extracting funds from rich backers of the royalist cause—funds that it could use to better advantage itself.[20]

The leaders of the Action Française still sought to gain some influence over the workers' organizations subsidized by rival reactionaries, but they did not have enough money to buy it. Certainly the "yellow unions" were not a numerous or imposing force. All the same, the Action Française tried to bribe them to abandon Biétry. Since it was unable to give them more money than they were currently receiving from other sources, they declined to serve Maurras' friends. Biétry, who was completely unscrupulous, warned these meddlers that his movement, which might under the proper conditions be a useful auxiliary, could also become a dangerous adversary. Although this type of blackmail did not intimidate them, it did convince them of the need to form their own "workers' groups." [21]

Some people in the League of the Action Française had worked with the Accord Social (a royalist Catholic social welfare club for workers) in 1908, and they had created simi-

[17] *Ibid.*, March 3, 1912.
[18] *Ibid.*, *Parti royaliste*, F⁷12861, April 9, 1906.
[19] *Ibid.*, *Action Française*, F⁷12862, December 17, 1908.
[20] *Ibid.*, April 22, 1908.
[21] *Ibid.*, November 10, 1908.

lar groups of their own in larger provincial cities. These "clubs" were usually sponsored by a local industrialist or nobleman. Their members gave lectures for the workers and distributed royalist leaflets at the gates of factories and mines. The Action Française also tried to revive Jules Guérin's antisemitic gang of packing-house employees and butchers in the La Villette district of Paris.[22]

In 1908 the movement's leaders established the Friendly Society of Royalist Employees.[23] Theoretically, the purposes of this organization were both political and professional. It was supposed to give its members a royalist education and to furnish them with practical training through courses in modern languages, accounting, and stenography. But its real goals were to secure employment for Camelots du Roi who had lost their positions after having been arrested and to obtain money from *bien-pensants* who were willing to sponsor charitable works but who were reluctant to join extremist movements.[24] The first of these objectives was soon abandoned, for the Friendly Society did not place more than ten Camelots in new jobs. It did provide help for workers who embraced royalism, and the Action Française could then advertise their "conversions" at its public meetings.[25]

The moving force of the Friendly Society was a man called Mahon, who had passed through the ranks of the revolutionary Socialist and the syndicalists. He was also one of the editors of the royalist-sponsored workers' weekly, the *Terre Libre*.[26] Although he was one of the most effective agents of the Action Française, he carried on his work discreetly and behind the scenes. The fact that the movement tried to conceal his activities shows the importance it ascribed to them. In fact, he was so highly esteemed that he was given complete

[22] *Ibid.*, April 22, 1910.
[23] *Ibid.*, September 27, 1908.
[24] *Ibid.*, March 15, 1912.
[25] *Ibid.*, March 22, 1912.
[26] *Ibid.*, March 25, 1912.

control of a monetary fund for recruiting followers for the
Action Française from the working class.[27] The main con-
tributors to this fund were the Marquise de MacMahon, the
Comtesse de Courville, and Madame Lebaudy.[28]

* * *

Beginning in 1909 the leaders of the Action Française in
Paris tried to proselytize openly among workers already under
the influence of the Socialists and syndicalists. They carried
on this campaign for more than three years, until its lack of
success—plus the fact that it alienated many of their Catholic
backers—forced them to abandon it. During its heyday Daudet
and others made speeches attacking the corruption of the
parliamentary regime at public meetings on the Left Bank
and in working-class suburbs. Twelve hundred persons attended a typical gathering of this kind in the Hall of the
Learned Societies on March 15, 1912. Almost a thousand of
them were directly connected with the Action Française. Fifty
Socialists and fifty former followers of Paul Déroulède were
also in the audience; the remaining hundred or so had come
simply out of curiosity.[29]

The main technique of the movement in trying to win followers in syndicalist circles was to sponsor public discussions
at which opposition speakers could challenge statements made
by its own leaders. At one such meeting a syndicalist spokesman praised the Camelot who had slapped Briand in the face
at the time of the great railroad strike in 1910, but he swore
that his followers would never allow royalists or Bonapartists
to restore regimes that had fallen in the past.[30] Most of the
syndicalist workers present felt the same way. They were dis-
gusted with the existing government and Briand's brutal
methods in suppressing strikes. Though they wanted a change

[27] *Ibid.*
[28] *Ibid.*, March 15, 1912.
[29] *Ibid.*
[30] *Ibid.*, February 13, 1912.

and seemed curious about the Action Française, they refused to accept its reactionary outlook.

On a similar occasion another militant syndicalist asked Bernard de Vésins what the working classes could hope to gain from a mere change of the political regime. Vésins answered him by saying that the monarchy would be more solicitous of the interests of French workers than the Republic. The syndicalist "contradictor" then argued that the real enemy of the proletariat was capitalism. Vésins replied that the capitalists were also the enemies of the Action Française because they were all Jews; hence it would march with the workers against them.[31]

For the Action Française attacking the Jews as an economic group was a permanent habit.[32] A step in this direction had already been taken in France when Édouard Drumont had added a program for economic discrimination by the lower and middle classes to the social segregation that certain members of the upper class had long practiced against the Jews. Drumont, echoing the sentiments of the *déclassé* nobility, had denounced Jewish capital, which he called "unproductive." This line of attack then became attractive to middle-class victims of industrial development, especially since it was not discouraged by their social betters and economic overlords.

As long as the evils of capitalism were blamed on the Jews, non-Jewish capitalists could support this kind of antisemitism when it suited their purposes. Although it was not practiced on any appreciable scale in France before 1914, it was already common in Central Europe. The writers of the Action Française set the precedent for their own country by decrying the plutocracy in an effort to lure people from the lower middle

[31] *Ibid.*, November 14, 1912.
[32] In 1911 the leaders of the Action Française blamed "Jewish gold" for the temporary hostility of the pretender toward them. Thereafter, they transformed its alleged effect on themselves into a national calamity.

and working classes away from the Socialists. Their motives for doing so were based on a genuine reaction against a society in which money seemed to rule everything, but their arguments were eventually to serve the reactionary segments of the plutocracy itself.

The French workers were never taken in by this kind of propaganda. The renegade revolutionary Daudet was especially eager to attract them to the Action Française by stirring up their antisemitic responses. One of his tactics was to discredit the Socialist Party by accusing its leaders of taking money from "internationalist Jewish capitalists." [33] He also tried to turn French workers against their Jewish colleagues [34] and employers. "We will give you the Jews to do with as you please and you give us the king," he said.[35] This offer found no takers. Most Frenchmen did not consider the Jews as their competitors in the labor market, and they felt that a Jewish employer could be dealt with in the same way as any other. The Socialists were able to persuade them that antisemitism was "the socialism of imbeciles," and the official attitude of the syndicalist militants was one of opposition to the neo-monarchists.

*

Although the Action Française had no direct influence on the syndicalists in the French labor movement itself, it tried to work temporarily with their self-appointed intellectual spokesmen through a man who called himself Georges Valois (but whose real name was Alfred Georges Gressent). Valois was born in Paris in 1878. After having gone to school until he was fourteen, he left France and worked his way around

[33] Léon Daudet, *Vers le roi* (Paris: Nouvelle Librairie Nationale, 1921), p. 224.
[34] He tried to make the wage earners believe that the Jews were not only their capitalist masters but their competitors for jobs as well. He published figures giving the number of Jews employed in the clothing industry to prove this point (*Action Française*, October 1, 1912).
[35] Dimier, *op. cit.*, p. 124.

the world, spending two years in the East Indies and another two years as tutor to the children of a noble family in Russia. When he came back to Paris in 1904, he began working as a clerk in publishing houses.[36] During his free time he moved in revolutionary syndicalist circles and wrote articles on the condition of the working class. Valois read a great deal in the field of social thought with the eclecticism so characteristic of the self-educated intellectual. Then, in 1907, he wrote a book called *L'Homme Qui Vient, Philosophie de l'Autorité*, which was an attempt to synthesize all that he had learned from Proudhon, Georges Sorel, and Nietzsche.

Maurras, who liked the book's emphasis on an authoritarian ruler, interviewed its author and took him into his movement.[37] The Action Française found it advantageous to show off a young revolutionary syndicalist who had accepted the monarchical principle.[38] He, in turn, dedicated himself to the task of persuading other followers of Sorel to abandon the class struggle and to rally to the king as the arbiter on social issues.[39] Between 1907 and 1910 he tried to convince them that the idea of social revolution was subsidized by Jewish financiers and could lead only to the expropriation of the French middle class to the exclusive profit of the Jews. His real problem, though, was to reconcile syndicalism as a means of improving the condition of labor with the need for political change.

Within the Action Française itself Valois' activities were restricted. Maurras did not approve of his Sorelian ideas and refused to allow him to publish his syndicalist articles in the movement's periodicals until after the First World War.[40] His main function before that time was to make speeches at

[36] *L'Almanach de l'Action Française* (Paris: Nouvelle Librairie Nationale, 1923), pp. 171–172.
[37] Georges Valois, *Basile ou la politique de la calomnie*, p. x.
[38] *Ibid.*, p. xi.
[39] Georges Valois, *Histoire et philosophie sociales. La Monarchie et la classe ouvrière* (Paris: Nouvelle Librairie Nationale, 1924), p. 262.
[40] Georges Valois, *Basile*, p. xii.

the league's national congresses, in which he was supposed to assure the delegates that France's workers were ready to rally to the monarchist cause. At the 1910 congress he said that the syndicalists were being forced to abandon their former aloofness from politics and their desire to concern themselves exclusively with labor questions. Briand's repressive measures against the trade-unions were turning these people against the whole republican regime. Some of them, he claimed, were already beginning to understand that the only way to be rid of political problems once and for all was to overthrow the Republic and restore the king.[41] Needless to say, the last part of this statement was largely wishful thinking, but many of the old-line royalists at the congress were happy to hear of possible support from the working class and praised Valois for his activities.

Valois and several other writers in the Action Française persuaded Sorel himself and Édouard Berth (another syndicalist intellectual and the treasurer of the Public Hospital for Paupers in Paris) to found in 1910 a review called the *Cité Française*.[42] Its purpose was to attack democratic institutions and to call for their overthrow and replacement by a functional society based on cooperation between classes.[43] Although the *Cité Française* published only one issue and then disappeared, Valois continued his efforts to bring royalists and syndicalists together. He succeeded in doing so within a few months by launching the *Cahiers du Cercle Proudhon*.[44] (Fifteen years later he said that it had been the first fascist periodical in France.)

The *Cercle Proudhon* was a nonroyalist discussion group in which intellectuals from both camps exchanged ideas on

[41] *Revue de l'Action Française*, XXXIII (December 1910), 510.
[42] Georges Guy-Grand, *Le Procès de la démocratie* (Paris: B. Grasset, 1911), p. 86.
[43] Michael Freund, *Georges Sorel: Der Revolutionäre Konservatismus* (Frankfurt-am-Main: V. Klostermann, 1932), p. 223.
[44] Archives Nationales, *Action Française*, F⁷12862, March 25, 1912.

the evils of democracy and individualism and the need for a society based on the "natural order of things." They found their common ground in the notion of the family as an island of authority in an otherwise anarchic world. Since Proudhon had conceived of the family in this way, he was an acceptable prophet for both syndicalists and neomonarchists.[45]

People of different shades of political opinion came to the meetings of the *Cercle Proudhon* for about a year and a half, from late 1910 until 1912.[46] It even began to publish a series of books. But neither Maurras nor Sorel gave their whole-hearted support to its activities, and it soon became little more than a memory.[47] It should also be noted that Sorel and the other intellectuals among the syndicalists had almost no influence in the labor movement itself, so that their temporary *rapprochement* with a few representatives of the Extreme Right did not reflect the official attitude of the syndicalist trade-unions.[48]

Sorel's lack of a popular following put him in the same predicament as Maurras, but the two men were poles apart intellectually. It was true that they both hated Romanticism, individualism, and nineteenth-century liberalism in general, yet they could never agree on the new order that should replace the existing one. Maurras was working for a monarchical-hierarchical community based on the family, the guild, and the church, whereas Sorel wanted a society administered by the trade-unions. Here was the polarization between reaction and revolution. Although Sorel admired the monarchy and the church as institutions of social authority, he said that they were dead and that it was impossible to revive them.[49] He also felt that the leaders of the Action Française were too doctrinaire to be capable of the direct action implied in their

[45] Guy-Grand, *op. cit.*, p. 73.
[46] Archives Nationales, *Action Française*, F⁷12862, March 25, 1912.
[47] Dimier, *op. cit.*, p. 26.
[48] Lewis Lorwin, *op. cit.*, p. 159.
[49] Freund, *op. cit.*, p. 227.

movement's name. For him, Maurras' attempt to lead the masses by means of newspaper propaganda was doomed to failure, since violence alone could overthrow the existing regime.[50]

Maurras was even more hostile to the *Cercle Proudhon* than Sorel. Not only did he disagree with Valois' ideas, he also resented the way this man was disrupting his following. The Marquis de La Tour du Pin, for example, withdrew his patronage from the movement because he disapproved of its flirtations with the syndicalists. By allowing itself to be associated with the forces of the Extreme Left—even in harmless discussion group—the Action Française was losing support from the *bien-pensants*. In 1913 and 1914 Maurras temporarily deprived Valois of his influence in the movement in order to regain their favor.

* * *

During the First World War the Action Française had no organization or periodical devoted to labor questions. It opposed all union demands for higher wages and better working conditions through the period of the peace conference. Then, when the big strikes of 1919–1920 loomed as a Bolshevik threat, Maurras and his colleagues tried to resume their prewar response to the revolutionary danger by founding a corporatist group of their own. At first it was called the Confédération de l'Intelligence et de la Production Française. Its guiding principles were those that Georges Valois (now in favor again with Maurras) had expounded in his book *L'Économie Nouvelle.*

Early in 1924 this "confederation" was renamed the Union des Corporations Françaises, with Valois as president and Bernard de Vésins as vice president specializing in agricultural matters.[51] It was largely a paper organization of craft unions

---

[50] Georges Sorel, *Propos de Georges Sorel,* ed. Jean Variot (Paris: Gallimard, 1935), pp. 171–172.
[51] *Action Française,* January 6, 1924.

and professional groups in such fields as insurance, stock brokerage, architecture and the building trades, commerce, engineering, and publishing. Aside from its own officers, it had virtually no members. It never functioned as anything more than a kind of general staff for plotting economic reform—just as the Action Française itself dreamed of a political *coup de force* without ever trying to bring it about. The movement was beginning to sound like the Prohibitionist or Townsendite parties in this country with its panacea: "Bring back the monarchy and all your problems will disappear."

But labor was definitely lost to the Action Française and the other French reactionaries after the war. The only "unions" with which they had ever had any direct contact—the "yellow unions"—had become ineffective by 1914. Efforts by *bien-pensants* and conservative employers to win over the workers through paternalistic welfare organizations also failed, and the Social Catholics declined in importance during the 1920's. Most of the revolutionary syndicalists either remained in the C.G.T. or joined its rival the C.G.T.U. after 1920. Aside from the replacement of Socialist by Communist influence in the working class, the main new developments were the foundation of the French Confederation of Catholic Workers, the C.F.T.C. (Confédération Française des Travailleurs Chrétiens) in 1919 and the Catholic Workers Youth (Jeunesse Ouvrière Chrétienne) in 1927. In addition, thousands of progressive young priests gained new respect—even from the non-Catholic masses—by participating more actively than before in the daily lives of the people and by showing a genuine concern for their social and economic problems. Some of these priests established Catholic "cells" in the "Red Belt" around Paris, where they tried to win the victims of industrial capitalism back to the true faith with a missionary zeal rivaled only by that of the Communists.

The Jeunesse Ouvrière Chrétienne sought to infuse class consciousness and solidarity into the newer industrial unions of the C.F.T.C.[52]—the older stronghold of the C.F.T.C. had been mainly among white-collar employees. Its efforts met with vigorous hostility from Catholic employers—especially in the North [53]—who clung to an outmoded policy of paternalism. Actually, the C.F.T.C. wanted economic democracy and social justice not through class struggle but through cooperation with employers and the state. Though it opposed the general strike of 1920 because of its political overtones, the C.F.T.C. sponsored many individual walkouts in the twenties and it was to support the nationwide sit-down strikes in the spring of 1936.

Except for the Popular Front period, however, the bulk of the French working class continued to feel isolated from the rest of the nation, and the failure to integrate conflicting economic forces into a functioning industrial society contributed to the downfall of democracy almost everywhere in Europe, thus aiding the growth of fascism and communism. Indeed, Georges Valois thought that fascism was the only alternative to communism. Eight months before his messy break with the Action Française in October 1925 he began editing his own newspaper, the *Nouveau Siècle*, which was financed by the millionaire perfume manufacturer François Coty. It called itself fascist and was violently nationalist and syndicalist in its policies. The *Nouveau Siècle* included Henri Massis, Georges Suarez, and Jérome and Jean Thâraud among

[52] Even the anticlerical philosopher Simone Weil said: "The J.O.C. alone has concerned itself with the misfortune of working-class adolescence. The existence of such an organization is perhaps the only sure sign that Christianity is not dead among us" (*L'Enracinement* [Paris: Gallimard, 1949], p. 61).
[53] In 1924 a spokesman for the Roubaix-Tourcoing employers complained to Pope Pius XI that the C.F.T.C. was slipping into Marxism and stirring up class hatred. Its leaders suffered a good deal of anguish during the five-year wait before the Vatican cleared them of these charges (Jules Zirnheld, *Cinquante années de syndicalisme chrétien* [Paris: Spès, 1937], p. 159).

its regular contributors. They all admired Mussolini and founded the Faisceau des Combattants et des Producteurs in imitation of his corporatist organizations.[54]

Despite his numerous shifts in politics,[55] Valois seems to have remained faithful to his nationalist and syndicalist biases and was always seeking some person or group that would put them into practice. He had used the Action Française as much as it had used him. A dynamic, strong-willed person, well schooled in the art of political treachery and journalistic black-mail, he might have become another Joseph Goebbels if he had found the right party in which to operate. This was difficult to do in France, where the conventional distinctions between reactionaries and revolutionaries left no place—at least, until the 1930's—for an extremist who refused to identify himself wholeheartedly with either side.

* * *

By and large, neither the leaders of the Action Française nor the bulk of its supporters were ever interested in economic problems and their social consequences. In its formative, experimental period the movement had tried to court favor among discontented workers by using a form of social demagogy that was alien to its basic outlook. The workers, in turn, saw through the artificial slogans and rejected the doctrine behind them. They were instinctively repelled by the patterns of acting and reacting, working and living, and seeking and believing of the Action Française. Their image of it—especially after 1919—comprised boisterous and arrogant rich men's sons shouting "Vive le Roi!" and "Vive l'Armée!" on Joan of Arc's

[54] *Nouveau Siècle*, November 17, 1925.
[55] After 1934 Valois returned to his original Left-wing position and founded still another newspaper, the *Nouveau Age*, which he designed to appeal to industrial technicians. He was sent to the Buchenwald concentration camp when the Germans occupied France. His experience there was fatal to his health, and he died shortly after his release in 1945.

birthday, priests and pious old country ladies praying for the return of the king and the destruction of civil and political rights, and snobbish intellectuals lounging in cafés and disdaining manual labor.

10

❧ ❧ ❧ ❧ ❧ ❧ ❧ ❧ ❧

Nationalists and Fascists

Before the First World War the Action Française had tried to compete with reactionary Catholics, royalists, and even syndicalists for working-class support, but in the 1920's and 1930's it became increasingly hostile to the labor movement, and its clericalism and royalism gradually gave way to its intransigent nationalism. It had been as logical for reactionaries to court favor among discontented workers as it had been for them to exploit nationalism and antisemitism for their own purposes. The Action Française was always too exclusive to win over the masses in this way, and it never became a fascist movement. Yet throughout the interwar years it remained the training ground for many young intellectuals with authoritarian and national socialist leanings. Maurras was still the best known publicist of the Extreme Right, and his rivals had to cope with his influence on their converts. At the same time, the Action Française moved closer to the fascists on domestic issues, while its views on foreign policy were often indistinguishable from those of the conservative nationalists. Increasingly, it seemed to want what the Red-fearing upper middle classes wanted.

The apparent shift in the outlook of the Action Française was due partly to its disavowal by the pope in 1926 and the pretender in 1937, partly to Maurras' growing reluctance to translate his talk about a *coup de force* into action, and partly to the changing alignment of political forces in France. The heavy costs of the war and reconstruction plus the steady growth of industry had created new economic and financial problems, and the conflict between the industrial oligarchy and the workers assumed an ever greater importance in French politics. Those *rentiers* and professional people who suffered from the postwar inflation found little meaning in the shop-worn slogans of the traditional Left and Right, and some of them were eventually to turn against the republican regime itself. The growing conservatism of other sections of the middle and lower middle classes was reflected in the evolution of the Radical Socialists into a party of the Center and, by 1936, of the Socialists themselves into a *parti de gouverne-ment*.[1] Meanwhile, the wealthy bourgeois "dynasties" tried to increase their indirect hold on the Third Republic by control of the press, manipulation of the stock exchange, and pressure on legislators and government administrators. With the nobility and the clergy less influential than ever, it was a few rich industrialists who took over the sponsorship of antidemocratic movements on the Extreme Right.

* * *

As a result of these developments, the Action Française had to seek new backers if it were to thrive in the postwar period. Within the movement itself the provincial sections of the league raised their own funds, as in the past, by selling tracts

[1] Eugen Weber, *The Right in France*, *loc. cit.*, p. 561. Professor Weber's forthcoming book on the Action Française in the interwar years will analyze in detail many of the points in this chapter.

and by soliciting voluntary contributions from their members.[2] On the national level its daily newspaper conducted periodic subscription campaigns for spreading its message. These drives had various names: "Propagande! Propagande!,"[3] "Pour l'Action Nationale,"[4] "Pour Conserver la Victoire,"[5] or, simply, "Contributions Volontaires."[6] Contributions to the first and last of these averaged five to ten francs, with a few scattered donations of more than one hundred francs. The second and third types—which were related to election campaigns or the question of extending the 1905 laic laws to the Alsace (see p. 157)—attracted larger donations, averaging one hundred francs, with some as high as ten thousand francs. Finally, the Action Française sought new subscribers as a source of income.[7]

The Action Française differed from the Communists and the fascists in having no foreign subsidies and no consistent backing from French industrialists. In 1924 it did begin accepting monthly sums of one hundred thousand francs from François Coty.[8] But he wanted to reorient its propaganda to suit his own purposes, and if he had been able to break down Maurras' resistance he might have turned the Action Française into a fascist league.[9] (In the early thirties Coty founded his

[2] See the league's weekly Bulletin du Travail de propagande, Action Française, March 31, 1924 and February 26, 1925.

[3] Ibid., April 3, 1923, October 16, 1923, January 12, 1924.

[4] Ibid., March 31, May 15, August 25, 1924, January 29, 1925, April 21, 1927.

[5] Ibid., November 6, 1924.

[6] Ibid., March 30, 1930.

[7] Ibid., April 19, 1925, in which the figure of thirty-six thousand subscribers is given. This allegedly increased to thirty-nine thousand on May 17 and to forty-two thousand on June 29, 1925.

[8] Charles Maurras, La Contre-révolution spontanée (Lyon: Lardanchet, 1943), p. 119.

[9] In the Action Française of September 27, 1932, Maurras said that he and Coty visited each other regularly in 1924 and that he supported Coty until 1926, when they disagreed on the question of paying France's war debts to the United States (Coty wanted to maintain

own league, the Solidarité Française, and tried to turn the *Figaro* into a fascist daily. When this effort failed, he launched his own newspaper, the *Ami du Peuple*.) Other industrialists contributed funds from time to time, though their support was always uncertain. Even so, the larger contributions to the Action Française—especially after 1926—came from people who were more concerned with anticommunism and organized labor than with clericalism and royalism.

For many French reactionaries (and an increasing number of conservatives) the Communist threat did not come just from the C.G.T.; it was international. In 1919 the heavy hand of Moscow was certainly visible in Munich and Budapest when Kurt Eisner and Bela Kun set up short-lived soviets in these cities and when angry workers paralyzed Berlin and Milan with general strikes. Hungarian and Italian conservatives were so frightened by these events that they soon turned to authoritarian rulers, and German democracy was "saved" only by an unholy alliance between the Socialists and the militarists.[10] A year later the Russian Bolsheviks were invading Poland. Though other French nationalists were also concerned about Communist penetration in Central Europe, Maurras claimed that his newspaper was "the loud voice of national anxiety,"[11] and that he, along with Marshal Lyautey, persuaded Prime Minister Millerand to send General Weygand to help defend Warsaw.[12]

Thus in the 1920's the Action Française continued to pose

---

good relations between his country and the American public, which was a major market for his perfumes and cosmetics.) and Great Britain. The final break between the two men did not come until 1929, at which time Maurras ceased taking money from Coty.

[10] In 1919 the Social Democratic German government made "deals" with the army chief of staff, General Groener, and with the leaders of the *Freikorps* (paramilitary gangs of demobilized soldiers), whereby it would not interfere with their affairs if they helped to suppress the Communist uprisings.

[11] *Le Procès de Charles Maurras*, pp. 68–69.

[12] *Action Française*, August 14, 1920.

as the watchdog against France's foreign enemies. The Millerand cabinet satisfied it by temporarily disbanding the C.G.T. and by pursuing an imperialistic policy in Turkey and Syria. But it hated Millerand's successor, Aristide Briand, not only as an enemy from prewar days but as an internationalist and a pacifist. The fact that the Bloc National had accepted him at all as head of the government was bad enough but that it should tolerate his conciliatory policies toward Germany, the United States, and Great Britain was worse. Maurras and Daudet attacked him especially for having consented too easily at the Washington Conference [13] to reducing the size of the French navy. They also took the credit when President Millerand finally dismissed him in January 1922.[14] The new prime minister, Raymond Poincaré, was a better exponent of the reactionary nationalists' "go it alone" foreign policy, and the Action Française eagerly supported his effort to teach the Germans a lesson by occupying the Ruhr in 1923.

*

Ironically, the year in which a republican government came closest to satisfying the Action Française in its foreign policy was also the one in which the movement became most preoccupied with its own internal problems. In 1923 it suffered through the deaths of two martyrs: Marius Plateau, war hero and Camelot leader, and Léon Daudet's fourteen-year-old son Philippe.

On January 22, 1923, a wild-eyed young woman named Germaine Berton stormed into the office of the Action Française and shot Marius Plateau. Though she insisted that she was an anarchist, the editors of this newspaper called her action a "Germano-police murder." [15] Léon Daudet then published an

[13] Ibid., February 7, 1922.
[14] Ibid., March 23, 1922. This unconstitutional act on the part of the president of the republic won approval from many conservative nationalists but was bitterly opposed by the liberals.
[15] Ibid., March 23 and April 3, 1923.

article claiming that it was really the miscarriage of a plot by the "pro-German police" to kill the four national leaders who had urged the seizure of the Ruhr: President Millerand, Premier Poincaré, Maurras, and himself.[16] Mlle Berton admitted at her trial that she had indeed wanted to murder Maurras and Daudet (though not the president of the republic and the prime minister), and these two men persisted in blaming the regime and the police for having goaded her on. During the spring of 1923 they sent out the Parisian Camelots to avenge their slain leader by wrecking the offices of two Left-wing newspapers and physically attacking Joseph Caillaux, Marc Sangnier, and several Socialist deputies. These acts of violence may well have swayed the jury to acquit Mlle Berton in late December. Their ostensible reason was that she was demented. In any case, republican justice seemed to have been flagrantly remiss,[17] and the Action Française found new grounds for hating the regime it served, Poincaré notwithstanding.

Just before Germaine Berton's acquittal the Action Française experienced another shock, which seemed even more like a republican plot against it. On November 25, 1923, the excitable young Philippe Daudet was found dead in a taxicab with two bullets in his head, after having been missing for five days. The police called his death a suicide (he had allegedly wanted to assassinate a prominent member of the government, had been betrayed by some anarchist accomplices, panicked, and shot himself), but the *Action Française* charged them with negligence and even complicity in arranging the victim's murder.[18] The bereaved father of the boy launched a series of court actions against various witnesses to the affair during the next two years. Then, on November 15, 1925, he was convicted of libel, fined twenty-five thousand francs, and sentenced to five months in prison.

[16] *Ibid.*, April 14, 1923.
[17] The January 4, 1924, issue of the *Action Française* called for a nationwide protest against Mlle Berton's acquittal.
[18] *Ibid.*, almost every issue in December 1923 and January 1924.

After a year and a half of appeals Léon Daudet was finally called to serve his sentence on June 10, 1927. He decided, instead, to bring the whole "battle" between himself and the Republic to a showdown by barricading himself and a contingent of Camelots inside his newspaper's headquarters and defying the police to take him by force. Three days later several hundred of them beseiged the building in earnest. (Poincaré, alas, was again prime minister and Jean Chiappe was the prefect of police—but the regime had to be defied.) When it became clear that much blood would really be shed, Daudet and the prefect of police (who was on the scene in person) engaged in a dramatic verbal exchange culminating in Daudet's surrender "in order to avoid unleashing a civil war." [19]

Daudet was taken to the *Santé* prison, and the Republic seemed to have won. But two weeks later the dauntless Camelots robbed it of its victory by brilliantly engineering his escape by a mere phone call. Imitating the voice of the minister of the interior, one of the Camelots instructed the director of the prison to release Daudet and two other prisoners. When the director returned the call two minutes later, another voice, this time imitating the minister's secretary, confirmed the order. Thus, by tapping a telephone line, Daudet's friends saved him from serving his sentence. After his release he went into hiding temporarily and crossed the frontier into Beligum several weeks later. He remained there, still sending copy to his newspaper, until the French government granted him an amnesty in January 1930.

*

Even though the Action Française was mainly concerned with its internal problems during the mid-twenties (see Chapter 8 for its difficulties with the Vatican), it joined the other nationalists and the emerging fascist leagues in lambasting the Cartel des Gauches for its "sell-out" at Locarno, its mishandling of native uprisings in Morocco and Syria, and its

[19] *Ibid.*, June 15, 1927.

failure to solve the increasingly serious monetary crisis. When the Herriot cabinet fell on July 20, 1926, thousands of Parisians (including Pierre Taittinger's Jeunesses Patriotes and the blue-shirts of George Valois' Faisceau) rioted in front of the chamber of deputies in protest against the imminent collapse of the franc. France seemed to be facing its first postwar *crise de regime*. Two days later the *Action Française* headline was "The Alternative of the Day: Either the Action Française or Revolution." France got neither one, for President Doumergue asked Poincaré to form a "ministry of concentration" that would unite all the republican parties, end the cabinet crisis, and solve the financial problem. The Socialists refused to support the new coalition, but most of the Radicals, the Center, and the Right willingly placed their trust in the Man of the Ruhr.

It is doubtful that Poincaré could have straightened out the "mess" at home without the current relaxation of international tensions symbolized by the Dawes Plan and Locarno. He certainly could not have balanced the budget and stabilized the franc (at one fifth its prewar value) if France had had to continue the costly occupation of the Ruhr. The diplomatic truce and Poincaré's orthodox financial program also satisfied a general wish to avoid political and economic experiments in the mid-twenties, though the crisis might have continued if there had been no respected leader available.

Once the crisis was over the Action Française—like extremist movements in other democratic countries—languished until the early 1930's. A core of loyal followers still bought its periodicals, sent small contributions to its various fund-raising drives, and held meetings. But Maurras and his colleagues had little to offer to outsiders. Most Frenchmen believed that Poincaré had saved the franc and that Briand had secured lasting peace. The "good Germans" were not threatening the *patrie*, antisemitism was temporarily outmoded, tourists were spending unprecedented amounts of money in France, and foreign workers were helping to reconstruct the war-torn areas.

The Action Française had probably reached the peak of its
development in the mid-1920's, but its popular appeal was
limited then, as always, by the Left-Bank parochialism of its
leaders. Aside from their own affairs, what went on in the
French Academy, the faculties of the university, and the Hall
of the Learned Societies seemed more important to them than
anything else. When the first Herriot cabinet fell in April
1925, for example, their newspaper was mainly concerned
with the temporary suspension of the dean of the law school
at the University of Paris, M. Barthélemy. This man had
shown sympathy toward a demonstration by the Students of
the Action Française against the appointment of a Freemason,
Professor Georges Scelle, by Herriot's minister of public instruction. The day after Herriot resigned Professor Scelle withdrew from his post, and Dean Barthélemy was reinstated ten
days later. To the *Action Française* editors these events overshadowed the "innocuous question of finance" [20] (!) that had
caused the fall of the Herriot government.

As in prewar days, the leaders of the Action Française were
intellectuals who dabbled in politics—they were prime examples of what Julien Benda called *La Trahison des clercs*.
Many French intellectuals assumed an ideological position in
order to reach a certain audience or to obtain a coveted academic honor or appointment rather than because of real conviction. Although this was certainly not the case with Maurras
and his cohorts, they periodically made an issue of the bestowal
of such an honor or appointment. In 1913 they had opposed
the candidacy of Henri Bergson for the French Academy.
Twenty years later they launched another campaign of the
same kind when it was rumored that Albert Einstein was to be
offered a chair at the Collège de France.[21] The Action Française leaders vied with the Inquisition and the totalitarian
dictators in vilifying those intellectuals who were "racially un-

[20] *Ibid.*, April 21, 1925.
[21] *Ibid.*, April 15–28, 1933.

acceptable" or who did not adhere to their particular brand of orthodoxy.

*   *   *

It was not the antics of the Action Française in the world of the *clercs* that partially revived the movement's fortunes in the 1930's; it was the Depression and the growing danger of foreign aggression. These challenges undermined the very foundations of the "Republican synthesis," [22] which had flourished since the late nineteenth century and survived Boulangism, the Dreyfus Case, World War I, and the monetary crisis of the mid-twenties. During this whole period the bourgeoisie had retained its ascendancy in a society that accepted social mobility and industrialization as long as these new forms did not disrupt the country's traditional way of life too sharply. The French political system worked fairly effectively within the economic and social balance of this stalemate society. It provided temporarily strong and stable cabinets during the aforementioned crises. Otherwise, the state let most citizens alone, while providing them at the same time with a parliament and a highly centralized administrative authority that would make decisions after they had expressed their conflicting views on election day. Finally, the "Republican synthesis" rested on the assumption of France's undisputed rank among the other world powers. The threat to France's international position did not come until the mid-1930's, but the Depression challenged her economic and social equilibrium by the end of 1932.

As prices fell and unemployment became a problem for the first time in the twentieth century, old extremists came out

[22] Stanley Hoffmann introduces this concept—along with that of "stalemate society"—in "The Effects of World War II on French Society and Politics," *French Historical Studies*, Vol. II, No. 1 (Spring, 1961), 28–63 and in "Paradoxes of the French Political Community," which will form a substantial chapter in a forthcoming volume on contemporary France by a group of Harvard social scientists.

of their torpor, and new ones joined them in attacking the democratic regime. The response of most citizens to this regime was obedience without love, distrust without revolt. They accepted its muddling-through efforts to preserve their stalemate society—cuts in public spending, deflation, etc.— in preference to fascism, communism, or any form of the welfare state. Nevertheless, a significant minority turned to authoritarian nationalist movements, some of which were mistakenly called fascist by their liberal opponents. Fascism is most commonly described as the ideology of a party seeking to create a totalitarian regime by emphasizing "social justice," ethnocentrism, and militarism and parading itself as the only alternative to proletarian revolution. By these standards the Action Française and some of the other nationalist leagues of the thirties were not fascist.

The Action Française did not try to gain support from the "little men" by practicing social demagogy among small shopkeepers or veterans. (Its own small veteran's organization— the Association Marius Plateau—consisted mainly of those Camelots who had fought in World War I.) It appealed to down-and-out aristocrats, pious old ladies, and a few office clerks, but it also found friends among high-ranking military leaders such as Marshals Pétain and Franchet d'Espéry and General Weygand and eminent writers such as Henry Bordeaux, Pierre Gaxotte, and the Duc de La Force. These men were more interested in saving the Old France than in creating a new one, and they supported other reactionary groups as well.

The most important of these was the Croix de Feu. Organized in 1927 as a veteran's group restricted to men who had been decorated for bravery during the First World War, its following had been widened by the early thirties to include all types of ex-servicemen as well as "associates" and "friends." Its leader, Colonel de La Rocque, resembled a Prussian Junker more than a Hitler or a Mussolini. He dedicated his efforts to the restoration of authority, patriotism, and moral values, and he blamed materialism, corrupt democratic institutions, and foreigners for France's current weakness.[23] These views were close to those of the Action Française, and most of La Rocque's followers—like the Camelots du Roi—were well-dressed and well-washed youths from middle- and upper middle-class families. If the Croix de Feu seemed to border on fascism, it was because of its emphasis on action rather than ideas. La Rocque never tried to overthrow the Third Republic by force, though his movement posed the most serious threat to it.

Pierre Taittinger's Jeunesses Patriotes, François Coty's Solidarité Française, and Henri Dorgères' Front Paysan were the truly fascist leagues in the early thirties. Their members, like the fascists in other countries, were primarily discontented *petit-bourgeois* whose economic distress and moral bewilderment made them easy prey for unscrupulous demagogues. By the end of 1933 France seemed to be in the kind of atmosphere that had led to the Nazi triumph in Germany. The climax came in early 1934, when the public found out that a Russian-born Jew from Bessarabia had sold some bogus securities to insurance companies with the aid of certain government officials.

Alexandre Stavisky was not a big financier by French standards; the effect of his embezzlement on the average investor was unimportant, but he served as the symbol of the crooks who were supposedly profiting from the economic difficulties of the masses. The complicity of a few high civil servants and Radical deputies in his activities provided a visible scapegoat in the form of the parliamentary regime itself. For, in addition to the nationalists and fascists, millions of Frenchmen who accepted the current government in "normal" times seemed ready to "throw the rascals [Radicals] out."

The Action Française took the lead in exploiting this response. In early January 1934 it began "exposing" Stavisky's

[23] Lt. Col. François de La Rocque, *Service public* (Paris: Grasset, 1934), *passim.*

accomplices and attacking the cabinet of Camille Chautemps for harboring them.[24] It interpreted Stavisky's alleged suicide a week later as an assassination at the hands of his henchmen in the government, who feared what he might say at the forthcoming parliamentary inquiry concerning his activities.[25] Chautemps kept putting off this inquiry,[26] and the Action Française was joined by other nationalist leagues in demonstrating against him in various parts of the city. He finally resigned on the day after a particularly spirited mass meeting in the Place de l'Opéra on January 27.[27] Édouard Daladier formed a new Radical cabinet, but his dismissal of a few suspect officials did not reassure angry Frenchmen that justice would triumph and that all the culprits would be punished. When his government was to make its first appearance before the chamber of deputies on February 6, the antidemocratic forces in Paris were massed for a riot.

Although the main action occurred in the Place de la Concorde, not all the leagues took part in it. Colonel de La Rocque's Croix de Feu which was mobilized on the Left Bank near the Palais Bourbon, decided against an open charge on the police cordon separating them from the building where the deputies were voting on the Daladier ministry. On the other side of the river the Jeunesses Patriotes were at the Hotel de Ville—more than a mile away—waiting to install a provisional fascist government after the existing one had fallen. Maxime Réal del Sarte and a veteran journalist named Binet-Valmer were with Taittinger's forces as liaison agents of the Camelots du Roi,[28] but there was no effective cooperation between any of the leagues.

[24] Action Française, January 2 and 4, 1934.
[25] Ibid., January 9, 1934.
[26] In a personal interview Camille Chautemps told me that the parliamentary inquiry had begun in secret before he resigned. I offer this statement for what it is worth. It was made twenty years after the fact by an embittered ex-premier living in exile in the United States.
[27] Matin and Le Petit Parisien, January 28, 1934.
[28] Havard de la Montagne, op. cit., pp. 153–154.

In the Place de la Concorde itself a large contingent of Camelots,[29] the Union Nationale des Combattants (which had the largest representation on the spot), the Solidarité Française, several smaller fascist gangs, as antitax league (the Fédération Nationale des Contribuables), and the Communists were harassing the police guarding the bridge that leads to the front of the Palais Bourbon. In addition, about one hundred thousand Parisians were milling about in the vast square. Many of these people were merely onlookers; others believed that the nation was somehow in danger and were caught up in the spirit of protest and indignation against an ineffectual and corrupt government.[30] The sight of policemen using fire hoses, clubs, and gunfire to keep a crowd of indignant citizens away from their own representatives was indeed a demoralizing one for those who witnessed it. For the moment, then, the majority was on the side of the demonstrators who were trying to storm the chamber. The police succeeded in holding the bridge at the cost of twenty dead and hundreds of wounded on both sides.

Daladier resigned, but the Third Republic survived, and the rioters did not even get to throw the deputies into the Seine. Since they were supposed to have been fascist-inspired, it should be noted that Hitler and Mussolini did not gain power by sending war veterans and undisciplined college boys into the streets to hurl rocks at policemen. They succeeded because

[29] On page 120 of his book *French Royalism under The Third and Fourth Republics* (The Hague: Martinus Nijhoff, 1960) Samuel M. Osgood cites a former Camelot leader as saying that the bulk of the Action Française forces had been ordered to assemble at their usual meeting place on the Left Bank and that those who appeared in the Place de la Concorde did so on their own initiative. Although it is true that Maurras refused to sanction a *coup de force* on February 6, a considerable number of Camelots did take part in the riot of that day, and five of them were killed (of a total of sixteen for all the leagues).

[30] René Remond, "Le 6 Février mérite-t-il de rester dans l'Histoire?" *Le Monde, Sélection Hébdomadaire*, February 5–11, 1959), p. 3.

of their leadership qualities and their national parties, which were well represented in parliament. The hotheads in the Place de la Concorde had neither dynamic (or even well-known) leaders nor a unified plan of action.[31] They were mainly disgruntled nationalists and half-hearted fascists who preferred wearing arm bands and berets to storm-trooper boots, and hissing members of parliament to beating up Jews and Communists.

The Action Française legend about its behavior on February 6 maintains that the "conditions" were not favorable to its kind of *coup de force* and that Talleyrand himself would have agreed with Maurras on this point.[32] (Just how Talleyrand would have been mixed up with a band of powerless reactionary intellectuals is not clear—he usually served those men who actually ruled.) Surely the other leagues were also to

[31] According to the report of a parliamentary investigating committee in May 1934, each league followed its own leader and was often hostile to his rivals. None of the leagues was comparable to the Nazi storm troopers—in having its own military training program—and there was no proof that they had carried out a premeditated and coordinated plot.

The report also cites the following figures on the numerical strength of the principal leagues:

Action Française	60,000
Jeunesses Patriotes	90,000
Solidarité Française	180,000
Croix de Feu	700,000
Fédération Nationale des Contribuables	700,000

In most cases these figures were simply taken from each group's own estimate and were therefore exaggerated. (Chambre des Députés, Quinzième Législature, Session de 1934, Annexe au Procès verbal de la séance du 17 mai 1934, Nos. 3383–3393; *Rapport fait au nom de la commission d'enquête chargée de rechercher les causes et les origines du 6 fevrier 1934 et les jours suivants, ainsi que toutes les responsabilités encourus* (3 vols.; Paris: Imprimerie de la Chambre des Députés, 1934), No. 3385, pp. 6–27.

[32] Gérin Ricard, *op. cit.,* p. 189.

blame for the failure to destroy the Republic on that day. But some of the younger men in the Action Française became convinced that Maurras and his cronies—all fairly old by then—would never engage in the action its name promised. The leaders of the movement had made this clear when at the height of the insurrection they were in their newspaper office writing the next day's editorial.

*

Between February 1934 and January 1936 the Republic was again "safely"—though precariously—in the hands of conservative politicians. Former President Gaston Doumergue was called out of retirement to preserve the regime, though he could not reform it. His foreign minister, Louis Barthou, tried to revive France's Eastern European alliance system, but, unfortunately, he was assassinated in November 1934. Pierre Laval's policy of financial retrenchment failed to stimulate economic recovery, and his paper alliances with Italy and Russia merely divided public opinion without protecting France from a resurgent Germany. He and his colleagues resembled acrobats trying to juggle the affairs of state, keep smiling, and maintain their balance so that they would not fall into the Communist or fascist nets. The avoidance of these two pitfalls required a tightrope performance that exhausted those who attempted it and finally discredited them.

Meanwhile, the Left-wing parties and the trade-unions began to unite against the fascist danger. Some Communist militants had joined the Extreme-Rightist leagues in rioting against the Daladier cabinet and the republican regime on February 6, but they were already on the verge of switching partners. A few days later the workers in the C.G.T.U. were demanding permission to join the general strike sponsored by the Socialists and the C.G.T.[33] Reluctantly, the party leaders

[33] Daudet said that the general strike on February 12 was organized by the Sureté Générale aided by "Bela Blum" (*Action Française,* February 17, 1934).

allowed the rank and file to participate in this protest demonstration against fascism. These men had begun to understand
that the German Communists had probably helped Hitler to
gain power a year earlier by attacking the Weimar Republic
and the Social Democrats. They did not want this to happen
in France.

Soviet power considerations and the antifascist sentiment of
most French workers provided the Communists with the basis
for a change of mind, though not of heart.[34] They decided to
enter into a *mariage de convenance* with the liberals. First they
gradually softened their attacks on the Socialists, and in July
1934 the two Marxist parties concluded a "unity of action
pact" against fascism and war. Then they began courting
Catholic and bourgeois republicans. After Laval signed the
Franco-Soviet pact in May 1935, the party's deputies voted
for larger armament expenditures and a longer term of military
service. The Popular Front had finally been conceived. Its
birth was officially celebrated at a gigantic demonstration in
the Place de la Bastille on July 14, 1935.

The majority of French Rightists—both moderates and extremists—were opposed to everything the Popular Front stood
for: collective security against Germany and Italy, government
handouts to the poor, inflation, the destruction of the "200
families," and the fascist leagues. The Action Française and a
number of other reactionary nationalists still stressed the German threat to French security in 1935.[35] At the same time,
however, they denounced all efforts to work with the Soviet

[34] In April 1934 Maurice Thorez still condemned any kind of union
with the Socialists (*L'Humanité*, April 13, 1934) and persuaded
Moscow to expel Jacques Doriot from the party for favoring one.
Then Thorez suddenly reversed his position in June and adopted the
very policy for which Doriot had been expelled (Gérard Walter,
Histoire du parti communiste français [Paris: Somogy, 1948], p. 274).
[35] A week after Hitler had re-established military conscription Daudet
said: "To imagine that a nation in such a state of warlike fury will
not soon turn to acts when we try to calm her by words is pure folly"
(*Action Française*, March 22, 1935).

Union and said that France had no interest in fighting Germany to keep her from expanding eastward.[36] But only by sacrificing their eastern European allies could the French satisfy Hitler's appetite for *Lebensraum*. Thus the people who had condemned the Locarno agreements for giving Germany too much a decade earlier had reversed their view of what that country should be allowed to do.

When the Franco-Soviet Pact came up for debate in the chamber of deputies in early 1936, the Action Française leaders attacked it as a Communist ruse to drag France into a war against Germany to defend Russia. Bainville wanted to let Nazi Germany and the Soviet Union fight each other,[37] and Maurras would have had France intervene with her forces intact only after the two giants had exhausted themselves.[38] Maurras went on to say that France could escape the dilemma of a Russian or a German alliance. "If we make the effort to be strong, we shall be able, with our friends of Central Europe, to maintain between Russia and Germany the only position that is favorable to peace." [39] (Maurras' "loyalty" to Poland and Czechoslovakia was pure hypocrisy, as will be seen later.) This was already a defeatist position, for it implied that France was in no position to compete with the two continental superpowers.

In some ways the response of the Action Française to Hitler's seizure of the demilitarized zone of the Rhineland in March 1936 resembled that of the French Communists to the German invasion of Poland three and a half years later. Both extremist movements completely contradicted their earlier antiaggression policies when their other values were threatened. The Communists, at least, had to be forced to this by outside pressure; the Action Française did so voluntarily. Maurras declared that a stable and foreseeing national government would have

[36] *Ibid.*, February 12 and March 27, 1935.
[37] *Ibid.*, January 2, 1936.
[38] *Ibid.*, February 27, 1936.
[39] *Ibid.*

sent French troops into the Rhineland but that such action was impossible under "the present circumstances." Hence, he concluded, "there is only one public counsel to give the government of the Republic: first of all, no war!" [40]

"No war?" Could Maurras, Daudet, and Bainville have really believed that the Nazis did not threaten France's national security? Certainly not. They knew that "Eternal Germany" had not changed. But ten days earlier Prime Minister Sarraut had dissolved the League of the Action Française after a gang of Camelots had been accused of beating Léon Blum on a Paris boulevard.[41] The very arrangement of headlines in the March 8 issue of its newspaper indicated that this act was as important as the reoccupation of the Rhineland. Once again, the movement's internal troubles colored its response to broad national issues. Only this time the Action Française soon found itself in the company of almost all other Rightists in its renewed attacks on the Third Republic.

The Popular Front victory in the elections of May 4, 1936, followed by a series of nationwide sit-down strikes, created a situation that seemed revolutionary to millions of Frenchmen. For the momentarily reunited Left it was the revenge against the fascist threat two years earlier, but most of the Right viewed it as a prelude to a soviet regime. The Communists did not initiate or control the strikes,[42] but Maurras and Daudet accused them of seizing armaments factories with the com-

[40] *Ibid.*, March 10, 1936.
[41] This attack—whether the Camelots were the main culprits or not—had occurred when Blum's chauffeur had inadvertently tried to drive his automobile through the funeral procession of Jacques Bainville on February 13. The other nationalist leagues defended the Action Française, and members of the fascist Solidarité Française held a meeting in Wagram Hall two weeks later, at which they criticized the government ban on Maurras' league (*ibid.*, February 25, 1936).
[42] Henry W. Ehrmann, *French Labor from the Popular Front to the Liberation* (New York: Oxford University Press, 1947), p. 38; also, Val Lorwin, *The French Labor Movement*, p. 73.

plicity—as always!—of the authorities.[43] The crowning blow to the whole Action Française outlook was the appointment of Léon Blum as head of the government. "Blum-la-Guerre," it called him—the man who wanted to unleash civil war at home and Russia's war against Germany.[44]

But Blum's worst fault in the eyes of his enemies—mainly, though not exclusively, on the Right—was that he was a Jew. "La France sous le Juif!" cried the editors of the *Action Française* in their headline on June 5, and for the next two months they published vicious diatribes against the Jew Blum. Everything he did or stood for was anathema to them. On June 19 Roger Salengro, Blum's minister of the interior, ordered the dissolution of the Croix de Feu, the Jeunesses Patriotes, the Solidarité Française, and Marcel Bucard's Francists. From the reactionary-nationalist and fascist points of view the *pays réel* was truly illegal now.

This type of response was most unfortunate for France's national safety, for it came at a time when the country should have been united in the face of German and Italian aggression. Instead, all of the legal parties (except the Communists) became divided in their attitudes toward Ethiopia, Spain, and Czechoslovakia. Other issues had caused similar divisions since the late nineteenth century, but never when the nation faced such an obvious danger from its neighbors. The situation was aggravated after 1935 by the tendency of an increasing number of Frenchmen to adopt a particular position on foreign policy because their enemies at home held the opposite one. Many Rightists began to advocate appeasement or "neutrality" when they thought that the Leftists wanted to stand up to the aggressors. This became the view of the Action Française, the antiparliamentary nationalists, the fascists, most of the *bien-pensants*, and conservative republicans like Pierre-Étienne Flandin and Georges Bonnet. It was certainly an oversimplifi-

[43] *Action Française*, May 28, 1936.
[44] *Ibid.*, May 29, 1936.

cation to say that the Left monopolized the goal of collective security. Conservative republicans such as Louis Marin and Paul Reynaud also shared it, whereas many Socialists were pacifists. Still, at the time, the appeasing tendencies of the Extreme Right and the bellicism of the Communists seemed to divide France into two opposing camps.

These two groups of protagonists fought their own civil war vicariously through the events in Spain, beginning in July 1936. At first, most supporters of the Popular Front wanted to help their sister regime across the Pyrenees; the Right—with some notable exceptions—favored the counterrevolutionary insurgents. The Action Française was responding like millions of French (and foreign) reactionaries and clericals when it described the war in Spain as a struggle between nationalists and Communists.[45] Premier Blum sympathized with the Loyalists, but, in an effort to warm over France's alliance with Great Britain, and recognizing the strong pacifist sentiment at home, he agreed to a policy of nonintervention.

Most French reactionaries and many moderate conservatives continued to view General Franco as the champion of Order. In psychological terms, they "projected" their own feelings and interests into the rebel cause and "identified with" its leaders. Once this identification was made, they could rationalize the unsavory aspects of the Spanish Rebels: their illegal status, their authoritarian bias, their dependence upon help from openly fascist countries, and the atrocities committed by Moorish mercenaries and German and Italian "volunteers." The ardent campaign for nonintervention in the bulk of the press was further intensified by Communist demands for aid to the government in Madrid.

British and French neutrality helped to distort the character of the international civil war in Spain by making it appear exclusively as a struggle between local Communists and fascists. As a result, some Frenchmen became convinced that they had to choose not only between a pro-German or a pro-Russian

[45] *Ibid.*, July 23, 1936.

foreign policy but between a fascist and a soviet regime in France. The Action Française helped to confuse many patriots by insisting that to risk war meant to encourage the Communist menace. Then, to bolster its own feelings about the Spanish Civil War, it triumphantly printed the following statement of Cardinal Verdier, archbishop of Paris: "The war in Spain is really the struggle between Christian civilization and the false civilization of Soviet atheism." [46]

*

At home the Popular Front government faced increasing opposition by early 1937—from employers who wanted "revenge" for the Matignon Agreements, from lower middle-class people who feared communism, from the Communists themselves because of Blum's nonintervention policy in Spain,[47] and especially from the fascists. For the sit-down strikes had had a psychological effect similar to that of the more violent proletarian uprisings in 1848 and 1871. The June Days of 1936 were marked by celebrations in the streets and factories, where the workers raised their fists and sang songs of the Revolution to usher in a victory won without bloodshed and without barricades. Many wealthy citizens, in turn, viewed these events as a defeat, and they sought to avenge their hurt pride and to safeguard their threatened interests by supporting some form of authoritarianism. Once again they called up the Red specter as a means of alienating the peasant proprietors and the urban petty bourgeoisie from the cause of labor.

Fascism failed in France because of its inability to win mass support and because of the divisions within the Right as a whole. The Popular Front slogans, which were in the French

[46] *Ibid.*, September 8, 1937.
[47] In a personal interview in 1948 Léon Blum confirmed the widely held impression that his heart had been with the Spanish Loyalists but that his responsibility as premier in 1936 had forced him to seek closer relations with Great Britain by following her lead on nonintervention. This move satisfied neither the Communists nor the fascists.

revolutionary and democratic traditions, continued to appeal to millions of middle-class people and they strengthened the hold of the Communists on the workers until 1938. Petty bourgeois Frenchmen still cherished their liberties and were suspicious of authoritarian leaders, even plebeian ones. They were more sophisticated politically than their German and Italian counterparts, especially in suspecting the motives and financial resources of popular demagogues. The only one who seemed comparable to Hitler or Mussolini was Jacques Doriot, mayor of the working-class suburb of Saint-Denis. (Two renegade Socialists, Marcel Déat and Adrien Marquet, developed their own brand of national socialism in the mid-thirties. But their heyday was not to come until the German Occupation.)

Doriot had been expelled from the Communist Party in 1934 and had founded the Parti Populaire Français two years later. Like so many renegades from the fold elsewhere, he used his knowledge of that party's personalities and tactics to criticize his former comrades for their subservience to Russia. He also attracted support from wealthy reactionaries by asserting that the French Communists wanted to start a war between France and Germany for the benefit of the Soviet Union.[48] His party held frequent rallies in Saint-Denis, and his newspaper, L'Émancipation Nationale, printed articles by Bertrand de Jouvenal and Pierre Dominique (who was nominally a Leftist in 1936). But Doriot's relations with his rich backers were too widely known for him to hoodwink many people into seeing him as a champion of the "little man." If democracy were to be destroyed in France, it would have to be done by force.

The Cagoulard affair in 1937 showed that some important reactionaries and nationalists were ready to overthrow the Republic in the name of anticommunism. A few months after Blum's dissolution of the leagues in June 1936, dissidents and extremists from the Croix de Feu,[49] the Action Française, and

[48] Jacques Doriot, *Refaire la France* (Paris: Grasset, 1938), *passim.*
[49] La Rocque and Yves Ybarnégaray, the chief Croix de Feu spokesman in parliament, had formed the Parti Social Français in July

Doriot's Parti Populaire Français, as well as some high-ranking army officers, organized the Secret Committee of Revolutionary Action (Comité Secret d'Action Révolutionnaire). Although these men did not wear hoods (*cagoules*), as their opponents jokingly charged, they did seem to resemble the Ku Klux Klan in other ways. They held clandestine meetings and stored away arms,[50] ostensibly to prevent a Communist revolt but actually in preparation for a *coup de force*. In November 1937 the police raided their strongholds and broke up their organization. The generals and industrialists who backed it were, for the most part, not prosecuted. (Some of the generals in the Cagoule were to be instrumental in destroying the Third Republic in July 1940. Their successors were later to threaten the Fourth and Fifth Republics.)[51]

Although Maurras apparently had no direct contact with the Cagoulards, the fact that their military dictator was not to be a General Monk would probably not have mattered much to him in late 1937. For less than a month after the Cagoule was broken up, the pretender (the Duc de Guise) and his son (the Comte de Paris) definitively repudiated the support of the Action Française. This action was the climax of a growing rift between the Comte de Paris and Maurras' movement. For months the Camelots had been boycotting the new royalist network the young prince was building in order to spread his liberal social doctrine. Then, in December 1937, the Comte de Paris declared that Maurras' integral nationalism was incompatible with the traditions of the French monarchy.[52]

1936, but this new group was too tame for some of its more hotheaded members (Alexander Werth, *The Twilight of France, 1933–1940* [New York: Harper, 1942], p. 113).

[50] Alexander Werth maintains that most of these arms were supplied by Germany, Italy, and Franco Spain (*ibid.*, p. 130), though he gives no evidence for this charge.

[51] On the activities of the *Cagoule* and its successors since the mid-1950's see J.-R. Tournoux, *Secrets d'état* (Paris: Plon, 1960).

[52] For an authoritative treatment of this whole episode see Osgood, *op. cit.*, pp. 130–135.

The answer of the Action Française was, in Daudet's words: "The rallying cry of all French patriots must be, now more than ever, *Maurras au Pouvoir!*" [53] Poor Maurras could hardly have pictured himself in the Hotel Matignon or the Elysée Palace. He knew he was unsuited for public office, and so did everybody else.

Despite its tribulations, the Action Française managed to keep the allegiance of its older members [54] and even to attract a number of gifted young intellectuals. The orthodoxy of some of Maurras' younger disciples was far from complete, but they stuck with the movement until the war. Robert Brasillach, Dominique Sordet, and Lucien Rebatet continued to write articles for the *Action Française* even though they were already flirting with fascism. Thierry Maulnier (Jacques Talagrand) tried to convert his master's doctrine into a more up-to-date national socialism [55] without repudiating it altogether. The future social historian Philippe Ariès and the future political scientist Raoul Girardet also accepted Maurras' tutelage in the late thirties. All the movement's auxiliary organizations continued to function. The disbanded league carried on its work unofficially under the leadership of Baron François de Lassus Saint-Geniès, who succeeded the indomitable Admiral Schwerer after his death in November 1936. Even the defunct Camelots organized themselves into Vendeurs Volontaires de l'Action Française, and the number of subscribers to its daily newspaper apparently held at around forty thousand.[56]

Not only did the Action Française retain the loyalty of most

[53] *Action Française*, December 15, 1937.
[54] This was the impression of all the former leaguers and Camelots I interviewed in 1949 and 1958.
[55] Henri Massis, *Maurras et notre temps*, II, 88–91.
[56] Osgood, *op. cit.*, p. 153, estimates its total circulation (subscriptions and sales by street vendors) in the late thirties at one hundred and twenty-five thousand. He bases this figure on reports from police spies to the Sureté National; but, given the secrecy surrounding newspaper circulation in France, such guesses are always questionable. All that can be safely said is that the regular readers of the *Action Française* seemed to have continued buying it.

of its own followers in the late 1930's, it even had a limited appeal for republican conservatives who could not reconcile themselves to the "loss" of their indirect control of the regime.[57] There was, of course, a long historical tradition for the tendency of these people to turn to the Extreme Right when the social balance was threatened. As the oldest and best-known champion of counterrevolution, the Action Française won a few followers from their ranks. But renovation rather than reaction was what most of them wanted.

The host of new movements, doctrines, and reviews that sought to bring about this renovation did not really fit into the conventional political spectrum. Only their antiparliamentarianism seemed to place them all together on the Extreme Right. The fact that La Rocque and Doriot could attack the rottenness of French capitalism and still appeal to the middle classes showed that the labels of Right and Left had lost their older meanings on economic questions. Another theme among the advocates of renovation was their desire to replace the individualism of France's stalemate society with new forms of group organization (ranging from the Personalism of some of the Christian Democrats to the organized professions called for by the new Business Confederation to youth movements of all political stamps). In repudiating the heart of Alain's Radical doctrine, were its opponents moving to the Right or to the Left? Finally, the widespread lament about France's mediocrity and immobility led a number of Frenchmen who could not accept the Soviet solution to look to Germany, Italy, or Franco Spain for guidance in regenerating the moral climate of their country.

Although the Action Française attracted only a small share

[57] On the growth of the antiparliamentary Right in the middle and late thirties, see Jean Touchard's "L'Esprit des années 1930," in *Tendances politiques de la vie française depuis 1789* (Paris: Hachette, 1960); on André Tardieu's criticism of the parliamentary system, see his own works and Rudolph Binion's *Defeated Leaders: The Political Fate of Caillaux, Jouvenel, and Tardieu* (New York: Columbia University Press, 1960).

of these new malcontents, some of the traditional Extreme
Rightists moved closer to its general outlook. The law school
of the University of Paris and the École des Sciences Politiques
trained high government officials and judges whose views on
the bankruptcy of democracy were virtually indistinguishable
from those of Maurras.[58] He and Daudet were often invited
by these people to speak at their banquets in the late thirties.[59]
They also increased their old following in North Africa by in-
tensifying their praise of colonialism in a semimonthly
feature page of their newspaper.[60] Enough Right-wing intellectuals admired Maurras to elect him to the French Academy
in 1938. (Bainville had also been one of the "40 Immortals.")
Their gesture was both a tribute to this champion of French
"classical" standards in literature and an expression of contempt for the regime that had made him a jailbird. (Maurras
had been in prison from October 1936 to July 1937 for having
written an article [61] demanding the murder of more than a
hundred parliamentarians—including Léon Blum—who had
wanted heavier sanctions against Italy during the Ethiopian
War.)

As the danger of war increased in the summer of 1938, more
and more disabused conservatives agreed with Maurras in wanting to avoid it at all costs. They believed that a war would
result either in the certain defeat of their declining nation or
in prolonging the life of the regime that was responsible for
this decline—especially after the experience of the Popular
Front. (By 1938 the spirit of the Popular Front was dead and
Daladier was leading the government along a more conservative path. But conservatives and reactionaries alike could not
believe that the danger of social revolution had passed.) It was
certainly strange for the Action Française, which had fought

[58] Pierre Tissier, *I Worked with Laval* (London: Harrop, 1942), p. 17.
[59] Gérin Ricard, *op. cit.*, p. 192.
[60] E.g., *Action Française*, February 10, 1936.
[61] *Ibid.*, January 13, 1936.

pacifists in the streets a quarter of a century earlier, to be shouting "Down with War" on the eve of the Munich Conference.[62] Maurras did not flinch at abandoning the country that he himself had called France's staunchest ally in central Europe two and a half years earlier. Even after Hitler took over what was left of Czechoslovakia in March 1939, Maurras still wanted France to hold back from any action that might antagonize him.[63]

This kind of pacifism and defeatism was shared by most of the other reactionaries, the fascists, a growing number of anti-parliamentary conservatives, and even some Socialists. Maurras and his friends distrusted Great Britain and saw the Soviet Union as enemy number one. All that they could propose as a defense against the Germans was an illusory "identity of interests" [64] among the Latin nations (three of which already had authoritarian regimes). Even if an alliance between France, Italy, Spain, and Portugal had been possible in 1939, it would have been no match for Nazi power.

A few days before Hitler invaded Poland and France declared war on Germany these were Maurras' sentiments: [65]

We do not want France to suffer a new hecatomb. Between the alternative of allowing the greatest and most dangerous of Germanies to endure and grow stronger and the alternative of the immediate massacre toward which we are heading, I believe in fostering further delays.

He later said that France's entry into the war was "absurd in itself, ill-considered, unconstitutional, and in the blind rut prescribed by a foreign power [Great Britain] at a time when everyone advised against it." France was too weak to help the

[62] Ibid., September 27, 1938.
[63] Ibid., March 17, 1939.
[64] Ibid., April 26, 1939. This line was taken by many reactionary intellectuals, including Henri Massis—editor of the Revue Universelle —who had begun advocating it twelve years earlier in his book Défense de l'occident.
[65] Ibid., August 28, 1939.

unfortunate Poles, "whereas a wise inaction would have allowed her to save them a little later and ourselves with them.[66] Maurras' talent for rationalization was wearing thin.

* * *

Unlike the French fascists, the Action Française leaders were neither open apologists for the Nazis nor traitors. They were would-be patriots confused by a view of the world that blinded them to the real issues confronting them. On the eve of the Second World War they were closer to the general outlook of the *bien-pensants* and the antiparliamentary nationalists than at any time since the Dreyfus Affair. Their antisemitism, their opposition to the Soviet Union and the Popular Front, and their defeatism were shared to some extent by perhaps a fourth of the total adult population. But the "two Frances" of 1939 were not the same as they had been at the end of the nineteenth century. The difference was especially striking among conservative republicans, who were split between defeatists and advocates of collective security and on the issue of antisemitism. Another new development was the attraction of national socialism for renegade Marxists.

The defensive—and ultimately defeatist—kind of nationalism that rode so high in the 1930's derived its strength from the temporary alliance between the conservative middle classes and those socially displaced persons who were dissatisfied with things as they were but who longed for something better than "proletarization." Since the time of the July Monarchy nationalists in France had periodically protested against the established regime for not satisfying their appetite for adventure and glory.[67] They ordinarily despised the complacency

[66] *Votre bel aujourd'hui* (Paris: Lanauve de Tartas, 1953), p. 103.
[67] E.g., Barrès in the 1890's, Drieu La Rochelle in the interwar years, Jean Dutourd in the 1950's; for further insight into this point of view, see Jean Dutourd's *The Taxis of the Marne* (London: Secker and Warburg, 1957) and Pierre Drieu La Rochelle's posthumous *Récit secret* (Paris: Gallimard, 1961).

of the bourgeoisie, and they were not necessarily Rightists by temperament. In fact, the Bonapartists of the 1840's, Gambetta, and even Déroulède (in his early career) were men of the Left.

By the 1930's the dominant feeling of French nationalism was a nostalgia for unity and grandeur in the face of disunity and decline. The Action Française was too doctrinaire and too static to compete successfully—especially in Paris itself—with the other nationalist leagues and the fascists for the support of the *déracinés* members of the lower middle class or of those bourgeois who feared for their property. Yet, its *Ni Berlin, Ni Moscou* line contributed to the general demoralization of those Frenchmen who wanted their country to be a great power but who were unwilling to fight for it on the same side as Jews, Communists, and other "un-French" groups.

In the late thirties it was not possible for the sons and daughters of former anti-Dreyfusards to accuse the Jews of being German agents, and in many cases their antisemitism or anticommunism made them admire Hitler secretly. The Nazis themselves exploited this response by subsidizing fascist propaganda and fifth columns in France. Although neither the Action Française nor the Croix de Feu ever got any money from them, Déat, Doriot, and the editors of the fascist weeklies did. Rightly or wrongly, being a French nationalist had meant seeing Germany as enemy number one for almost seventy years. When the Second World War broke out, the Action Française and a significant proportion of the so-called nationalists seemed to have forgotten this.

11

❧ ❧

Vichy

During the Second World War all traditional political distinctions in France were blurred by "the German question." Some *bien-pensants*, nationalists, and Socialists had already become defeatists in the late thirties. In addition, many workers had been confused by Communist slogans linking the forty-hour week with resistance to fascist aggression and by the division between *Munichois* and *Antimunichois* within almost all of the other major parties. Then the German-Soviet Pact of August 1939 forced the Communists to reverse themselves by denouncing France's war effort in terms harsher than those used by the Action Française and the fascists before the fighting had actually begun. The Daladier government declared their party illegal and persecuted their leaders, but the labor movement as a whole suffered as well, for his wartime regimentation of the country also expressed a vindictiveness toward the Popular Front. Though the penalties he imposed on the workers did not necessarily weaken their willingness to defend the fatherland, they made them feel that the social values they cherished were becoming more and more illusory.

Many of the Frenchmen who were most pleased with Daladier's conservatism at home were least enthusiastic for a war to the death with Hitler. After the fall of Poland some of these people began to reassert their belief that a peaceful settlement in the West would send Germany against the Soviet Union. They were right in viewing the Moscow Pact as resembling similar ones signed by the Nazis with other countries—that is, as a tactic to throw a potential victim off its guard before attacking it; they were wrong in assuming that Hitler would settle for anything less than the military collapse of France before invading Russia.

Aside from the Communists and a handful of fascist traitors, the majority of Frenchmen did not allow their political differences to blind them to the German menace. But the nine months of "phony war" before the *Blitzkrieg* in May 1940 gave the reactionaries and disabused conservatives time to reflect further on the sins of the Third Republic. The leaders of the Action Française continued to blame Daladier (within the limits allowed by the wartime press censorship) for the war and for France's lagging military preparedness.[1] They were happier when his successor, Paul Reynaud, appointed Marshal Pétain as minister of state and vice premier.[2] The Victor of Verdun was a symbol of hope for almost everyone, and, to Maurras and his sympathizers, he represented military leadership as a good in itself.

When the Germans were about to take Paris, Maurras agreed with General Weygand that the army had to be preserved at all costs.[3] Weygand is said to have favored an armistice so that France's military forces could put down a Communist uprising, which he allegedly feared.[4] The Action

[1] *Le Procès de Charles Maurras*, p. 87.

[2] *Action Française*, May 9, 1940.

[3] *Ibid.*, June 10, 1940; Maxime Weygand, *Memoirs* (3 vols.; Paris: Flammarion, 1950–1953), Vol. III: *Rappelé au service*, p. 216.

[4] Paul Reynaud, *In the Thick of the Fight* (New York: Simon and Schuster, 1955), p. 459.

Française also favored some sort of cease-fire because it shared this fear. Although Maurras expected no quarter from Hitler,[5] he seemed willing to pay any price in order to avoid the internal revolution he had been warning against since the mid-thirties.

After having opposed the decisions of the *pays légal* for two decades, the Action Française voiced its approval at the news that Pétain—who replaced Reynaud as head of the government on June 16—had requested an armistice. Maurras said: "It would have been anarchic to substitute our will for the will of the Chief." [6] Actually, Pétain was a prime minister of the Third Republic until early July, but Maurras and other reactionary opponents of democracy looked upon him as their "man." They saw him primarily as a champion of Order, though, at the time, Maurras stressed the importance of "unity." "Everything can come to life again in unity. But if we have the misfortune of becoming divided—even with the illusion of resisting the victorious enemy—this division will never benefit anyone except him." [7]

* * *

In July 1940 France had indeed become an incoherent mass of individuals and families seeking to go on living with some semblance of order and decency. Her people were too stupefied by their sudden defeat to think clearly about any political decisions. They watched silently when, under pressure from Pierre Laval and certain generals, the constitution of the Third Republic was suspended and Pétain was invested with personal power. He assumed the offices of chief of state and prime minister and named Laval, who became vice-premier, as his successor. The new regime had been established by a vote of 569 of a total of 649 deputies and senators in their final meeting. These men had been hastily rounded up in the converted

[5] *Action Française*, June 10, 1940.
[6] *Le Procès de Charles Maurras*, p. 92.
[7] *Action Française*, June 26, 1940.

gambling casino of a town whose springs were famous for their curative powers. Unfortunately, the waters of Vichy could not cure the ills of forty million disillusioned Frenchmen.

The fact that the majority of Leftist deputies had voted the Third Republic out of existence on July 10, 1940, did not mean that they approved of the regime that succeeded it. (On June 2 and 3, 1958, a smaller majority—but with stronger Socialist support—voted the Fourth Republic out of existence and—again under pressure from certain generals—gave extraordinary powers to a war hero. Their action did not make them Gaullists any more than that of their predecessors had made them Pétainists.) Their self-effacement expressed their awareness of their inability to prevent the military disaster. It also seemed to acknowledge the temporary disillusionment of millions of Frenchmen with parliamentary institutions. But these people were repudiating a foreign policy that had failed, not a political system. In their minds the politicians of both the Right and the Left who had championed collective security and resistance to aggression had been wrong and the defeatists had been correct. At first, then, almost everyone looked to Pétain as a stern but benevolent patriarch whose dignity and prestige would shield his people from the barbarian invaders. Even some leading Radicals viewed him in this way [8] without thinking about such issues as civil liberties, electoral methods, or social justice.

Pétain tried to maintain this image of himself for almost four years, but he had no consistent program of his own, and his regime was never more than a congeries of divided and opposed groups surrounding a feeble, vain old man. The following description of it by Alfred Cobban is most revealing.[9]

[8] Édouard Herriot, president of the chamber, and Jules Jeanneney, president of the senate, expressed their "veneration" and "gratitude" toward the marshal when they voted to give him dictatorial powers on July 10 (*Le Figaro*, July 11, 1940).

[9] "Vichy France," in *Survey of International Affairs, 1939–1946*, eds. Arnold and Veronica Toynbee, Vol. IV: *Hitler's Europe* (London: Oxford University Press, 1954), p. 344.

Its history is not the history of a government by Pétain, or by anyone else, but of intrigues and struggles of conflicting factions, fighting for power in what was left to them of France, but confused and constrained on all sides by the conditions of a world at war and the dictates of the Germans. The impression its history gives is that of some ramshackle copy of an eighteenth-century court, with Pétain as an aged and puritancial Louis XV, appointing his courtiers to office, or dismissing them, with a singular detachment for personal affections, allowing one group to cancel out another, and giving his full confidence to nobody, or if to anyone then to his personal medical attendant, Dr Ménétrel. . . . All this formed the makeshift political reality to which the idealism of what was termed the National Revolution provided an imposing but detached façade.

Perhaps even this appraisal is too kind, for Laval, Flandin, and Darlan resembled ambitious Near Eastern court eunuchs more than the fancy aristocrats who fawned over Louis XV. And Pétain's political position was really closer to that of the Sultan of Morocco in the early twentieth century than to that of an independent European monarch. In 1912 and in 1942 the "protecting" power occupied the whole country in order to prevent "aggression" by a rival. Thereafter, in each case, the chief of state was to play a purely ceremonial role.

From July 1940 until at least the end of 1943 the Vichy regime was a pluralist dictatorship rather than a bloc, or two antagonistic and successive systems (nationalist and *attentiste* at the beginning—fascist and collaborationist at the end). The main reason for the rival policies and tendencies within it was the sudden access to power of all the forces the defunct parliamentary Republic had held in abeyance.[10] Since 1934—and especially after the Popular Front electoral victory in 1936—many French conservatives had felt that they had lost their

[10] Stanley Hoffmann, "Aspects du regime de Vichy," *Revue Française de Science Politique*, Vol. VI, No. 1 (January–March, 1956), 47f. Much of my interpretation of the politics of the Vichy regime comes from this excellent article. Professor Hoffmann expands on its themes in his forthcoming book on the road to Vichy and the Vichy regime.

social and economic dominance in the Third Republic. These people included an important faction of the well-to-do farmers, shopkeepers and artisans, owners and managers of business enterprises, and a lesser fraction of white-collar workers in the government and in private concerns. They had turned against the Republic because the growth of the Socialist and Communist Parties, the seeming triumphs of the working class, and the financial crises and scandals of the thirties had threatened to subvert the traditional social order. Between 1936 and 1940 some of them had sought to regain direct political control of the regime through men like Doriot, La Rocque, and even Daladier—always without success. Then, with its demise, all the Right-wing minorities were finally able to take their revenge.

The antirepublican conservatives were in agreement with the Maurrassian reactionaries and the fascists only in their common desire to regain political power in a regime that would not be of the classical representative type. If fascism itself is a revolt of the *déclassés*, the policies of Vichy in 1940–1941 were largely the creation of people who wanted to avoid becoming *déclassés*.[11] But the fascists differed violently with the other two groups in their desire to use totalitarian methods to make the state all-powerful. The Germans took little interest in Vichy's efforts to turn the clock back, but their Parisian henchmen constantly criticized its reactionary and clerical orientation. Maurras, in turn, charged that Marcel Déat (before he became editor of *Le Cri du Peuple*) was a "false convert" to the National Revolution and that his intrigues were more dangerous than the underground conspiracies of the Communists.[12] Until the Nazi censors stopped him in November 1942, Maurras carried on a running verbal squabble with Déat and Jacques Doriot (editor of *L'Œuvre*).

Maurras' bitterness toward the Paris fascists was intensified by the continuing attraction they had for the younger, more

11 *Ibid.*, p. 52.
12 *Action Française*, October 23, 1940.

dynamic members of his movement. Many former Camelots in the Occupied Zone were joining the Parti Social Français, the Parti Populaire Français, and the Francistes.[13] Robert Brasillach had already begun writing for the fascist weekly *Je Suis Partout* while he was still the literary critic of the *Action Française* in the late thirties, and he became one of its editors under the German Occupation. He also contributed articles to *Deutschland-Frankreich* and was a member of the Association des Journalistes Antijuifs.[14] Dominique Sordet was fired by Maurras when he went over to the pro-German news bulletin *Inter-France* in August 1940.[15] After embracing fascism, he wrote a book called *Les Décombres*, in which he attacked Maurras' movement for its reactionary and anti-German bias. Even a few older Action Française stalwarts deserted temporarily to the fascists, as in the case of Firmin Baconnier—the movement's main spokesman for corporatism—who became a regular contributor to Déat's *Le Cri du Peuple*.[16]

But the Paris fascists had little influence in the Unoccupied Zone before 1942 so that the field was open to the reactionaries and the conservatives who had broken with the liberal side of the Orleanist tradition. These conservatives were willing to cooperate in reducing the power of the state to general police functions and in creating an "organic" society of autonomous, hierarchical, disciplined communities with regulatory authority. On the other hand, they rejected the reactionary goals that seemed too utopian or too sectarian. They wanted organizations of professional men, not corporatism; they did not take the restoration of the monarchy or of France's ancient provinces and dialects seriously; they refused to deny the whole heritage of 1789, which had made the bourgeoisie the dom-

---

[13] *Le Procès de Charles Maurras*, pp. 128–129.
[14] Office of Strategic Services, Research and Analysis Branch, R. and A., N. 2344, A *Selected Who's Who in Vichy France* (Washington, D. C., 1944)—hereafter referred to as OSS—pp. 145–146.
[15] *Le Procès de Charles Maurras*, p. 103.
[16] OSS, p. 96.

inant class in France. Aside from these qualifications, the authoritarian conservatives were willing to go in the same backward direction as the traditional reactionaries.

It is an oversimplification to say that the Vichy regime put into practice the ideals of the Action Française,[17] but a number of men from this movement were Pétain's closest advisers and helped to shape government policy. The most prominent was Raphaël Alibert, the minister of justice from June 1940 to January 1941.[18] It was he who with Laval organized Vichy's political institutions along authoritarian lines. Other members and fellow travelers of the Action Française who were close to the chief of state and who helped to write many of his speeches included René Benjamin, Henri Massis, René Gillouin, Henri du Moulin de Labarthète, and Admiral Fernet.[19] Maurras himself held no official position in the government, nor was he the gray eminence he had always hoped to be under a monarchy. He said that he wanted to preserve his "independence" as a journalist and social critic.[20] Though Pétain once called him "the most French of Frenchmen," there is no evidence that he ever asked for Maurras' advice.

Despite the influence of some of its prominent members and disciples on Vichy policy, the Action Française declined as a movement in 1940–1942. Its Paris headquarters was permanently closed when the Germans arrived, and its organizations virtually ceased to function in the Occupied Zone. All the former leaders of the dissolved league and the Camelots—except Maurice Pujo—were dead by the summer of 1940. (Léon Daudet was already living in semiretirement and was to die of a cerebral hemorrhage in July 1942.) After temporary sojourns in Poitiers and Limoges, Maurras and Pujo took up residence in Lyon, where they resumed the publication of their

[17] E.g., Robert Aron, *Histoire de Vichy*, 1940–1944 (Paris: Fayard, 1954), p. 198; Cobban, *op. cit.*, p. 350.
[18] OSS, p. 110.
[19] Robert Aron, *op. cit.*, p. 202.
[20] Gérin Ricard, *op. cit.*, p. 213.

daily newspaper. It carried frequent reports of the movement's local activities in the Unoccupied Zone. But with the bulk of its membership in the Occupied Zone and with its central organization gone, the Action Française became little more than a coterie of Parisian refugees living in Lyon, a daily newspaper whose circulation was limited primarily to the southern third of the country and a shrunken group of provincial sympathizers.

This remnant of the faithful accepted Maurras' dictum: "Our worst defeat has had the good result of ridding us of democracy." [21] He and his friends undoubtedly wished that Pétain, like Franco, would promise to restore the monarchy eventually. They never persuaded the Marshal to do so, but, until the Liberation, they persisted in hoping that the legal "reforms" of the National Revolution would develop into a full-fledged reactionary regime. This hope, more than anything else, explains their dogged support for Pétain until the end. For the Action Française and its sympathizers the *"armistice sauveur"* created the opportunity for the destruction of the institutions they opposed and the persecution of the groups they despised.

But the *"armistice sauveur"* was not a peace settlement, and the attitude of the Vichy government toward both Germany and Great Britain was far from clear at first. Until the beginning of 1941 most of Pétain's advisers favored the wait-and-see policy (*attentisme*) advocated by Maurras. He was therefore elated when a group of influential conservatives persuaded the chief of state to dismiss Laval—who seemed too eager to tie France's future to Germany's—in December 1940 and to appoint Pierre-Étienne Flandin in his place.[22] By late February, however, Admiral Darlan had taken over the office of vice-premier. He obtained Pétain's permission to renovate his cabinet, eliminate the men who had engineered Laval's ouster, and assume more power than his predecessors had ever had.

[21] *Action Française*, January 15, 1942.
[22] *Ibid.*, December 15, 1940.

The reactionaries and conservatives tried to carry out their National Revolution at home while Darlan was forced to collaborate more closely with the Germans, but, as the war dragged on, their position went from the tenuous to the untenable.[23] Under such conditions the country's ultimate fate depended on the side that won in the end. Consequently, the basic reason for the failure of the National Revolution—aside from the presence of the occupying armies and the economic exploitation of the country by the enemy—was that the bulk of the population could not take it seriously. Most people were to trust the Marshal's personal leadership at least until the end of 1941, but they understood the futility of building a new social and economic order in the midst of a world war.

*

Even without the war, the effectiveness of the National Revolution would have been limited by the diverse—and sometimes contradictory—tendencies among the men who conceived it and tried to implement it.[24] In 1941 the secretary

[23] This was especially so after the Germans occupied southern France in November 1942 and the French scuttled their fleet at Toulon. The following appraisal of Vichy foreign policy before that date is the most recent and the best one available: "During the years when it was still free to act, Vichy, by its dangerous pursuance of a policy based on false premises [namely that France's greatness could be restored by collaborating with the Germans], constantly courted disaster. But thanks to the Germans who, because they understood the hostility of the French and their real aims far better than the English and Americans did, neither wanted nor dared to exploit the possibilities of the situation, Vichy did not commit the irreparable mistake of allowing France to become the enemy of her natural friends" (Adrienne Doris Hytier, *Two Years of French Foreign Policy, Vichy 1940–1942* [Geneva: Librairie Droz, 1958], p. 360). For a good exposition of the reactionary view of a neutral France mediating in the war, see Thierry Maulnier, *La France, la guerre et la paix* (Lyon: Lardanchet, 1942).

[24] The examples in this paragraph come from Hoffmann, *loc. cit.*, pp. 46–47.

of the youth ministry wanted to unite all France's young people into a single, politically oriented organization, but he allowed the Compagnons de France to become a mere imitation of the boy scouts at an older age level, and he tolerated the activities of the École des Cadres d'Uriage, whose directors were disciples of the Personalist philosopher Emmanuel Mounier and poles apart from the Maurrassian outlook of Pétain's chief advisers.[25] The secretary of labor wanted to transform the unions into a state agency and make syndicalism the basis of French society. At the same time, other cabinet ministers were trying to destroy the labor movement altogether. The theoreticians of a peasant corporation wanted to restore agriculture as the economic and social foundation of France. Meanwhile, the committees of organization for industry and commerce were reinforcing the power of big business.[26]

The authoritarian conservatives and the reactionaries were caught up in a basic contradiction. They wanted a revolution without dirtying their hands with revolutionary tactics. (They seemed like Right-wing versions of Sartre's hero in *Les Mains sales*.) In order to transform the modern France of 1940 into the ancient France of their dreams, they would have had to set up a totalitarian state and a monolithic party that would have rallied the masses to its support, either by consent or terror. Louis XIV could ignore the masses; Pétain could not. An absolute but limited state simply would not work in a twentieth-century setting.

With the abolition of parliament and the prewar parties, the French people were left without any means of political expression. At first Pétain was content to have it so, but the Paris fascists were not. In January 1941 a group of them—including

[25] The last class of the Uriage school joined the Maquis. See Janine Bourdin, "Des Intellectuels à la recherche d'un style de vie: L'École nationale des cadres d'Uriage," *Revue Française de Science Politique*, Vol. IX, No. 4 (December 1959), 1031–1032.
[26] See Henry W. Ehrmann, *Organized Business in France* (Princeton, N. J.: Princeton University Press, 1957), Ch. II.

Déat, Doriot, and Jean Luchaire—founded the Rassemblement National Populaire, which was supposed to be a mass
party along Nazi lines. Its goals included the absorption of
France into Hitler's European Order and a kind of authoritarian national socialism at home. The Germans encouraged its
leaders and gave them a monopoly over the mass media of
communication, but their effort to work together was not successful. Each of the participating leagues clung to its independence and to its own distinct legion.

After several unsuccessful attempts to create some sort of
mass movement to counteract the Rassemblement National
Populaire, the Vichy government in August 1941 converted
the Légion Française des Anciens Combattants into a national
"party" called the Légion Française des Vétérans et des Volontaires de la Révolution Nationale. The Legion had branches
in North Africa and two subsidiaries: the Amis de la Légion
and the Légion des Jeunes. Members of these groups had special privileges, such as extra food and clothing rations, cheap
meals in restaurants, and free medical care. The movement's
newspaper, Le Légionnaire, sold more than a million copies per
issue, and its membership, including auxiliaries, was more than
one and a half million. But since the leaders of the Légion,
like those of Vichy's youth movements (Chantiers de la
Jeunesse, Mouvement des Compagnons de France), were dedicated to the repudiation of political action, they were unable
to organize the masses and to persuade them to support an
ideology that deprived them of any voice in public affairs.

Aside from the Légion there was an "armistice army" of one
hundred thousand men in the Unoccupied Zone. Like the
paramilitary groups just described, it held frequent parades and
public displays. Never had military pomp been so highly cherished as during this period of defeat. The braiding and white
gauntlet gloves that had hitherto been the prerogative of the
Garde Républicaine were now worn by the smallest regimental
bands. Members of the Légion and its branches sported caps
with colored tops, and they decorated their chests with medals

the size of a man's hand. Except for its pathetic aspects, this kind of martial theatrics made the Vichy regime look like some imaginery kingdom in an operetta.

Insofar as the National Revolution showed any real consistency it was in building up the conservative forces whose organizations had been weak under the Third Republic and in trying to destroy the groups that had gained strength during the last few years of its existence. On the one hand, organizations of business and professional men, managers, and peasants were strengthened. On the other hand, the civil servants' union was suppressed and the labor movement was deprived of its independence. The Vichy regime tried to revive the church's conservative role in French society by making religious instruction compulsory in the public schools and restoring the subsidies (which had been abolished in 1905) to those operated by religious orders. Maurras was especially gratified when the government abolished the state teachers' colleges,[27] which all *bien-pensants* viewed as hotbeds of atheistic radicalism. He would also have liked to see the public schools decentralized, but—like other reactionary intellectuals[28]—he first wanted to suppress their "corrupt" republican textbooks and remove their politically "unhealthy" teachers and administrators.

The authoritarian conservatives and Maurrassian reactionaries wanted the "organic," pluralist society they were planning to be ruled by a dictatorship of men who shared their outlook. With this end in mind, they not only destroyed the institutions of the Third Republic—parliament, parties, elections (except in communes with less than two thousand inhabitants)—but they tried to get rid of its personnel as well. A few "safe" conservative politicians held posts in early Vichy gov-

[27] *Action Française*, September 4, 1940.
[28] See Serge Jeanneret, *La Vérité sur les instituteurs* (Paris: Flammarion, 1941); Pierre Dominique's article on education in *Candide*, September 18, 1940; and Henry Bordeaux, *Les Murs sont bons: nos erreurs et nos espérances* (Paris: Fayard, 1941).

ernments, but most political leaders of the fallen Republic were forced into retirement. "Undesirable" members of the national and local administrations were also eliminated from office. Many of these people were Freemasons, whom the reactionaries had long accused of conspiring to take over the Third Republic and whom the Action Française charged with sabotaging its successor.[29] The historian Bernard Faÿ took over the "crusade" against them and saw to it that several thousand of them lost their jobs in the civil service.

In the place of the dispossessed republican enemies, Vichy tried to substitute "healthy," "uncontaminated" people. Army and navy officers gained an extraordinary influence in the government and the youth groups of defeated France. (Maurras called these men the incarnation of the *pays réel*.)[30] Conservatives in the high civil service got special consideration for promotion and sometimes became cabinet ministers. Finally, local *bien-pensant* notables who could never have won an election were appointed heads of communes and *départements*.

Disillusionment with prewar allies, the military defeat, the Occupation, and Vichy's diplomatic impotence had made most Frenchmen approve, at first, of their government's nativist bias. Normally the French took pride in their tolerance of non-French peoples and even non-Europeans. France was a traditional haven for refugees from political, racial, and moral persecution. In 1939 there were hundreds of thousands of recent arrivals from Central Europe and Spain. Along with the Communists, they had been put into internment camps by the Daladier government. A few of them managed to go into hiding, but after the Armistice there was little public sentiment to relax the wartime restrictions on "enemy" aliens. *Fraternité* was now reserved for the natives, though not all of them were considered safe.

While reactionary intellectuals tried to restore a "conscious-

[29] *Action Française*, September 27, 1941.
[30] *La Seule France* (Lyon: H. Lardanchet, 1941), p. 19.

242 ❧ The Action Française

ness of the native essential," the Vichy government decided
that it had to do something about "the Jewish problem." [31]
In December 1940 it forbade French Jews from engaging in
certain occupations. Later it restricted them in other ways as
well. Maurras not only approved of Vichy's antisemitic laws
(which were written by his disciple Raphaël Alibert) but he
eventually began criticizing the government for its laxity in
enforcing them.[32] He was especially pleased when, in March
1941, Pétain created a Commissariat-General for Jewish Affairs and named Xavier Vallat, a long-time reactionary and
friend of Léon Daudet, as its chief.[33]

As with everything else, the "housecleaning" activities of
the National Revolution were already, in the summer of 1941,
being hampered by German economic, military, and political
pressure on the Pétain regime to abandon the last vestiges of
its *attentisme.* Hitler had no need of French military help in
his attack on the Soviet Union, but the Paris fascists, led by
Doriot, tried in August to organize still another legion—the
Légion des Volontaires Contre le Bolchevisme. Pétain decided
to break off diplomatic relations with Moscow without an
open declaration of war. At the same time, he praised the
French "volunteers" against Bolshevism and said that the
Nazis were engaged in the defense of civilization. Although
many reactionaries shared this view, Maurras' response illustrated once again his preference for counterrevolution at
home to any kind of foreign undertaking. He said that France
must put the battle for the *patrie*—that is, the Old France—
before a crusade against Communism.[34]

Pétain agreed with this stand, but as chief of state he had

[31] Even the Right-wing nationalist Resistance movement, Organisation Civile et Militaire, concerned itself with "the Jewish problem"
in its *Cahier* of June 1942 (Arthur Calmette, *L'O.C.M." Organisation
civile et militaire* [Paris: Presses Universitaires Françaises, 1961],
pp. 52–54).
[32] *Action Française,* November 27, 1942.
[33] *Ibid.,* March 30, 1941.
[34] *Ibid.,* July 3, 1941.

to placate the Nazis with public denunciations of the Soviet Union. In November 1941 he dismissed General Weygand as commander of French forces in North Africa, again under German pressure. His last effort to forestall the Germans— short of taking Laval back into his government—was to agree to their demand that France's "war criminals" be tried. The Vichy government also hoped that the Riom trials would give judicial sanction to its policies of revenge against the politicians of the Third Republic.

The Action Française enthusiastically supported the prosecution of Blum, Daladier, Reynaud, Gamelin, and Mandel.[35] It had accused them of being warmongers in the thirties and it rejoiced at seeing a legal French government try them in open court. Ironically, the defendants turned the tables on the prosecution by shifting the charge from "Who made France go to war against Germany?" to "Whose fault was it that France lost the war?" In these terms the Riom trials not only convinced Hitler that the French were unrepentant, they also damaged the reputation of Marshal Pétain, since he had been minister of defense in 1934. The proceedings were summarily suspended on April 11, 1942. A week later the Germans forced Pétain to replace Darlan with Laval as head of the government, this time with virtually dictatorial powers.

After that the Action Française rapidly lost its influence over Vichy policy, and the royalist cause also suffered a series of setbacks. The Comte de Paris had repudiated Maurras' movement and he never openly backed the Vichy regime. (By the end of 1942 he was supporting General de Gaulle.) Although he did have several talks with Pétain in August 1942, the Marshal was not a monarchist and he did not intend to jeopardize his own shaky position any further by committing himself to a man without a following.[36] When the Allies invaded North Africa three months later, the pretender approached General Eisenhower, who also turned him down.

[35] *Ibid.*, February 28, 1942.
[36] Osgood, *op. cit.*, pp. 169–170.

Maurras expressed his regret that some of the French officers who had facilitated this invasion were not executed.[37] Admiral Darlan had not worked with the Allies before they landed (indeed, he had just "landed" in Algiers himself), but he became their "stooge" as soon as they established themselves in Morocco and Algeria. His brief career in this role ended on December 24, when he was shot to death by a young royalist named Bonnier La Chapelle. The Comte de Paris did not sponsor this assassination,[38] and there was probably no direct connection between it and Maurras' article a few weeks earlier. Nevertheless, it destroyed royalist hopes in North Africa, just as the German Occupation of all of France in November made it impossible for the Vichy regime to carry out its counter-revolution at home.

*

The rigors of the Occupation also hastened the disintegration of the Action Française throughout the country after November 1942. Only its daily newspaper continued to function without interruption until August 1944, and it was subject to German censorship. It still printed occasional news items about the study circles, fund-raising drives, and religious celebrations in the few surviving sections of the league. In 1943 and especially in 1944 many Action Française militants and sympathizers were abandoning these genteel activities and Maurras' unrealizable ideal of La Seule France. Some of them joined the Resistance; others became open collaborators. In Maurras' eyes both groups were deserters. Although the Nazis continued to view Maurras with disfavor,[39] they never molested him. (They took Pujo into custody for nineteen days in June 1944 and then released him.) Their only demand was that he

[37] Action Française, December 7, 1942.
[38] Osgood, op. cit., p. 176.
[39] Ibid., p. 165, n. 3. Osgood cites the Dossier Maurras and the Dossier Maison de France of the Sureté Nationale on this point.

refrain from attacking the fascist enemies of Vichy. He was
free, of course, to attack its antifascist enemies.

Maurras and his associates became increasingly bitter toward the Allies as the prospect of Liberation threatened the
imitation Old Regime they thought Pétain had restored. Their
main fear was that the Gaullists, Communists, and Christian
Democrats—rather than the Americans and the British—
would undo the Marshal's noble work. For Maurras the im-
pending Liberation would be a second 1789, since it would
destroy "the only France" worth preserving. When he said
"don't assassinate France," [40] he meant "don't destroy what
Vichy has tried to build." Despite his hatred of the Germans,
he seemed to prefer their continued occupation to a "Gaullo-
Communist" regime sponsored by the victorious Allies.

As early as August 1941 Maurras had boasted that "the
toughest and most enduring anti-Gaullist campaigns are
ours." [41] Henceforth, his newspaper denounced the Fighting
French movement and its sympathizers in France for divid-
ing the nation morally without aiding in its "true liberation."[42] The *Action Française* called those Frenchmen who had
joined the Allies traitors and servants of Moscow [43] and said
that if the death penalty were not a sufficient deterrent to
them then hostages from their families should be seized and
executed.[44] Until the Liberation Maurras insisted that the followers of De Gaulle were "armed partisans" and that they
should be "shot on sight." [45]

When Joseph Darnand organized the notorious *Milice* [46]

[40] *Action Française*, June 1, 1943.
[41] *Ibid.*, August 9, 1941.
[42] *Ibid.*, December 24, 1942, October 18, 1943.
[43] *Ibid.*, also November 25, 1943.
[44] *Ibid.*, September 1, 1943.
[45] *Ibid.*, April 27, 1944.
[46] The Service d'Ordre Légionnaire was founded by Darnand in 1942
as a paramilitary subsidiary of the Vichy Legion. In January 1943
this organization was given a separate status and renamed the

in early 1943 to supplement the regular police in maintaining order, Maurras responded with unqualified praise: "Great benefits can come of it, no bad effects could possibly result from it." [47] Then, when the *Milice* became an arm of the *Waffen SS* in September, Maurras advised his followers not to join it.[48] He said that he wanted to avoid a civil war between this organization and those people who resisted collaboration, but he still urged other Vichy agencies to execute members of the Resistance forces and take hostages among them.[49]

Maurras and his coterie also seemed to see nothing wrong in forcing hundreds of thousands of their compatriots to work in Germany under conditions that—despite good wages —were an ill-disguised form of slavery. Not only did he justify Laval's forced-labor levy, he made vicious attacks on young Frenchmen who joined the *maquis* in order to escape it.[50] At first he declared that these partisan fighters were bandits led by the Communists and that the "government" should repress them by force.[51] Later he said that ordinary judicial proceedings were too slow and should be replaced by courtsmartial that would execute these "criminals" in forty-eight hours.[52]

By early 1944, with Darnand running France like a police state and with the Paris fascists in Laval's government, the realization of a National Revolution was impossible. Still, to the bitter end Maurras opposed and denounced those Frenchmen who tried to hasten the Allied victory. What could have

---

Milice Française. Darnand's boss was no longer Pétain but Laval, the head of the government. Thereafter, until the Germans left the country, Darnand and his militia worked for them in repressing the growing Resistance movements and killing Jews.

[47] *Action Française*, March 2, 1943.
[48] *Le Procès de Charles Maurras*, pp. 130, 233.
[49] *Action Française*, January 4, 1944.
[50] *Ibid.*, July 10, 1943.
[51] *Ibid.*
[52] *Ibid.*, October 12, 1943.

been his vision of the French political scene after the Germans left France and the puppet regime fell? Could he possibly have believed that Pétain's honor and past prestige would have kept him in power?

The situation in France in 1943 and 1944 was something like that of a prisoner-of-war camp. Maurras was like the prisoner who denounced those of his comrades who opposed their jailors and the "stool pigeons" in their own midst. His reason was that these comrades were goading the authorities into punishing everyone for their acts. In modern prisoners' compounds the authorities often give the inmates some sort of administrative structure for handling their own affairs but keep its power restricted to routine matters. Such was the puppet regime of Laval and Pétain. When liberation from the outside becomes possible, those inside who try to hasten it are the true patriots.

* * *

In 1944 and 1945 most people seemed to believe that the Resistance was exclusively a movement of the Left; recent research has shown that this impression was illusory. The earliest Resistance organizations—Organisation Civile et Militaire in the Occupied Zone and Libération-Sud in the Unoccupied Zone—were formed by reserve army officers and technocratic-minded administrators from industry, government, and the unions. By the end of 1941 a group of Christian Democrats with a more liberal orientation turned against Vichy and organized their own Resistance movement, but they differed in many ways from the old parliamentary Left. General de Gaulle and his closest associates in London were not Leftists either. Only in 1943 did Communists and Socialists begin to submerge the other Resistance forces at home—by sheer numbers and by flooding the country with clandestine newspapers and tracts. The Communist-led Front National often acted independently and was viewed with suspicion by De Gaulle. The F.F.I. itself was staffed in part by conservative military officers from the Organisation Civile et Militaire. Yet by late 1943 De Gaulle was accepting support from Communist politicians in Algiers, and the Charter of the Conseil National de la Résistance proposed to renovate France with a more extreme version of the Popular Front. Many conservative *résistants* did not approve of this goal, but they (unlike those conservatives who remained loyal to Pétain) temporarily subordinated some of their principles in order to present a united stand against the enemy.

As the Resistance forces took over various parts of France during the summer of 1944, they initiated a "purge" of collaborators, which the Provisional Government continued for more than a year. Communists and other Left-wing extremists confiscated property illegally and killed some innocent people, but these executions resembled ritual murders more than atrocities in a civil war. It should also be remembered that De Gaulle was eager to bring his country back into the war against Germany as well as to punish his Vichyite enemies. Besides, the majority of the French people wanted to forget that they had once been defeatists. Their search for scapegoats and their haste to climb aboard the bandwagon of the Allied victory were the two means by which they sought to regain their self-respect. Finally, the purge helped to reunite Frenchmen from all political camps (including conservatives who had put their faith in Pétain and the National Revolution in 1940–1941) by implementing the Resistance myth that the collaborators were a tainted minority and that the rest of the nation had recovered its patriotic purity.

Laval's execution in October 1945 marked the climax of the "purge." At Pétain's trial three months earlier Laval had already shown his ability to defend himself at the expense of France's most prominent political and military leaders. Obviously these men were anxious to silence him, and almost everyone else hated him as the incarnation of their worst responses during the Occupation. This hostility was apparent in the viciousness of the court, the jury, and the audience at

Laval's own trial. He was shouted down when he tried to speak in his own defense, and, after his attempted suicide, he was brutally executed. In the true biblical tradition, the French people—Rightists and Leftists alike—projected all their sins onto this scapegoat and sent him off to another world.

Pétain's case was more complex. Aside from the minority that had opposed him from the beginning, most people had once looked upon him as a visible justification for their own wartime behavior. Of Laval they were able to say: "I couldn't have been like that!" It was different with Pétain. He, too, had to be sacrificed, not as a scapegoat but as a beloved sovereign who had gone astray. Though the death sentence seemed to be a necessary symbolic gesture condemning the regime he represented, it was subsequently commuted to life imprisonment.

*

The Liberation "purge" also brought an end to the history of the Action Française. On August 24, 1944, the last issue of its daily newspaper appeared in Lyon. When the Germans departed ten days later, the Resistance forces took over the city. Maurras went into hiding in order to escape their vengeance, but on September 4 he could not resist giving an interview to four newspaper reporters attached to the American army. Not only did he thus reveal his whereabouts to the authorities of the new Provisional Government, but his remarks themselves were self-incriminating. He said, for example, that Pétain was "the most *résistant* of all Frenchmen" [53] (a slap in the face to De Gaulle) and that the restoration of democracy in France would be a disaster (a defiance of the prevailing Resistance spirit).

Four days after this interview Maurras and Pujo were arrested. Soon thereafter the property of the movement was seized and its organizations were proscribed. Maurras remained in jail for more than four months before being brought

[53] Havard de la Montagne, *op. cit.*, pp. 221–222.

to trail. During this time the Liberation press and radio clamored for his head while some of his remaining sympathizers put up posters proclaiming his innocence on walls throughout Lyon. Maurras' attorney demanded a change of venue, and the authorities considered postponing the trial beyond its scheduled date.

The trial of Maurras and Pujo finally took place in Lyon between January 24 and 27, 1945, and was highly publicized by the press, radio, and newsreels. Both the prosecution and the defense produced newspaper quotations, affidavits, and character witnesses. But the main event was Maurras' hundred-and-ten-page (in print) review and justification of his behavior since his childhood. He insisted on answering all questions about his "collaborationist" activities by repeating his life history and political philosophy.[54] Pujo spoke very briefly and said that he did not remember specific acts attributed to him. Maurras was full of fire and persistence. Though old and deaf, he read on and on for two days.

In a sense, both Maurras and his prosecutors made the trial a mockery. The latter did so by condemning him for his principles rather than for treasonable acts. Maurras, on the other hand, claimed, as always, that his views were infallible, hence incapable of leading him to betray the national interest. After both sides had stated their cases, the jury convicted the two defendants, and the court sentenced Maurras to life imprisonment in isolation and to national degradation. Pujo received a five-year prison term and was fined twenty thousand francs and deprived of his civic rights.

There was no proof that Maurras had commited treason, but there was ample evidence that his public statements during the occupation had demoralized the nation and—inadvertently or not—helped the enemy. Maurras persisted in claiming that he was anti-German, and this he certainly was. (In a book written in prison six years later he argued that "our anti-Gaullist polemics themselves had an anti-German

[54] *Le Procès de Charles Maurras*, pp. 27–28.

meaning that enabled us, by a thousand allusions, to remind the people that our number one enemy was in Berlin.") [55] Even so, his denunciations of Frenchmen from all sections of society and all political movements that did not share his outlook had caused a great deal of harm. In any case, he had alienated the majority of his countrymen, who momentarily rallied behind the Resistance. In their eyes he was an intellectual Judas who had betrayed his country out of pure spite against the enemies of Vichy.

When informed of his conviction, Maurras cried: "This is the revenge of Dreyfus!" He was wrong, as he had always been wrong, in evaluating the motives of his enemies. It was Maurras, not his prosecutors or the majority of Frenchmen, who was still responding to the Dreyfus Affair. The history of the Action Française lay between these two trials, to be sure, but Maurras' attempt to link them directly was only a supreme act of self-dramatization. (During his seven years in prison Maurras' friends were to try to create an image of him as the Dreyfus of the Right and to clamor for a revision of the judgment that had convicted him—*this* time unjustly—of treason.) The real significance of Maurras' condemnation was the repudiation by the French people of the counterrevolutionary tradition he stood for. The Action Française had prepared the way for Vichy, defended it when almost everyone else abandoned it, and suffered the same fate as its spiritual offspring.

[55] *Les Mensonges de "l'expert" Verdenal au procès de Lyon* (Paris: Éditions de la Seule France, 1951), p. 23.

12

❧ ❧ ❧ ❧ ❧ ❧ ❧ ❧ ❧ ❧ ❧ ❧ ❧

Reactionaries: A Family Portrait

Twentieth-century French reactionaries have had many faces and appeared in many guises. In education, manners, and dress a prelate such as Cardinal Baudrillart bore no resemblance to a Jew-baiting army sergeant. The rowdy Camelot du Roi who had been raised in an orphanage moved in a different world from that of the fashionable Marquise de MacMahon. Pierre Gaxotte—brilliant historian and member of the French Academy—had little in common with a bigoted housemaid. Yet they all shared the reactionary outlook. For some of them it was a custom or tradition, for others it was acquired out of sentiment, interest, or ideals.

If enough of these people could be interviewed and tested by a team of social scientists, some statistical correlations might be revealed; another procedure would be to construct an ideal type. The evidence at my disposal is insufficient to meet the standards of the first method, and—in view of the variations in age, sex, background, and motives of French reactionaries over a period of fifty years—the second one would yield an inadequate and artificial result. I shall therefore limit myself to showing a pattern of attitudes and personality traits in the form of a family portrait.

*

Reactionaries everywhere think that life was more congenial in an earlier age, and they want to restore a vanished *status quo*. From Calabria to Alabama, from Philadelphia to Vienna, there are people who miss the old distinctions between masters and servants, rulers and subjects, the upper classes and the masses. When they say "the country is going to the dogs" they mean that "upstarts" of one kind or another are changing its traditional way of life. Their aristocratic ancestors (if they had any) prided themselves on being cosmopolitan, but they themselves are usually afraid of anyone or anything foreign. They especially detest minority groups that were once outcasts and are now trying to "assimilate." If everybody were as good as everybody else, nobody would be anybody.

To the followers of the Action Française and other French reactionaries, returning to the past meant everything from church-run schools to the preservation of local dialects. It required the elimination of such "un-French" distortions of their culture as the "German" Romantic movement, the "Jewish" credit economy, "English" parliamentary government, and the egalitarianism that was part of the "Judeo-Masonic conspiracy" known as the French Revolution. The traditionalist also condemned the impersonal and cosmopolitan aspects of the modern city and self-consciously praised the simple virtues of rural life. This attitude was sheer pose on the part of the Parisian café intellectuals who held it—Saint-Germain-des-Prés was as close to the country as they cared to live. On the other hand, a nonintellectual reactionary such as General Giraud sincerely believed that France could be "regenerated" only by going back to a predominantly agricultural economy.[1]

[1] General Giraud expressed this view in the press and on the radio

Like their counterparts in most societies, French reactionaries have defended the established church against its modern enemies. They have wanted to restore it as an institution representing and teaching social and political order, conventional behavior, and obedience to authority. Their clericalism became increasingly articulate as the Third Republic tried to foster individual liberty, universal suffrage, the separation of church and state, and a system of lay education that encouraged freedom of thought. Speaking before the branch of the League of the Action Française in eastern Brittany a naval commander said that public secondary schools for girls were corrupting Christian womanhood.[2] Although this gentleman was ostensibly opposed to education by the state because it was irreligious, he also seemed to favor the obscurantism that is so dear to the nonintellectual reactionary.

Some clericals believed that it was impossible to serve God and be a republican at the same time. One provincial priest said that only the traditional monarchy could remove "the yoke of the monstrous politicians of the Judeo-Masonic republic."[3] In a letter to Henri Vaugeois a provincial dowager maintained that the policy of *ralliement* was detrimental to the interests of the church. "Just as there must be a God in heaven and a pope at the head of the church," she said, "so there must be a king at the head of the nation." For, according to her, "both the church and the king contribute to the general order of society, and each must have a share of the political power that maintains order."[4]

As the twentieth century progressed, an increasing number of reactionaries lost hope for the return of the king, but

when he was the supreme commander of French military forces in North Africa after the Allied landing there in late 1942.

[2] Ligue de l'Action Française. Section d'Angers. *Conférence faite par M. Le Commandant d'Argenton le 15 Juillet 1913* (Angers, 1913, pamphlet).

[3] Letter cited in the *Revue de l'Action Française*, XXI (August 1908), 230.

[4] *Ibid.*, XVI (March 1905), 329.

those who had reached adulthood before 1900 were usually royalists.[5] Of those who had grown up since then, some were monarchists because of family background, others by persuasion. The country nobility, especially in the West, was the most ardent traditional royalist group in France. Even their young daughters often followed the publications and lectures of the Action Française and pledged themselves to "work with all their ardor for the French monarchy." [6] Sixteen of these girls accompanied a donation of three hundred francs to the movement with the following remarks: [7]

We are no longer living in the time when the women sewed for the ransom of Duguesclin. Certainly women still work with the spindle and the needle—thus you see the fruit of our labors in the small sum we are sending to you—but something else is needed. Today everyone, even women and girls, must fight against lies and serve the truth. We study this truth in the *Revue de l'Action Française*, where it appears complete and clear to us, separated from the clouds of romanticism and liberalism.

In another letter, a young man from the Languedoc said: [8]

I have always been a royalist, and I remember that when I was a child I could not imagine that one could have a different opinion, which proves that traditionalism still has profound and living roots in our region.

Although this youth went on to thank the Action Française for giving him arguments with which to defend his beliefs, he was still a monarchist by tradition. The following letter to Charles Maurras came from a convert.[9]

[5] Some former royalists like Albert de Mun and Jacques Piou changed into conservatives at the turn of the century; others, like Marshal Lyautey, had served the Comte de Chambord and were later to serve the Republic, while always preserving a strictly reactionary outlook. In more recent times the Comte de Paris and some of his followers adopted a liberal program of social and economic reform.
[6] Letters in the *Revue de l'Action Française*, XXII (July 1906), 153.
[7] *Ibid.*
[8] *Ibid.*, XVI (February 1905), 248–249.
[9] *Action Française*, December 28, 1910.

You have made a royalist out of me, the son of the principal of a state school. I used to read the *Enquête sur la Monarchie* in my room while my father was at the meetings of the Union République. What delightful evenings I spent reading your works, which I bought with difficulty from my paltry savings! When I move to a neighboring town next year to continue my studies I will have more freedom and I hope to take part in the demonstrations of the Camelots du Roi there.

Although all twentieth-century reactionaries in France have not been monarchists, they have all had an authoritarian bias. By the 1930's they would have settled for a man like Franco or Pétain as a substitute for the king. Their main desire was to restore some form of authority as the basis of interpersonal relations at all levels. The following lament from an indignant father illustrates this attitude.[10]

According to the principle in force in old France, rights were but the counterpart of duties accomplished, and privileges were the remuneration for services rendered. There was no doubt then that this good citizen [the *père de famille*] should have an important role in the management of public interests.

Under the monarchy he was called a "notable."

Under democracy his legal political capacity is worth exactly one unit, that is to say, it is mathematically equal to that of any of his four sons who can vote.

Having arrived almost at the end of a long and active career, I find that my experience of men and things does not count any more than the limited experience of my children!

Such is the monstrous and unbearable lack of reason in a democracy that so many imbeciles consider a gain.

The petty country nobleman, the *petit-bourgeois* clerical, and the reactionary army officer felt more at home in a world where tradition could be counted on to make human relations comfortable than in one where the law forced them to be equitable. These people were not opposed to all laws— their passion for order and legality was very strong. They complained about the abstract character of the French legal code,

[10] Letter cited in the *Revue de l'Action Française*, V (October 1901), 587–588.

but they really hated it because it represented an outlook that was not theirs. What they wanted was a law that protected status and privilege, not one that enforced contracts and rights. They looked back to the time when property meant land (and mortgages were unheard of), bill collectors used the back door, and everyone knew his "place" and behaved in a predictable way.

Many reactionary intellectuals, in turn, were nostalgic for the days when writers and artists were patronized by the royal court and by the elegant ladies who kept salons. In the early twentieth century the court was dead, and, according to them, the few remaining salons were being taken over by Jewish social climbers. Today, Maurras said, the writer is the servant of money and public opinion.[11] Maurras was expressing in an extreme form the concern of many conservative writers for the cultural crisis brought about by the ubiquity of modern industrial capitalism. He agreed with John Ruskin and with Jakob Burckhardt's charge that "art and science have the greatest difficulty in preventing themselves from sinking into a mere branch of urban money-making and being carried away on the stream of general unrest." [12]

The majority of the reactionaries shared Maurras' criticism of the vulgarity of the modern world. They thought this vulgarity was new, and they blamed it on the democratic political system. A man who gave Maurras half a million francs once said: "I hate nothing so much as optimism, individualism, and to say everything in one word, democracy, which in the eyes of all serious-minded people, can obviously end only in the triumph of mediocrity and charlatanism." [13] Burckhardt and Ortega y Gasset were also worried about the apparent decadence of cultural standards in an "ant-heap age." Nevertheless, they understood that the Revolt of the Masses

[11] L'Avenir de l'intelligence (Paris: A. Fontemoing, 1909), p. 59.
[12] Force and Freedom: Reflections on History (New York: Pantheon Books, Inc., 1947), p. 297.
[13] Maurras, Tombeaux, p. 304.

was due not to democracy but to industrialism and the omnip-
otence of the state, regardless of its political structure. As
Burckhardt put it: [14]

> This Power State was initiated on a big and small scale as far as
> it lay in men's ability to do so, and persisted even when Reason
> and Revolution had given it quite a new meaning and its name was
> no longer Louis, but Republic. . . . The modern version of the
> Rights of Man includes the right to work and subsistence, for
> men are no longer willing to leave the most vital matters to Society,
> because they want the impossible and imagine that it can only be
> secured under compulsion from the State.

Writing in the 1850's Burckhardt believed that the regime
of Louis XIV, which Maurras admired so, was as detrimental
to individual creative effort in the arts and sciences as the
Third Republic. But in more recent times many sensitive
intellectuals became so alarmed by the blurring of all distinctions based on social responsibility and intellectual merit, as
well as the spread of vulgarity and mediocrity through the
mass media of communication and universal education, that
in their zeal to end this intolerable situation [15] they advocated
a return to authoritarian rule by an elite. For some of them
Maurras' brand of reaction had a certain appeal. Others, in
France as elsewhere—for example, Ezra Pound, William
Butler Yeats—turned to fascism, which, ironically, outdid
both Louis XIV and the mass democracies in its destruction
of independent cultural activity.

Maurras' advocacy of what Carlton J. H. Hayes called "cultural nationalism" appealed to reactionary and conservative
intellectuals alike. Many educated Frenchmen became cul-

[14] *Op. cit.*, pp. 180, 228.

[15] In Germany the conservative revolutionary attack against urbanism,
industrialism, rationalism, and Jewry was fully formulated and widely
popularized before 1914. See Fritz Richard Stern, *The Politics of
Cultural Despair; A Study in the Rise of the German Ideology*
(Berkeley, California: The University of California Press, 1961),
in which the examples of Paul de Lagarde, Julius Langbehn, and
Arthur Moeller van den Bruck are treated.

tural nationalists in the face of their country's declining power and refused to see greatness outside the prescribed limits of the French classical tradition. They associated the true genius of France with the seventeenth century,[16] when she had been supreme both politically and in the arts. According to them, Germany had not only caused France's political eclipse but German educational techniques were ruining her universities, and the spirit of Kant and Goethe was turning young French minds away from the glory of their own cultural heritage.

These people have a sincere and profound understanding of France's classical authors, but they will not allow themselves to appreciate the literature of most other nations. When one talks with them, one gets the impression that they are cultured and sophisticated. They are extremely sensitive to the beauties of Ronsard, Racine, and Stendahl, yet they seem to lose their capacity to be moved when confronted with Shakespeare, Dostoevsky, Goethe, or Ibsen. According to them, the writings of these men lack French clarity and order and are little more than examples of refined barbarism. Indeed, in their desire to assure themselves that anything that is not French should not be taken seriously they often use the words barbarous and non-French—or non-Latin—synonymously. They even include modern art-forms created by Frenchmen under these labels.

With few exceptions, France's reactionary intellectuals have also been opposed to the spirit of modern science. The Action Française claimed as its "masters" such enthusiasts of scientific progress as Comte, Taine, and Renan, and Maurras considered himself a "positivist." But the majority of France's educated reactionaries shared the Fundamentalist hostility of the uneducated ones to the disturbing new theories in the biological and social sciences and to what they called "scientism." In England and the United States the Fundamentalists were mainly nonintellectuals, and the educated classes were not antiscientific after the turn of the century; in France

16 Maurras, *L'Avenir de l'intelligence*, p. 27.

they have had cultivated and articulate spokesmen such as Paul Bourget and Léon Daudet.[17] These writers expressed in an extreme form the feelings of millions of *bien-pensants*. Many university students came from this background and tended to share their parents' indifference to or contempt for scientific achievement.

* * *

The other major attitude of French reactionaries—aside from their *passéisme*—has been "out with the upstarts!" They felt that since the world they wanted no longer existed its demise must have been brought about by a conspiracy of usurpers who were not truly French. In their minds the Revolution had put France in the hands of a sinister clique of Jews, Freemasons, Protestants, and foreigners. Like most reactionaries everywhere, they were nativists in believing that only people with deep roots in the fatherland could be true patriots.[18]

Maurras claimed that naturalized citizens (*métèques*), along with Jews, could never be Frenchmen, and that they should therefore be denied political rights.[19] This view of the *patrie* as something to which one was attached by physical roots was popular among provincials, especially in the West and the Midi, where local patriotism had a long tradition. It expressed a feeling that the *patrie* was really a patrimony—in a way almost a tribe—with the king as the father of his people. As a man from Toulouse once wrote to the editors of the *Action Française*: "More than ever, I, an old royalist by tradition, reason, and out of hatred against everything that is not *us*, feel myself closely bound to all of you." [20]

[17] See Bourget's novel *Le Disciple* and Daudet's articles: "L'Agonie de l'évolutionisme" (*Action Française*, October 15, 1923), "Un Bobard dangereux: freudisme et psychanalyse" (*ibid.*, February 4, 1921), and "Le Danger des sérums" (*ibid.*, November 19, 1926).
[18] Maurice Barrès, *Scènes et doctrines*, p. 137.
[19] Maurras, *Au Signe de Flore*, p. xiv.
[20] Letter cited in the *Action Française*, December 24, 1910.

This type of nativism evolved in France and other nations of the Western world by the end of the nineteenth century as industrialization transformed the traditional cultural pattern.[21] People brought up according to the standards of expectation of an earlier age had difficulty finding a place in the new society. Many of them felt that the nation was becoming foreign to them and that they were somehow aliens in the land of their birth.[22] They often blamed the Jews, immigrants, and what they considered "foreign" techniques of political and economic organization for robbing them of their birthright. Not only did they develop intense feelings of local and national "patriotism," but they were suspicious of any idea or group that was new or different.

Some Frenchmen felt that their country attracted uncouth visitors from other lands because of its superior culture and wealth, and that these foreigners, like the German invaders of Italy in the Middle Ages, were bleeding her dry. Maurras himself often attributed the German invasions of France in modern times to this motive. Another expression of this response in the early twentieth century came from a reader of the *Action Française*, who said [23] that at the University of Montpellier

... a horde of Russians, men and women, has invaded the schools, especially the Faculties of Medicine and Letters. These individuals are ridiculously dressed, speak hardly any French, and affect a rudeness toward their French comrades that is typical of their native land. To be sure, everything is for their benefit. . . . The whole educational machine built by our fathers is now functioning for the benefit of the foreigner.

[21] For similar developments in the United States, see John Higham, *Strangers in the Land* (New Brunswick, New Jersey: Rutgers University Press, 1955), *passim*, and Richard Hofstadter, *The Age of Reform* (New York: Alfred A. Knopf, 1955), Chapter II.
[22] In the mid-twenties, for example, the Action Française held a big protest meeting against "the enslavement of France by foreigners" (*Action Française*, November 6, 1926).
[23] Letter cited in *ibid.*, January 6, 1909.

Another man claimed that thirty-five per cent of the candidates who passed their examinations in the Faculty of Law at the University of Paris were *métèques*.[24] Under this heading he included French Jews, naturalized aliens, and foreign students.

The Action Française directed its nativist prejudices especially against those "foreigners" who were competing with Frenchmen in the professions, in research, and on the labor market in general. Its leaders lamented the fact that French doctors, workers, and employees had to fight an "economic war for survival" against these outsiders.[25] One of its readers complained that the National Library in Paris was "infested with *métèques* with black finger nails and filthy hair," while it was closed to French students, who had to use the university libraries.[26] In the late 1930's the Action Française intensified its attacks against educated immigrants—especially Jews—when thousands of refugees from Nazi persecution in Central Europe sought asylum in France.

Antisemitism has long served the function of providing people with an escape from a reality that has become intolerable—whether this reality is a personal weakness or a hostile environment. Representatives of the formerly dominant classes who were living to a large extent in genteel poverty by the turn of the century directed their contempt for money making and the spirit of bourgeois capitalism against the age-old symbol of the new rich. The following lengthy quotation from a letter written by a *déclassé* nobleman, the Vicomte de Bruc, should suffice to illustrate this attitude.[27]

Just a few years ago there were only a dozen Jews in high society, and they got in because of some horse-racing deal. In the salons, pretty fund-raisers occasionally authorized the Jew to disinfect his gold by coming to deposit it in the fund for the poor—and that was all. Now, if you take the trouble to open a fashionable news-

[24] Letter cited in *ibid.*, November 12, 1908.
[25] *Ibid.*, July 6, 1912.
[26] Letter cited in *ibid.*, June 17, 1912.
[27] Cited in the *Revue de l'Action Française*, III (November 1900), 834–837.

paper, you will find that there are no more receptions except at the homes of Jews, and there you will see the best names of France.

One observes the nobles—formerly servants of the kingdom and Empire—at the end of their resources and as servants of the Jew! When one is indebted to a Jew, one inevitably becomes his servant. For the Jew does not obligate in the truly French sense of the word, he pawns. Once they are ruined many of our nobles turn to the government, the banks, to what one calls business; and there the Jew reigns. In exchange for a long-awaited position it is necessary to present the powerful protector in such and such a circle or salon. Behind him other hooked noses creep in whom, alas! some noble young ladies who no longer have any dowry but the vocation of celibacy allow themselves to marry.

When a Jew asks one of our daughters or sisters in marriage it is not love that pushes him; it is because he expects to use our honorable past as a shield against the general contempt for him. He knows very well that he raises himself by lowering others to his level. . . . In the eyes of the Jew, we represent a value. When he will have taken that value from us—destroying it by just touching it—we shall no longer be worth anything to him. Then he will push us into the gutter with our disgrace as a pickpocket tosses an empty wallet into a sewer.

The arguments in this letter are particularly forceful because they contain certain half-truths. Very often a nobleman allowed himself to get into debt to a Jew and eventually ruined himself, though any other professional moneylender (provided that the impecunious nobleman could find one who did not consider him too poor a risk) would have treated him in the same way. It was also true that many Jews tried to climb the social ladder by contributing large sums of money to fashionable charities and by marrying into impoverished noble families. Again, such behavior was not restricted to the Jews; it was typical of the *nouveaux riches* in general. But the Vicomte de Bruc was too prejudiced to admit these other possibilities. His phobia against Jews marrying into the ranks of the aristocracy smacks of the racism of the Comte de Gobineau, Houston Stewart Chamberlain, Madison Grant, and the Nazis.

Most well brought up reactionaries were more subtle than

the Vicomte de Bruc when expressing their hostility toward Jews who had already "arrived" in some sense. The Jew who had managed to get accepted into gentile social circles by virtue of conversion, marriage, or fame was never completely safe from their slights and their thinly veiled derisive remarks. It was not so much the individual Jew as things "Jewish" that the reactionary antisemites hated. They could make a book, a play, a scientific theory, or a scholarly treatise lose a little of its value—no matter how good it was—by applying this label to it. (In all fairness it should be noted that many Leftists use labels like "Catholic" and "fascist" in the same way.) For them too, the failings of the Jews were racial: "Jews are not creative"; "Jews do not blush when insulted," etc.

In addition to believing that the Jews held France in bondage, the typical reactionary maintained that they were all alike, hence all evil. Some people even claimed that all French Jews were related to each other—and, consequently, to Captain Dreyfus—and held them responsible for Dreyfus' "treason." In the 1930's many *bien-pensants* still refused to accept socially anyone who said that this unfortunate man was not a traitor.[28] As in the prewar period, they accused the Jews of wanting France's military power destroyed so that they could consolidate their already strong hold on the country's wealth and administration.[29]

Reactionaries of all classes and ages agreed that "true Frenchmen" should have nothing to do with Jews, no matter how well "assimilated" they seemed to be. One "native" housemaid told the editors of the Action Française that she had refused an offer of employment from a Jewish family that had been in France since the fourteenth century.[30] In another letter two high school students described a fight between them-

[28] Yves Simon, *op. cit.*, p. 70; the author cites his own personal experiences to support this observation.
[29] Letter cited in the Action Française, February 9, 1909.
[30] *Ibid.*, January 26, 1910.

selves and a Jewish classmate. They said that they had hissed their victim as an informer for complaining to their professor, but at the same time they had protested to this man that they had only defended themselves. When he asked them why they had not reported the incident, their reply, "in good French," was "No sir, I am not a dirty Jew!" [31] The interest of such stories is not only in their content but also in the fact that Maurras and his colleagues printed them as worthy examples of how reactionaries should behave.

The response of the people who wrote letters like these was in some ways a distorted version of the feelings of patriots in an occupied country toward members of the occupying forces. Only the Jews for them were worse; they were an accursed race of parasites and bloodsuckers, lacking the moral integrity of the "Aryan race." [32] Xavier Vallat candidly admitted that he was anti-Jewish because he was a "xenophobe." [33] As Commissioner for Jewish Affairs in 1941, he dealt with "assimilated" French Jews and refugees from Nazi-controlled territories differently, to be sure. (He was even willing to send the refugees from their concentration camps in Unoccupied France to their "homeland" [34]—which from 1941 on meant Buchenwald and Auschwitz!) Even so, the laws he administered—and strengthened—treated French Jews like some sort of Maffia, which was trying to control the country for its own sinister purposes.

During the German Occupation the impetuous and less "respectable" people who had broken away from the Action Française in the 1930's to join the fascist leagues put pressure on French reactionaries to condone official persecution and mass extermination of the Jews—just as the Nazis had done in Germany. In this connection, it is important to remember

[31] *Ibid.*
[32] Jules Soury, *Une Campagne nationaliste, 1899–1901* (Paris: Plon-Nourrit, 1902), p. 91.
[33] Vallat, *op. cit.*, p. 221.
[34] *Ibid.*, p. 253.

that many people embraced the Action Française and the fascist movements in admiration for one particular value—such as political order—or as a solution to a specific problem—such as national security.[35] Their wishful thinking led them to believe that these movements would drop their more distasteful aspects. The dictators, once in power, dispelled such illusions.

Since the end of the nineteenth century France's die-hard reactionaries have claimed to be the true defenders of the national interest, but their conception of it has often been limited by ideological considerations. Just as the Jacobins had given the world "patriotism" a revolutionary connotation, so Maurras gave "nationalism" a reactionary one. For this reason it was not possible to combine nationalist slogans with promises of social justice in France as the fascists had done in Germany and Italy. Those Frenchmen who preferred Mussolini to Herriot in the twenties and Hitler to Blum in the thirties had a very small following, yet they compromised the patriotic reputation of the whole Extreme Right when the country was threatened by the Axis. In contrast to them, the national loyalty of the Action Française and the Croix de Feu was sincere, even though they opposed the legal government. For these reactionaries the "true France"—the *pays réel*—was what counted, and its interests required an authoritarian political system. The descendants of the *émigrés* viewed the twentieth-century *sans-culottes* as subversive "upstarts" who wanted to seize the *pays légal* and transform it into a soviet regime.

At first glance the militarism of most French reactionaries also seemed to be based on patriotic motives. Faith in the army was widespread at the time of the Dreyfus Affair, and many people were reluctant to believe that members of the general staff had deliberately martyred an innocent man. A

[35] This kind of self-justification was expressed to me by numerous people in personal interviews.

professor at the École Normale Supérieure expressed this faith in the following way: [36]

I am less moved . . . by political matters than by questions of race and national conscience. . . . At Rennes, before the officers of the tribunal, and especially when listening to our generals, I had the revelation of a world of superior spirits, of upright and essentially noble beings.

The Extreme Rightists were also sincere in their desire for a strong army that would defend the country from foreign aggression. Yet many of them continued to view it as an instrument for preventing proletarian disturbances, as it had done so often until 1871. Since then it had played the role of *La Grande Muette* in politics, but individual officers had joined the Action Française, the Croix de Feu, and the Cagoulards in hatred for democrats, Jews, Socialists, Communists, and the undisciplined masses in general. Thus militarism was partly an expression of the authoritarian-nativist desire to rid the "true France" of its "upstarts."

*   *   *

Harold D. Lasswell once said that "political movements derive their vitality from the displacement of private affects [feelings] upon public objects." [37] Some theories maintain that childhood maladjustments lead to this kind of displacement; others say that people who were seemingly well adjusted as children can become quite disorganized under conditions of personal stress caused by social, political, and economic factors. Whatever its origin may be, personal discontent often turns people into cranks and fanatics. Political movements certainly do not rely on them alone for support and enthusiasm. Altruism, guilt feelings, ambition, and sheer physical

[36] Soury, *op. cit.*, p. 76.
[37] *Psychopathology and Politics* (Chicago: The University of Chicago Press, 1930), p. 173.

energy seeking a socially approved outlet infuse these movements with life as much as frustration does.

The most important "private affect" of reactionaries is a
fear of freedom that attracts them to authoritarianism. Some
people of this kind emphasize the authority of religion, the
clergy, or the military; others devote themselves to perpetuat-
ing traditional social and cultural values. The more modern
authoritarians, especially in the lower middle and lower classes,
seek to identify their interests with a strong popular leader and
a policy of aggressive nationalism. Even the avowedly revolutionary Communist Party has authoritarian appeal. Despite
these varieties of expression for authoritarian personalities,
they have certain psychological characteristics in common.

Most authoritarians are afraid of their own weakness. A
person may have been hindered in some way from working out
his own problems, hence prevented from developing a feeling
of confidence in his ability to adjust to new problems and situations. He is afraid of himself, his impulses, his responsi-
bilities, and his ability to act freely. Though he does not
like to be alone, he fears society and the world, for they re-
quire adjustments and sacrifices that he is not prepared to
make. In a word, he is a coward who does not want to admit
his cowardice to himself. Occasionally he will overcompensate
for this basic cowardice by acts of superficial daring. More
often he projects his own weakness onto others and fights
it in them rather than himself. For this purpose he can usually
find socially acceptable scapegoats, such as women, pacifists,
and various minority groups.

Unconsciously, this kind of person is aware of his own
weakness, but he relieves himself of the necessity of consciously admitting it by identifying himself with a symbol of
authority—an authority that will be powerful and make his
decisions for him. He participates in the wielding of power
vicariously, and his anonymity in such a relationship renders
him relatively safe from the consequences of his leaders' acts.
The church, the army, the bureaucracy, the "company" (the

"organization man" is basically an authoritarian), a strong leader, or a combination of these attract him. A monarchy, a dominant social class, and intellectual or artistic "masters" also have authoritarian appeal.

Certain kinds of experience tend to make some people unable to love their fellow human beings. They conceive of the world as a jungle, and they can no more love and respect others than animals can be said to love and respect one another. In a world so conceived, the basic drive is fear born of a feeling of insecurity. Other people are thought of as objects to be exploited and manipulated, catered to or kept in their places. Under such conditions genuine spontaneity of affection is impossible, especially since it may lead to rejection or betrayal. Furthermore, the authoritarian attributes his own exploitive and manipulative motives to others and refuses to accept their expressions of friendship or love at their face value. He views kindness, pity, charity, humanitarianism, and mutual affection as signs of weakness.[38] Because of his own inability to love, he faces the world with hostility, suspicion, and cynicism.

But inability to love is not the only reason for the reactionary's dreary view of human nature; it is sometimes inspired by what has been called the Revolt of the Masses. The reactionary resents the sight of people of "low descent" imposing their standards everywhere—in politics, the arts, entertainment, and social behavior. Even though Christ predicted it, he does not want to see the meek and the poor inherit the earth. Things may be different in the kingdom of heaven, but *here* the elite should rule, for *here* birth (or "blood") distinguishes a "noble" minority from the mean and vulgar mob.

Although the French reactionary is usually a practicing Catholic, his views about the masses are not inherent in

[38] Léon Daudet once called Jean Jaurès and Jacques Piou "two sister spirits" because of their "sentimental" liberalism (*Action Française*, August 19, 1908).

Catholicism. There are two kinds of believers: those who stress the Crucifixion and man's baseness in killing Christ and those who point to the Resurrection and the possibility of salvation for all sinners. One critic has called the first group "Good-Friday Catholics" and the second one "Easter-Sunday Catholics."[39] The former tend to be reactionaries or conservatives, the latter liberals.

The reactionary is cynical and pessimistic, but since he cannot stand alone he seeks refuge in an easily identifiable "in-group." A social class, a military platoon, a geographical region, a religious sect, or an extremist political movement may give him the illusion of security and impregnability he craves. Most often he chooses his own nationality or "race." He is loyal to it because he depends on it for protection, not because he loves it. Such a person is not really patriotic; he is a chauvinist. Just as he is blind to his own weakness and imperfections, he also refuses to admit the existence of these defects in the group with which he has identified himself. Instead, he projects these undesirable qualities onto "out-groups."

Another aspect of this "in-group-out-group" orientation is a tendency to regard differences between the two as signs of superiority and inferiority. The authoritarian constructs for himself a hierarchy in society with his "in-group" and its power symbols at the top. Those "out-groups" that resemble his most closely—or that threaten it least—are placed next below it, while "inferior races," "foreigners," "the masses," and any groups that appear to be weak are relegated to the bottom.

The man who is afraid to see himself as he really is often refuses to see how the world is made. He does not want the prejudices that comfort him to be shaken, and any attempt to question his beliefs or to analyze the values of his "in-group" arouses his hostility. His stereotyped responses to the external and superficial aspects of people and events relieve

[39] Pierre-Henri Simon, *Histoire de la littérature française au XXe siècle* (2 vols.; Paris: Armand Colin, 1957), I, 205.

him of the task of thinking things through and of the
anxiety that such thoughts might cause him. As a result, he
rejects books, plays, and people that deal with personality
problems or unpleasant social phenomena as being "too serious." An intellectual such as Maurras may spend much time
in solitude constructing pseudorational theories, but the typical
reactionary avoids introspection and situations that might in-
duce it. Even in his leisure time he tries to keep himself occupied with routine activities, preferably in the company of
others.

Mental rigidity is the dominant feature of the authoritarian
personality. Parts of the following quotation from Jean-Paul
Sartre apply to doctrinaire extremists of all kinds, but it is a
particularly good summary of the reactionary mind.[40]

How can one choose to reason falsely? Because one feels the
nostalgia of impermeability. The rational man seeks the truth
gropingly; he knows that his reasoning is only probable, that other
considerations will arise to make it doubtful; he never knows too
well where he is going, he is "open"; he may even appear hesitant.
But there are people who are attracted by the durability of stone.
They want to be massive and impenetrable, they do not want to
change: where would change lead them? This is an original fear of
oneself and a fear of truth. . . . Nothing but a strong emotional
bias can give instant certitude.

Charles Maurras was the most effective purveyor of "instant certitude" that the French reactionaries have had in the
twentieth century. As he himself once said: "It is true that
a great friend, the Certainty of having the political Truth,
lived, walked, sat, and conversed familiarly with us." [41] This
"great friend" was a comfort to the militants and the bien-
pensant followers of his movement, and it filled a special
need for young intellectuals. After having rejected all the
gods-that-failed [42] of their predecessors, today's educated youth

[40] Jean-Paul Sartre, "Portrait of the Antisemite," *Partisan Review*,
13 (1946), 166.
[41] *Au Signe de Flore*, pp. x–xi.
[42] This reference is to the book *The God that Failed* (ed. Richard

—in France, as elsewhere in the Atlantic world—has difficulty in finding a "cause" and a creed to go with it. But many French students of a generation ago found both in the Action Française.

Some of the militants in this movement satisfied their personal need for certainty by behaving like missionaries. One young girl wrote to Maurras that she had become the problem child in the charity organization for the Catholic schools of her community by spreading his ideas at its fund-raising affairs. Finally, according to her, the ladies put her behind the refreshment counter, where she would "compromise the Catholic schools less." [43] A more extreme example of such behavior was that of a young man who said,[44]

> I distributed five hundred Action Française leaflets in my neighborhood. . . . I also seek out discussions. I talk everywhere about our principles and of the king. I speak about them to workers; I speak about them to priests; I speak about them in people's drawing rooms between dances [!] In the street I always have several copies of the Action Française with me. I pretend to read it, and if someone looks at the title attentively, I offer it to him.

Reports on the league's activities in the provinces also mentioned public demonstrations, the sale of tracts, and the "fruits" all of these would bear.[45]

Pedantry and an obsessive devotion to formal reasoning are additional signs of the insecure person's quest for certainty. He transforms his deep doubts about himself into doubts about the world and tries to allay them there by means of an ostentatious preoccupation with truth. The dogma of Maurras allowed many people to project their own difficulties

---

Crossman; New York: Harper, 1950), which described the disillusionment of six European and American intellectuals with communism. Other "gods" of the thirties and forties included fascism, antifascism, and pacifism.

[43] Letter cited in the *Revue de l'Action Française*, XVIII (August 1905), 305.

[44] Letter cited in the *Action Française*, April 16, 1908.

[45] E.g., *ibid.*, January 6, 1934.

onto the republican regime, which they could then condemn with his (to them) irrefutable logic. They also considered themselves members of an exclusive intellectual aristocracy for having adopted his line of reasoning and they expressed their contempt for everyone who questioned it. The political consequences of their antidemocratic feelings were not without significance in a country like France, where respect for intellectuals was still strong and where men of letters have sometimes been the objects of cults.

An interesting example of pedantry and intellectual snobbery can be seen in the predilection of Maurras and other writers of the Action Française for archaic and regional words. Their affectations, which others might regard as merely old-fashioned, were perfectly consistent with their general outlook. Within the movement the only heretic in matters of literary style was Léon Daudet. He seems to have thought of himself as a reincarnated Rabelais in his use of pungent slang and original words. Although Daudet's unorthodox efforts to put the language of the gutter and the brothel into print could never measure up to those of Louis-Ferdinand Céline— the self-crowned lyricist of profanity—they too represented a kind of intellectual snobbery.

The members of the Action Française and other French reactionaries sometimes carried literary pedantry into their everyday speech, where they employed the imperfect subjunctive and other rarely used grammatical forms. Another of their somewhat strained usages was *un sieur* instead of *monsieur* in reference to political adversaries and members of "out-groups." The ordinary Frenchman would not think that *monsieur* had an affective connotation any more than the average American letter writer would interpret "Dear Sir" as anything other than a purely mechanical form of address.

Snobbery is a common defense mechanism for many people who are frustrated in their effort to maintain their feelings of self-regard. A person's ego encompasses not only his ideal of himself but also his status, preferences, and possessions—

anything that he identifies as *his*. Hence, when society as a whole does not seem to recognize what he considers his proper social position or his superior artistic tastes, he often joins an organization with values similar to his own. In this way his own ideas are reinforced and he can assume an air of superiority toward the uninitiated.

In addition to attracting intellectual snobs, the Action Française appealed to people who were anxious to maintain their social status. One middle-class woman insisted that the French might be amiable, hospitable, and a little unconstrained but that was as far as their democratic spirit went. In her opinion France was really a nation of aristocrats.[46] Even so, she gave herself an additional claim to exclusiveness by joining the Dames de l'Action Française. These ladies were socially oriented, and in the 1930's they were more interested in the pregnancies of the Comtesse de Paris than in the doctrines of Maurras.

Personal discontent can also manifest itself in the form of outward aggressiveness and an apparent love of physical violence. The Camelots du Roi and the Students of the Action Française were neither an iron brigade nor a praetorian guard. They were twentieth-century Muscadins who liked to hiss republican politicians, heckle "liberal" university professors, and beat up pacifists and Socialists. For students who had to study hard and who had little opportunity for athletics, for office clerks who led inactive, humdrum lives, the possibility of shouting and fighting in the streets had much appeal.

In some ways the die-hard reactionary cause—especially as it was represented by the Action Française—resembled a cult. It had its dogma, its prophet, its saints, and its martyrs. Good and Evil were personified in the minds of the reactionaries by two women—Joan of Arc and Marianne. They called Marianne (who symbolized the Republic) *La Gueuse* and they often said that when their day arrived they would "hang

[46] Letter cited in the *Revue de l'Action Française*, XVI (March 1905), 33.

the slut." When they felt that Joan of Arc had been insulted, they reacted as if a sacred cow had been pushed off the road or a tribal god profaned. At a public meeting held in protest against Professor Thalamas, François Coppée said,[47]

For all of us, believers and unbelievers, she is the ideal personification, the very symbol of the French Fatherland. . . . Thus, when a professor charged with teaching history to high-school students pronounced some ignoble words against her, the national conscience experienced a sensation of rape and outrage, and every day for a week now the magnanimous youth of the schools has not ceased to protest energetically in the streets and in front of Joan's statue and has made itself the spokesman of the nation indignant at this sacrilege and this profanation.

Like the members of other cults, people in the Action Française considered themselves "privileged characters" and believed that they were entitled to special consideration when they broke the law. They claimed that their "principles" justified behavior that would be reprehensible in other people —such as informing on their fellow countrymen to the fascist *Milice* during the Second World War—but when something happened to one of *them* their indignation knew no bounds. After the demented girl who had shot Marius Plateau in 1923 was acquitted, the editors of the *Action Française* ascribed their own indignation to the nation as a whole with their heading, "*La Réaction Nationale.*"[48] In 1936 they called Léon Blum's effort to drive through Jacques Bainville's funeral procession a *crime de lèse-majesté.*[49] A few years after Maurras was convicted as a collaborator his friends demanded that his prosecutor be brought to trial for perpetrating this injustice.

Another characteristic of the Action Française and French reactionaries in general has been their periodic feeling of being persecuted. Their belief was justified at various times during the twentieth century. Whether it was true or not, it gave

[47] Speech cited in *ibid.*, XV (December 1904), 409–410.
[48] *Action Française*, January 4, 1924.
[49] *Ibid.*, February 14, 1936.

them an illusion of self-importance. In 1905, for example, a government decree temporarily forbidding all religious processions brought the following response from a cousin of Henri Vaugeois: "We took our legal revenge at the Château of X. That was the occasion of a sensational demonstration." [50] Two decades later those priests and laymen who remained loyal to the Action Française after the pope had condemned it were constantly complaining about being victimized for following the dictates of their conscience. Finally, the Right as a whole suffered its most devastating persecution since the Terror in the years 1944–1946.

*

Although its "features" are mainly those of the Action Française, the portrait of attitudes and personality traits I have tried to create represents all reactionaries in twentieth-century France. Whatever their temperament or status, the members of this "family" think of themselves as the true Frenchmen and everyone else as outsiders. In some situations they divide into feuding factions, in others they unite in the face of a common enemy. One branch may be particularly concerned with the church, another with the arts and intellectual matters; Uncle Jean is a lecher, Aunt Marie is a prude. But they are all authoritarian, antidemocratic, antisemitic, and certain that their thinking alone is right.

[50] Letter cited in the *Revue de l'Action Française*, XVIII (August 1905), 305.

Epilogue

S ince the end of the Second World War, France's "family" of die-hard reactionaries has changed in many ways. Until 1940 the Action Française had been the main school for the nation's *déclassé* intellectuals of the Extreme Right and had attracted sympathy from other social groups that felt their status and their way of life threatened by economic and social change: the clergy, the petty aristocracy, *bien-pensant* army and navy officers, and older middle-class professions such as law and medicine. After the Liberation the ranks of the Maurrassian reactionaries were decimated by purges and the natural deaths of older stalwarts, and those authoritarian conservatives who had joined them in supporting Pétain turned to the M.R.P., the R.P.F., and, by 1951, the rejuvenated Center in parliament. In addition, two postwar movements, the Poujadists and the Gaullists, organized rival "families" on the antiparliamentary Right, the Poujadists recruiting among shopkeepers and peasants, the Gaullists among the new middle classes of engineers, modern businessmen, and white-collar workers. Finally, since the mid-1950's, a new version of the prewar Cagoule has gained the allegiance of "intoxicated" army officers in that last refuge of the Old France—her overseas possessions.

*

With its organization and name proscribed, its ranks reduced, and its master in jail, the Action Française ceased to be a political force under the Fourth Republic. In his prison cell Maurras wrote poems, a semiautobiographical novel (*Le Mont de Saturne*), commentaries on the current political scene, and several books attacking the judges who had sentenced him. Meanwhile, on June 10, 1947, a group of his disciples began publishing a new weekly, *Aspects de la France*. Their main concern was to vindicate Maurras and to remain faithful to his teachings. They tried to make their newspaper resemble the defunct daily of the same initials as much as possible, not only in its rigid *La Seule France* line but even in its vocabulary and format. After he was released from prison on medical grounds in March 1952, Maurras contributed an article each week until his death eight months later. (The fact that he asked for the last rites of the church on his deathbed was probably little more than a cultural reflex on the part of a sick, old Frenchman—like that of another lifelong agnostic, Édouard Herriot, in 1957.) But the informal organizations that sprang up in support of the weekly in the late forties and early fifties were mere relics of the prewar movement. Neither Maurice Pujo (who became the director of *Aspects de la France* after his release from prison in 1949) nor his successor Georges Calzant (another militant from the old days) were able to attract a permanent following of more than twenty-five thousand readers.

However, these people were not the only Maurrassians left. A rival weekly, *La Nation Française*, began to appear in late 1955 and to attract almost the same number of readers. Its guiding force has been Pierre Boutang, the most dynamic and intelligent claimant to Maurras' mantle since the master's death. Boutang had broken with *Aspects de la France* after a series of disagreements with the senile Pujo. In the first issue (October 12, 1955) of his new periodical he announced that its general line would foster integral nationalism, opposition to democracy, sympathy to monarchism, and "courtesy" in discussions with its opponents. It has generally lived up to this program, although it can be virulent when attacking the Christian Democrats.

Both the editorial staff and the readers of *La Nation Française* are more heterogeneous and less doctrinaire than those of *Aspects de la France*. Its regular contributors include men who had left the Action Française after 1940 (Philippe Ariès and François Léger), older traditionalists who had never joined it (Gabriel Marcel, Émmanuel Beau de Loménie, and Daniel Halévy), members of the "young Right" (Roger Nimier and Antoine Blondin), erstwhile "Leftists" who had become nationalists (Jules Monnerot and Jacques Despuech), a former Vichyite (Gustave Thibon), and a former Gaullist (Colonel Rémy—pseudonym of Gilbert Renault-Rouhier). In its first two issues of January 1957 *La Nation Française* published the results of a "survey" of the social, economic, and political composition of its readers. It showed that forty-one per cent were under thirty years of age, that the majority were students, engineers, civil servants, or school teachers, and that they all differed considerably among themselves on specific issues— such as the E.D.C., the Suez Crisis, and colonial policy.

La Nation Française prides itself on its "modernism" as opposed to the "passéism" of its rival. Its editors abjure the political quarrels of the past but they maintain that the traditions that inspired them still have a certain value. Philippe Ariès says that [1]

. . . the current positions of Left and Right no longer have any meaning. . . . Our mission, then, is to orient our efforts and our studies in the two following senses: to protect and to call forth the rebirth of a new political spirit, which will express itself in the moral outlook of the people who have become indifferent to the *res publica*, and to regenerate old traditions in those places where they are still confused with an absurd conformism.

This goal of renewing old moral and political traditions, albeit without nostalgia, looks like a return to the position of De Bonald and Le Play. In general, however, *La Nation Française* is more up-to-date than *Aspects de la France* in its acceptance of a technical civilization and in its renunciation of antisemitism and hatred for Germany.

In addition to these two direct "heirs" of the Action Fran-

[1] *La Nation Française*, May 20, 1957.

çaise, its continuing influence has been apparent in other quarters. The fascist-inclined, Extreme-Rightist weekly *Rivarol* and the die-hard Vichyite review *Écrits de Paris* [2] are staffed mainly by Maurrassian reactionaries who deviate little from the orthodox counterrevolutionary line. Another group of epigones consists of certain young writers—including Jacques Laurent, Michel Déon, Roger Nimier, and Antoine Blondin— who call themselves the "new-" or "young-Right." Their dandyism and their apolitical stand, though seemingly opposed to the *politique d'abord* of the old Action Française, are closely related to that movement's traditional antiparliamentarianism, its mockery of party politics, and its flaunting of the official standards of republican society. [3] Finally, a number of "integrist" Catholic reviews—*Verbe, L'Homme Nouveau,* and *Les Nouvelles de la Chrétienté*—show a marked sympathy for Maurras' condemnation of democracy in all its forms. [4]

*

It is beyond the scope of this Epilogue to analyze all of the other movements of the antiparliamentary Right since 1945, but a few words are necessary in order to show the extent to

[2] The following estimates of circulation figures in 1957 come from Raoul Girardet, "L'Héritage de 'l'Action Française,' " *Revue Française de Science Politique,* Vol. VII, No. 4 (December 1957): *Aspects de la France,* 20,000–25,000 (p. 768); *La Nation Française,* 20,000 (p. 769); *Rivarol,* 45,000 (p. 772); *Écrits de Paris,* 26,000 (p. 771).

[3] Roger Nimier expresses this outlook in the following way: "Nous sommes quelques-uns dont les traits communs sont un certain sérieux, un besoin de vérité, un air sombre. Mais les choses sont établies de telle sorte que nous faisons figure d'esprits légers. Nous ne respectons ni les lois ni les êtres qui nous gouvernent. . . . Nous sommes les libertins du siècle." (*Le Grand d'Espagne* [Paris: Éditions de la Table Ronde, 1950], p. 234.)

[4] But another "integrist" review, *Itinéraires,* condemns Maurras' "positivism" and his placing of political values above spiritual ones. In the winter of 1956–1957 this disagreement led to a series of attacks and counterattacks—verbal, of course—between *Itinéraires* and the strictly Maurrassian *Les Libertés Françaises,* which had been founded by the

which they have transformed the counterrevolutionary tradition in France. The Gaullism of the years 1947–1953 was authoritarian-progressive, with elitist undertones. Because its original function had been to rally a disparate mass of nationalists against the Communist menace, the R.P.F. disintegrated when the Center coalitions of the early fifties showed their ability to "contain" the Communists by legal means. Most of of its parliamentary representatives then found their way into existing progressive and conservative groupings until the advent of the Fifth Republic, when they formed the U.N.R.

The other mass movement of the antiparliamentary Right, the Poujadists, represented a different set of values. These were reactionary-defensive. The program of Pierre Poujade was essentially an exasperated protest against an overcomplicated world symbolized by an incomprehensible fiscal system, a hollow political jargon, and inaccessible—hence dangerous—technical experts. Poujade himself resembled the fascists in his demagogy and his glorification of action for action's sake. Most of the marginal shopkeepers and artisans who momentarily backed him were simply resisting Mendès-France's efforts to modernize the French economy in the mid-1950's. They wanted to return to an idealized golden age when little Frenchmen cultivated their little garden in little towns and when the local notary was the only "technical expert" they needed. (When the Poujadist party gained forty-four parliamentary seats in the 1956 election, General de Gaulle quipped: "De mon temps, les épiciers votaient pour les notaires. Aujourd'hui, les notaires votent pour les épiciers.")

Besides these two organized movements, there was another form of antiparliamentarianism on the Right, which expressed the outlook of the elusive but still powerful "bourgeois dynasties" and other vested interest groups such as the army and the upper ranks of the civil service (some of whom were authoritarian technocrats). These people supported the exist-

Daudet family a year earlier as a postwar version of the old *Revue Universelle*.

ing political system as long as it insured order and stability. They had "rallied" successively to the Orleanist Monarchy, the Second Empire, the Third Republic, and Vichy, but they had been ready to overthrow one another when it no longer served their purposes. When the Fourth Republic seemed to be failing them in the spring of 1958, they "rallied" to General de Gaulle. This kind of behavior was especially noticeable among the Algerian *colons,* who became Gaullists in 1958 for the same reason they had been Pétainists in the early 1940's— in order to preserve what was theirs.

Since the mid-1950's Frenchmen from the more marginal and insecure sections of society have found new appeal in the fascist outlook. Its nationalism has expressed a rage of humiliation at France's declining status, an obsession with decadence, and a call for direct and violent action against the "false" elites of both the Fourth and Fifth Republics. The military and diplomatic defeats suffered by France since Dien Bien Phu have especially discredited these regimes in the eyes of many young veterans who had fought their losing battles. Ex-legionnaires and ex-paratroopers felt humiliated and frustrated at having been forced to "sweat it out" in hot, unfriendly outposts in Indochina, Morocco, and Tunisia, only to see these territories "abandoned" by "cowardly" politicians. These young men had been trained to think of themselves as elite troops, which, indeed, they were. They wanted battles, glory, and power. As they came to despise governments that would not let them do their job properly, some of them were taken in by fascist demagogy and preserved their *esprit de corps* in exclusive veterans' organizations and the Organisation de l'Armée Secrète.

Fascism also became attractive again to students who wanted to express their nonconformism and their defiance toward a world they had not made. Some of them praised the super-patriotism and bravado of Jean Dutourd in his *Taxis de la Marne.* Others rediscovered the prewar writings of Pierre Drieu La Rochelle, Robert Brasillach, and Louis-Ferdinand

Céline. These men had glorified virility, daredevil feats of courage, dictatorship, and the "Aryan" race at one time or another. (Brasillach had been executed as a collaborator, Drieu La Rochelle had taken his own life in 1945, and Céline was living in exile.) A number of their youthful admirers joined the Jeune Nation, a frankly fascist movement founded by the son of a former *Milicien* in 1957. During the 1958 crisis these young rowdies hawked their movement's newspaper, shouted "Algerie Française," and clashed with the police in much the same way as the Camelots du Roi a generation earlier.

It was in Algeria that the new fascism gained the largest following, especially among the young activists. The war there has revitalized and transformed France's antidemocratic forces. After more than half a century of playing the role of *La Grande Muette*, the army once again began claiming to know more about what was good for the national interest than the government. Only now, if it should gain power, it has officers who would like to use modern totalitarian techniques in order to keep their "subjects" in line. These militarists, the Organisation de l'Armée Secrète, the civilian counterterrorists on both sides of the Mediterranean, and the neofascists have little in common with the Action Française and the other leagues of the thirties.

*

The most dangerous force on the Extreme Right in France since the mid-1950's has been a secret organization that closely resembles the prewar Cagoule. Its leaders are difficult to identify, but they have apparently infiltrated the highest levels of the civil service and the military hierarchy, even to the point of being able to remove compromising evidence about themselves from the files of the security police.[5] When one of them is arrested or forced to flee the country, he is simply replaced by someone else. The main goal of these people has been to overthrow the *pays légal*—which they see as controlled by

[5] Tournoux, *op. cit.*, p. 194.

Freemasons and atheists and serving foreign interests—before it succumbs to communism at home. Since the only way they can do this is by a *coup de force*, their chief agents have been dissident army officers (now mainly fugitives in the Organisation de l'Armée Secrète) who view their own attempt to keep Algeria French as part of a guerrilla war against international communism.

Although only a few of the masterminds of the new Cagoule have been directly influenced by Maurras, the sort of regime envisaged by its "praesidium" in the late fifties [6] had everything Maurras wanted except a king. Their state would be Christian, corporatist, and decentralized. It would borrow authoritarian techniques from Portugal and Vichy; it would make the family the nucleus of society; it would "depolitize" elections and hold them in the "natural" communities of the nation—the professions, the cities, and the provinces. And, like Maurras in the early 1940's, the current counterrevolutionaries have been violently opposed to General de Gaulle.

Just as only a fraction of France's intellectuals had engaged in the *trahison des clercs* advocated by the Action Française, so only a few of her army officers are carrying out what might be called the *trahison des hobereaux*. Among the suspects arrested in connection with the attempted assassination of De Gaulle in September 1961 there were petty noblemen with names like Martial de Villemandy, Cabanne de la Prade, Barbier de Blignières, and Boucher de Crèvecoeur. But the social background and general outlook of most French officers have changed markedly since the early 1900's (when Maurras first proposed the idea of a military *coup de force*). Today they represent a much wider cross section of society. Instead of being an elite, they now see themselves as uprooted (many of them have spent most of their time outside France since 1940), betrayed by their government, and viewed with suspicion in respectable bourgeois circles. At the same time, a significant group of those in Algeria—"intoxicated" by their

[6] *Ibid.*, p. 187.

mission and their feeling of superiority over decadent republican politicians—see themselves as the only true saviors of the
pays réel. They are a far cry from the ideal colonial officer
personified by Marshal Lyautey forty years ago—a monarchist
by sentiment but a faithful, apolitical servant of the Republic
and a respector of the "natives'" rights.

The *purs* among today's army officers (including reservists
and renegades in the O.A.S.) have become a new kind of *bien-
pensants*, for all their emphasis on terror, political assassination, and "brainwashing" the "natives." Their counterrevolution is more plebeian in its techniques and its goals than that
of their predecessors. They have learned much from the Viet
Minh guerrillas and the F.L.N. *fellaghas* and they have little
use for the Europeans whose rights they are defending in
Algeria or the capitalists who covet the oil of the Sahara. The
Cross and the Heart symbolize their ideals. In their own way,
they are the last important group of die-hard reactionaries in
France.

Appendix

Better than any other single document, the marching song of the Camelots du Roi summarizes the Action Française pattern of response and the movement's attempts to appeal to various groups in French society. Hence it is reproduced here in full and without comment.

Chant d'Assaut

La France Bouge

Le Juif ayant tout pris
Tout raflé dans Paris,
Dit à la France:
—Tu n'appartiens qu'à nous:
Obéissance.
Tout le monde à genoux!
           Refrain
—Non, non, la France bouge
Et voit rouge.
Non, non!
Assez de trahison!

—Tant pis dit le rabbin
Je tiens tout dans ma main,
J'ai la police
Et, pour violer la loi
Une justice
De magistrats sans foi.

—Non, non. . . .

—De brûler vos vaisseaux
Avec vos arsenaux
Le Juif est maître.

Sous les canons prussiens
Dreyfus le Traître
Pousse vos citoyens

—Non, non. . . .

Les travailleurs ont faim . . .
Le Juif dit:—Pas de pain,
Mais, à rafales,
Pour sauver nos écus,
Voici les balles.
Peuple, ne bouge plus!

—Non, non, la France bouge,
Et voit rouge.
Non, non!
Assez de trahison.

Juif insolent, tais-toi,
Voici venir le Roi,
Et notre race
Court au devant de lui:
Juif, à ta place!
Notre roi nous conduit!
                    Refrain
Un, deux, la France bouge
Et voit rouge,
Un, deux,
Les Français sont chez eux.

Assez de Panamas!
Assez de Thalamas
Toute ta clique
De pédants, de brigands,
O République,
Nous la mettrons dedans!

—Un, deux. . . .

Le Roi revient d'exil:
—O France, dira-t-il,
Reine du monde,
Te voilà donc aux mains

Du Juif, immonde
Coureur de grands chemins?

—Un, deux. . . .

—Oui la France aux Français,
À mes loyaux sujets!
Je prends le glaive
Pour que le travailleur
En paix achève
Son honnête labeur.

—Un, deux. . . .

Notre jeunesse en fleur
Vous a donné son coeur,
Roi magnanime!
Menez la jusqu'aux cieux
De cime en cime
Sur vos pas glorieux.

—Un, deux. . . .

Hardi! France d'abord!
Français, mieux vaut la mort
Que l'esclavage.
Gloire à qui tombera!
Tous à l'ouvrage!
La France renaîtra.

—Un, deux. . . .

Demain sur nos tombeaux
Les blés seront plus beaux.
Formons nos lignes!
Nous aurons cet été
Du vin aux vignes,
Avec la royauté.

—Un, deux, la France bouge
Et voit rouge
Un, deux,
Les Français sont chez eux.[1]

[1] *Action Française,* February 9, 1909.

Bibliography

PRIMARY SOURCES

1. *Personal Interviews*

Léon Blum, Camille Chautemps, Albert Bayet, Georges Valois, Émile Buré, Alexandre Zévaès, Jacques Kayser, Georges Lefebvre, Charles Morazé, Henri Massis, Maurice Pujo, and dozens of French men and women in the Action Française and kindred movements.

2. *Unpublished Police and Government Records*

(a) Thanks to the Ministry of the Interior and the Director of the French National Archives, I was able to consult the following series of manuscript documents of the Sureté Générale up to 1917. Ordinarily such items may not be seen until fifty years after their date of issue.

France. Archives Nationales. *Police Générale*, F⁷12452, F⁷12453.

———. *Sureté Générale*, F⁷12431, F⁷12444, *Surveillance des relations du Duc d'Orléans avec Ninon Desmelay*, 1904–1908 (mainly copies of telegrams, 1904–1908).

———. *Sureté Générale*, F⁷12459, *Mouvement antisémitique*.

———. *Sureté Générale*, F⁷12476, *l'Affaire des fiches*, 1904–1907.

———. *Sureté Générale*, F⁷12553–12559, *Meetings, réunions publiques, etc.*, 1899–1913.

———. *Sureté Générale*, F⁷12715–12716, *Application de la loi de séparation, résistance aux inventaires, agitation cléricale*, 1908–1913, *dossier de la Croix de Paris, procès des assomptionistes*, 1899–1900.

———. *Sureté Générale*, F⁷12719, *Action Libérale*.

———. *Sureté Générale*, F⁷12842–12843, *Dossiers des journaux*, 1909–1914 (circulation figures, facts on editorial staff, information on foreign and domestic subsidies).

———. *Sureté Générale*, F⁷12844, *Dosiers des journaux*, 1917.

———. *Sureté Générale*, F⁷12862, *Action Française*.

———. *Sureté Générale*, F⁷12863–12864, *Camelots du Roi*.

France. Archives Nationales. *Sureté Générale, F⁷12861, Parti Royal-iste.*

(b) Office of Strategic Services. Research and Analysis Branch, R. and A., No. 2344, *A Selected Who's Who in Vichy France.* Washington, D.C., 1944 (mimeographed).

3. Pamphlets

Argenton, Commandant d'. *Ligue de l'Action Française. Section d'Angers. Conférence faite par M. le Commandant d'Argenton. Le 15 juillet 1913.* Angers, 1913.

———. *Ligue de l'Action Française. Section d'Angers. La franc-maçonnerie, conférence faite au groupe ouvrier René D'Anjou. Le 5 juillet 1913.* Angers, 1913.

Barrès, Maurice. *Quelques lettres inédites de Maurice Barrès sur l'Action Française.* Paris, 1924.

Beau, Ferdinand, Lur-Saluces, Comte Eugène de, Firmin Baconnier, and Henri Vaugeois. *Ligue de l'Action Française (Section de l'Orne). Grand réunion privée donnée à Alençon, le 21 octobre 1906.* Alençon, 1906.

Brun, Émile. *Révélations sur les organisations de l'Action Fran-çaise.* Paris, 1936.

Buisson, Ferdinand (pseudonym, Le Pic). *La Ligue de la Patrie Française.* Paris, 1902.

———. *Une Campagne de l'Action Française, en chalonnais, 1912–1913.* Chalons-sur-Saône, 1913.

———. *Une Campagne royaliste en Franche-Comté; compte-rendu des travaux de la fédération régionale des Camelots du Roi du Doubs et de la Haute Saône.* Besançon, 1911.

Cleuziou, Alain Raison du. *L'Action Française; conférence faite à la première réunion de la section de l'Action Française des Côtes-du-Nord, Le 29 janvier 1906.* Saint-Brieuc, 1908.

Congrès 11 de l'Action Française. Rapport des groupes de dames, Le 19 Novembre 1924. Blois, 1924.

Congrès régional royaliste de l'Action Française tenu à Montpelier les 5 et 6 juin 1909. Montpelier, 1909.

Copin-Albancelli, A. *La Conspiration juive contre le monde chrétien.* Paris, 1908.

Courcoural, Paul. *La Fin de la querelle.* La Rochelle, 1929.

Dolle, A. *Section laonaise de l'Action Française. (1) Comment je suis devenu royaliste (conférence). (2) Aux Combattants de 1870 (discours). (3) Les Ligueurs de l'Aisne chez le Duc d'Orléans (al-locution).* Reims, 1913.

Durand, Bruno. *Les Origines. de l'Action Française.* Aix-en-Provence, 1920.

Gonnet, Louis. *L'Affichage et le colportage devant la loi. Textes de jurisprudence et instructions pratiques destinés aux Camelots du Roi et aux ligueurs de l'Action Française.* Paris, n.d.

Hilaire de Barenton. *L'Action Française et l'œuvre de Charles Maurras.* Paris, 1916.

La Rocque, François de. *Les Croix de Feu, leur chef, leur programme.* Paris, 1935.

Le Mercier d'Erm, Camille. *La Question bretonne nationaliste et l'Action Française.* Rennes, 1913.

Ligue de l'Action Française, groupe picard. *"Ce que nous voulons."* Amiens, 1912.

Ligue de l'Action Française, Section champenoise. Reims, 1912.

Longin, M. *Action Française, allocution du président de la section de Dijon au Punch le 5 Janvier 1912.* Dijon, 1912.

———. *Action Française, allocution du président de la section de Dijon à la réunion du 9 décembre 1909.* Dijon, 1911.

Meunier, Lucien Victor. *Camelots du Roi et Camelots du Pape.* Bordeaux, 1909.

Morel, André. *Les Exécutions nécessaires. Rapport sur les incidents de décembre 1910. Section toulousaine de l'Action Française.* Toulouse, 1911

Note sur l'association des dames de l'Action Française. Paris, 1911

Pitollet, Camille. *Sur un Universitaire qui a mal tourné, ou l'affaire Syveton et les méthodes historiques de l'Action Française.* Paris, n.d.

Pujo, Maurice. *L'Action Française contre l'Allemagne.* Paris, 1946.

———. *Comment La Rocque a trahi.* Paris, 1937.

———. *Le Problème de l'union.* Paris, 1937.

Vaugeois, Henri. *L'Action Française, conférence du 20 juin 1899 à la salle de la Rue d'Athènes.* Paris, 1900.

4. Published Government Documents and Court Proceedings

Chambre Des Députés, Quinzième Législature, Session de 1934, Annexe au Procès-Verbal de la Séance du 17 Mai 1934, Nos. 3383–3393. *Rapport fait au nom de la commission d'enquête chargée de rechercher les causes et les origines du 6 fevrier 1934 et les jours suivants ainsi que toutes les responsabilités encourus.* 3 vols. Paris: Imprimerie de la Chambre des Députés, 1934.

Les Evénéments survenus en France de 1933 à 1945, No. 2344, Assemblée Nationale, Session de 1947. 2 vols. Paris: Presses Universitaires De France, 1947.

Journal Officiel de la République Française, débats parlementaires, chambre des députés and *sénat*.

Le Procès de Charles Maurras: compte rendu sténographique. Paris: Albin Michel, 1946.

Le Procès du Maréchal Pétain: compte rendu sténographique. 2 vols. Paris: Albin Michel, 1946.

Le procès de Pierre Laval: compte rendu sténographique. Paris: Albin Michel, 1946.

For annuals and biographical dictionaries used to identify Action Française members, see footnote 20, p. 125.

5. Newspapers and Periodicals

L'Action Française (every issue from 1908 to 1944).
Revue de l'Action Française (every issue from 1899 to 1914).
Le Gaulois.
Le Matin.
La Libre Parole.
Le Temps.
Le Monde (post-1945).
Le Journal.
Le Jour.
L'Écho de Paris.
Le Nouveau Siècle.
Candide.
Gringoire.
Je Suis Partout.
La Nation Française.
La Croix.
Le Petit Parisien.
L'Humanité.
Le Figaro.
L'Osservatore Romano.
Le Populaire.
La Gazette de France.
Aspects de la France.
Rivarol.
Revue des deux Mondes.

Revue Critique des Idées et des Livres.
Revue Universelle.
L'Almanach de l'Action Française.

6. Books and Articles

Articles in the *Revue de l'Action Française* and the daily *Action Française* are not listed by their authors. My purpose in this study has been to show the outlook of the movement, not to identify ideas with individual writers. Most of the articles taken from these two periodicals were written by Maurras, Daudet, Bainville, and Vaugeois.

Adam, Juliette. *Nos Amitiés politiques avant l'abandon de la revanche.* Paris: A. Lemerre, 1908.

Baconnier, Firmin. *Le Salut par la corporation.* Paris: Les Œuvres Française, 1935.

Bainville, Jacques. *Comment est née la révolution russe.* Paris: Nouvelle Librairie Nationale, 1917.

————. *Les Conséquences politiques de la paix.* Paris: Nouvelle Librairie Nationale, 1920.

————. *Les Dictateurs.* Paris: Denoël, 1935.

————. *Histoire de deux peuples. La France et l'empire allemand.* Paris: Nouvelle Librairie Nationale, 1915.

————. *Historie de la troisième république.* Paris: Fayard, 1935.

Bardèche, Maurice. *Les Temps modernes.* Paris: Les Sept Couleurs, 1956.

Barrès, Maurice. *L'Appel au soldat.* Paris: Plon-Nourrit, 1926.

————. *Les Déracinés.* Paris: Plon-Nourrit, 1922.

————. *Le Jardin de Bérénice.* Paris: E. Paul, 1910.

————. *Un Homme libre.* Paris: E. Paul, 1912.

————. *Mes Cahiers.* 4 vols. Paris: Plon, 1929–1931.

————. *Scènes et doctrines du nationalisme.* Paris: Juven, 1902.

Bernanos, Georges. *La Grande peur des bien-pensants.* Paris: Grasset, 1931.

————. *Nous autres français.* Paris: Nouvelle Revue Française, 1939.

————. *Scandale de la vérité.* Paris: Nouvelle Revue Française, 1939.

Biétry, Pierre. *Les Jaunes de France et la question ouvrière.* Paris: Paclot, 1907.

Blum, Léon. *L'Exercise du pouvoir: discours prononcés de mai 1936 à janvier 1937.* Paris: Gallimard, 1937.

Blum, Léon. *For All Mankind.* New York: Viking, 1946.

———. *Souvenirs sur l'Affaire.* Paris: Gallimard, 1935.

Bourget, Paul. *Le Disciple.* Paris: Fayard, 1946 (definitive edition).

Bouthillier, Yves. *Le Drame de Vichy.* Paris: Plon, 1950.

Brasillach, Robert. *Notre avant-guerre.* Paris: Plon, 1941.

———. *Portraits.* Paris: Plon, 1935.

Caillaux, Joseph. *Devant l'histoire, mes prisons.* Paris: Aux Éditions de la Sirène, 1920.

Carcopino, Jérome. *Souvenirs de sept ans, 1937–1944.* Paris: Flammarion, 1953.

Céline, Louis-Ferdinand. *Bagatelles pour un massacre.* Paris: Denoël, 1937.

Chenu, Charles. *La Ligue des patriots. Son programme, son passé, son avenir* (with a preface by Maurice Barrès and extracts from speeches by Paul Déroulède). Paris: L. Tenin, 1916.

Clemenceau, Georges. *Grandeur and Misery of Victory.* New York: Harcourt, Brace, 1930.

Daladier, Édouard. *In Defense of France.* New York: Doubleday, Doran, 1939.

Daudet, Léon. *La Pluie de sang. Nouveaux souvenirs (1914–1918).* Paris: Grasset, 1932.

———. *Souvenirs des milieux littéraires, politiques, artistiques, et médicaux.* 2 vols. Paris: Nouvelle Librairie Nationale, 1920.

———. *Vers le roi.* Paris: Nouvelle Librairie Nationale, 1921.

De Gaulle, Charles. *Mémoirs de guerre.* 3 vols. Paris: Plon, 1954–1959.

Dimier, Louis. *Vingt ans de l'Action Française et d'autres souvenirs.* Paris: Nouvelle Librairie Nationale, 1926.

Dimnet, Ernest. *France Herself Again.* London: G. P. Putnam's Sons, 1914.

Doriot, Jacques. *Refaire la France.* Paris: Grasset, 1938.

Drault, Jean (pseudonym Alfred Gendrot). *Drumont la France juive, et la Libre Parole.* Paris: Malfère, 1935.

Drieu La Rochelle, Pierre. *Gilles.* Paris: Nouvelle Revue Française, 1939.

———. *Récit secret.* Paris: Gallimard, 1961.

Drumont, Édouard. *La Dernière bataille.* Paris: E. Dentu, 1890.

———. *La France juive.* 2 vols. Paris: E. Dentu, 1886.

———. *Le Testament d'un antisémite.* Paris: E. Dentu, 1891.

Dutourd, Jean. *The Best Butter.* New York: Simon and Schuster, 1955.

———. *The Taxis of the Marne.* London: Secker and Warburg, 1957.

Foch, Ferdinand. "Du Malaise mondial," *Revue de France*, Vol. VIII (January 1928).

France, Anatole. *Monsieur Bergeret à Paris*. Paris: Calmann-Levy, 1923.

Freycinet, Charles-Louis de Saulces de. *Souvenirs*. 2 vols. Paris: Delagrave, 1912–1913.

Gérin Ricard, Lazare de, and Louis Truc. *Histoire de l'Action Française*. Paris: Fournier-Valdès, 1949.

Guérin, Jules. *Les Trafiquants de l'antisémitisme*. Paris: F. Juven, 1905.

Halévy, Daniel. "Apologie pour notre passé," *Cahiers de la Quinzaine*, Vol. 10, Series 11 (1910).

Havard de la Montagne, Robert. *Histoire de l'Action Française*. Paris: Amiot-Dumont, 1950.

Isorni, Maître Jacques. *Quatre années au pouvoir*. Paris: La Couronne Littéraire, 1949.

Lamy, Étienne. "L'Action Française et 'Le Correspondant,'" *Le Correspondant*, Vol. CXCIII (December 10, 1907).

La Rocque, François de. *Service public*. Paris: Grasset, 1934.

Lasserre, Pierre. "Georges Sorel, théoricien de l'impérialisme," *Cahiers de la Quinzaine*, Vol. 18, Series 17 (1914).

La Tour du Pin Chambly de la Charce, René de. *Aphorismes de politique sociale*. Paris: Nouvelle Librairie Nationale, 1909.

Martin du Gard, Maurice. "Le Testament de Pierre Lasserre," *Nouvelles Littéraires*, October 17, 1931.

Massis, Henri. *Défense de l'occident*. Paris: Plon, 1927.

———. *Les Idées restent*. Lyon: Lardanchet, 1941.

———, and Alfred Tarde (writing under the joint pseudonym of Agathon). *Les Jeunes gens d'aujourd'hui*. Paris: Plon-Nourrit, 1913.

———. *Maurras et notre temps*. Paris: La Palatine, 1951.

Maurras, Charles Marie Photius. *L'Action Française et religion catholique*. Paris: Nouvelle Librairie Nationale, 1913.

———. *Les Amants de Venise: Georges Sand et Musset*. Paris: Flammarion, 1926.

———. *Anthinéa*. 5th edition. Paris: Juven, 1926.

———. *Au Signe de Flore*. Paris: Collection Hier, 1931.

———. *L'Avenir de l'intelligence*. Paris: A. Fontemoing, 1909.

———. *Le Chemin de paradis*. Paris: E. de Boccard, 1921.

———. *La Contre-révolution spontanée*. Lyon: Lardanchet, 1943.

———. *Corps glorieux, ou la vertu de la perfection*. Paris: Flammarion, 1929.

Maurras, Charles Marie Photius. *La Démocratie religieuse*. Paris: Nouvelle Librairie Nationale, 1921.

———. *De Démos à Cesar*. 2 vols. Paris: Éditions du Capitole, 1930.

———. *Dictionnaire politique et critique*. Paris: Cité des Livres, 1933.

———. *Le Dilemme de Marc Sangnier*. Paris: Nouvelle Librairie Nationale, 1907.

———. *Enquête sur la monarchie*. Versailles: Bibliothèque des Œuvres Politiques, 1929.

———. *L'Étang de Berre*. Paris: E. Champion, 1915.

———. *Gaulois, germains, latins*. Paris: Nouvelle Librairie Nationale, 1926.

———. *Kiel et Tanger*. Paris: Nouvelle Librairie Nationale, 1916.

———. *Maîtres et témoins de ma vie d'esprit: Barrès, Mistral, France, Verlaine, Moréas*. Paris: Flammarion, 1954.

———. *Le Mauvais traité: de la victoire à Locarno—chronique d'une décadence*. Paris: Éditions du Capitole, 1928.

———. *Les Mensonges de "l'expert" Verdenal au procès de Lyon*. Paris: Éditions de la Seule France, 1951.

———. *Mes Idées politiques*. Paris: Fayard, 1937.

———. "Les Métèques," *La Cocarde*, December 28, 1894.

———. *La Musique intérieure*. Paris: Grasset, 1925.

———. "Le Nationalisme intégral," *Soleil*, March 2, 1900.

———. *Quand les français ne s'aiment pas*. Paris: Nouvelle Librairie Nationale, 1926.

———. *La seule France*. Lyon: Lardanchet, 1941.

———. *Si le coup de force est possible*, in 1929 edition of the *Enquête sur la monarchie*.

———. *Tombeaux*. Paris: Nouvelle Librairie Nationale, 1921.

———. "Trois idées politiques," in *Romantisme et révolution*. Paris: Nouvelle Librairie Nationale, 1925.

———. *Votre bel aujourd'hui*. Paris: Lanauve de Tartas, 1953.

Meyer, Arthur. *Ce que je peux dire: la Comtesse de Loynes*. Paris: Plon-Nourrit, 1912.

Montard, Charlotte. *Quatre ans à l'Action Française. Ce que j'ai vu. Ce que j'ai entendu*. Neuilly-sur-Seine: Éditions Lori, 1931.

Montherlant, Henry de. *Le Solstice de juin*. Paris: Grasset, 1941.

Mun, Albert de. *Ma Vocation sociale*. Paris: P. Lethielleux, 1911.

Paléologue, Maurice. *An Intimate Journal of the Dreyfus Case*. New York: Criterion Books, 1957.

Péguy, Charles. "Notre jeunesse," *Cahiers de la Quinzaine*, Vol. 12, Series 1 (1910).

———. *Notre patrie.* Paris: Nouvelle Revue Française, 1915.

Proust, Marcel. *À La Recherche du temps perdu.* 15 vols. Paris: Gallimard, 1919–1927.

Pujo, Maurice. *Les Camelots du roi.* Paris: Flammarion, 1933.

Rebatet, Lucien. *Les Décombres.* Paris: Denoël, 1942.

Rey, Étienne. *La Renaissance de l'orgueil française.* Paris: Grasset, 1912.

Reynaud, Paul. *In the Thick of the Fight.* New York: Simon and Schuster, 1955.

Roux, Marie de. *Charles Maurras et le nationalisme de l'Action Française.* Paris: Nouvelle Librairie Nationale, 1926.

———. *Réforme républicaine ou restauration monarchique?* Conférence faite Par MM. Henri de Kérillis et Marie de Roux aux Grandes Conférences des Ambassadeurs à Paris, Le 30 Mars 1935. Paris: Éditions des Ambassadeurs, 1935.

Sembat, Marcel. *Faites un roi, si non, faites la paix.* Paris: Figuière, 1913.

Sorel, Georges. *Propos de Georges Sorel*, ed. Jean Variot. Paris: Gallimard, 1935.

———. *Réflexions sur la violence.* Paris: Rivière, 1910.

———. *La Révolution dreyfusienne.* Paris: Rivière, 1911.

Soury, Jules. *Une Campagne nationaliste, 1899–1901.* Paris: Plon-Nourrit, 1902.

Taittinger, Pierre. *Les Cahiers de la jeune France.* Paris: Éditions du National, 1926.

Uzès, La Duchesse d'. *Souvenirs de la Duchesse d'Uzès.* Paris: Plon, 1934.

Vallat, Xavier. *Le Nez de Cléopatre: souvenirs d'un homme de droite.* Paris: Éditions "Les Quatre Fils Aymon," 1957.

Valois, Georges (pseudonym for Alfred Georges Gressent). *Basile: ou la politique de la calomnie.* Paris: Georges Valois, 1927.

———. *Histoire et philosophie sociales. La Monarchie et la classe ouvrière.* Paris: Nouvelle Librairie Nationale, 1924.

Vaugeois, Henri. *La Fin de l'erreur français.* Paris: Librairie d'Action Française, 1928.

———. *Notre pays.* Paris: Nouvelle Librairie Nationale, 1916.

Viau, Raphaël. *Vingt ans d'antisémitisme.* Paris: E. Fasquelle, 1910.

Weygand, Maxime. *Mémoirs.* 3 vols. Paris: Flammarion, 1950–1953.

SECONDARY SOURCES

Aron, Robert. *Histoire de Vichy, 1940–1944.* Paris: Fayard, 1954.

Auriac, Jules d'. *La Nationalité française.* Paris: Flammarion, 1913.

Bankwitz, Philip C. F. "Maxime Weygand and the Army-Nation Concept in the Modern French Army, *French Historical Studies,* Vol. II, No. 2 (1961).

Beau de Loménie, Émmanuel. *Les Responsabilités des dynasties bourgeoises.* 3 vols. Paris: Denoël, 1943–1954.

———. *Maurras et son système.* Bourg-en-Bresse-Paris: Éditions Touristiques et Littéraires, 1953.

Beik, Paul. *The French Revolution Seen from the Right: Social Theories in Motion, 1789–1799.* Philadelphia: American Philosophical Society, 1956.

Benda, Julien. "Note sur la réaction," *Nouvelle Revue Française,* Vol. VIII (1929).

———. *La Trahison des clercs.* Paris: Grasset, 1927.

Binion, Rudolph. *Defeated Leaders: The Political Fate of Caillaux, Jouvenel, and Tardieu.* New York: Columbia University Press, 1960.

Bloch, Marc. *L'Étrange défaite.* Paris: Société des Éditions Franc-Tireur, 1946.

Bosworth, William. *Catholicism and Crisis in Modern France.* Princeton, New Jersey: Princeton University Press, 1962.

Brogan, Denis W. *France under the Republic.* New York: Harper, 1940.

———. *French Personalities and Problems.* New York: A. Knopf, 1947.

Buthman, William Curt. *The Rise of Integral Nationalism in France.* New York: Columbia University Press, 1939.

Byrnes, Robert F. *Antisemitism in Modern France.* Vol. I: The Prologue to the Dreyfus Case. New Brunswick, New Jersey: Rutgers University Press, 1950.

———. "Édouard Drumont and *La France juive,*" *Conference on Jewish Relations.* New York, 1948.

Cairns, John C. "Along the Road Back to France, 1940," *American Historical Review,* Vol. LXIV (1959).

Carli, Ferruccio de. *Pio X e il suo tempo.* Florence: A. Salmi, 1951.

Carroll, E. Malcom. *French Public Opinion and Foreign Affairs, 1870–1914.* New York: The Century Co., 1931.

Chapman, Guy. *The Dreyfus Case: A Reassessment.* New York: Reynal and Co., 1955.

Chastenet, Jacques. *La France de M. Fallières*. Paris: Fayard, 1949.

Chevalier, Louis. *La Formation de la population parisienne au XIXe siècle*. Paris: Presses Universitaires de France, 1950.

Cobban, Alfred. "Vichy France," in *Survey of International Affairs, 1939–1946*, eds. Arnold and Veronica Toynbee. Vol. IV: *Hitler's Europe*. London: Oxford University Press, 1954.

Cot, Pierre. *The Triumph of Treason*. Chicago: Ziff-Davis, 1944.

Coudekerque Lambrecht, Ade. *Léon de Montesquiou*. Paris: Nouvelle Librairie Nationale, 1925.

Curtis, Michael. *Three Against the Third Republic: Sorel, Barrès, and Maurras*. Princeton, New Jersey: Princeton University Press, 1959.

Curtius, Ernst Robert. *Maurice Barrès und die geistigen Grundlagen des französischen Nationalismus*. Bonn: F. Cohen, 1921.

Dansette, Adrien. *Du Boulangisme à la révolution dreyfusienne*. Vol. I: *Le Boulangisme, 1886–1890*. Paris: Perrin, 1938.

———. *Histoire religieuse de la France contemporaine*. 2 vols. Paris: Flammarion, 1948–1951.

———. "L'Église et l'Action Française," *Esprit*, Vol. XIX (September and October 1951).

Daric, Jean. "La Structure économique et sociale de la population française," *Les Cahiers Français*, No. 10 (October 1956).

Earle, Edward Mead (ed.). *Modern France*. Princeton, New Jersey: Princeton University Press, 1950.

Ehrmann, Henry W. "The Blum Experiment and the Fall of France," *Foreign Affairs*, XX (October 1941).

———. *French Labor from the Popular Front to the Liberation*. New York: Oxford University Press, 1947.

———. *Organized Business in France*. Princeton, New Jersey: Princeton University Press, 1957.

Einaudi, Mario, and Jean-Marie Domenach. *Christian Democracy in Italy and France*. Notre Dame, Indiana: University of Notre Dame Press, 1952.

Elbow, Matthew H. *French Corporative Theory, 1789–1948*. New York: Columbia University Press, 1953.

Farmer, Paul. *Vichy: Political Dilemma*. New York: Columbia University Press, 1954.

Fauvet, Jacques. *La Quatrième république*. Paris: A. Fayard, 1959.

———, and Jean Planchais. *La Fronde de généraux*. Paris: Arthaud, 1961.

Fontaine, Nicholas. *Saint-Siège, "Action Française," et "catholiques intégraux."* Paris: J. Gamber, 1928.

Forges, Roger Joseph, and Jean Forges. *Biblio-iconographie de*

Charles Maurras. 2 vols. Roanne, Loire: Les Amis du Chemin du Paradis, 1954.

Freund, Michael. *Georges Sorel: der revolutionäre Konservatismus.* Frankfurt-am-Main: V. Klostermann, 1932.

Galtier-Boissière. *Le Bourrage de Crânes.* Paris: Crapouillot, 1937.

Géraud, André (pseudonym Pertinax). *The Gravediggers of France.* Garden City, New York: Doubleday, 1944.

Girardet, Raoul. "L'Héritage de 'l'Action Française,' " *Revue Française de Science Politique,* Vol. VII, No. 4 (December 1957).

————. "Pour une introduction à l'histoire du nationalisme français," *ibid.,* Vol. VIII, No. 3 (September 1958).

————. *La Société militaire dans la France contemporaine, 1815–1939.* Paris: Plon, 1953.

Goguel, François. *Géographie des élections françaises de 1870 à 1951.* Paris: A. Colin, 1952.

————. *Histoire des institutions politiques de la France de 1870 à 1940.* Paris: Cours de Droit, 1951–1952.

———— (ed.). *Nouvelles études de sociologie électorale.* Paris: A. Colin, 1954.

Gurian, Waldemar. *Die politischen und sozialen Ideen des französischen Katholizismus, 1789–1914.* Munich-Gladbach: Volksvereinsverlag, 1929.

————. *Die Integrale Nationalismus in Frankreich.* Freiburg-im-Breisgau: Herder, 1931.

Guy-Grand, Georges. *Le Procès de la démocratie.* Paris. Grasset, 1911.

Halévy, Daniel. *Essais sur le mouvement ouvrier en France.* Paris: Société Nouvelle de Libraire et d'Édition, 1901.

Hayes, Carleton J. H. *France: A Nation of Patriots.* New York: Columbia University Press, 1930.

Henriot, Émile. *À Quoi rêvent les jeunes gens?* Paris: H. and E. Champion, 1913.

Hoffmann, Stanley. "Aspects du régime de Vichy," *Revue Française de Science Politique,* Vol. VI, No. 1 (January–March 1956).

————. "The Effects of World War II on French Society and Politics," *French Historical Studies,* Vol. II, No. 1 (Spring 1961).

————. *Le Mouvement Poujade.* Paris: A. Colin, 1956.

Huddleston, Sisley. *France: The Tragic Years, 1939–1947.* New York: Devin-Adair, 1955.

Huntington, Frank C. "The Ideology of the Action Française." Unpublished Ph.D. dissertation, Yale University, 1954.

Hutchins, Merrill L. "The Relations between Church and State in France from 1905–1925." Unpublished Ph.D. dissertation, University of Chicago, 1949.

Hytier, Adrienne Doris. *Two Years of French Foreign Policy, Vichy 1940–1942.* Geneva: Librairie Droz, 1958.

Johnson, Harry M. "The Fall of France: An Essay on the Social Structure of France between the Wars." Unpublished Ph.D. dissertation, Harvard University, 1949.

Kayser, Jacques. *L'Affaire Dreyfus.* Paris: Gallimard, 1946.

Laberthonnière, L. *Autour de l'Action Française.* Paris: Bloud, 1911.

Lavau, G.-E. *Partis politiques et réalités sociales.* Paris: A. Colin, 1953.

Lecanuet, R. P. *L'Église de France sous la troisième république.* Paris: Alcan, 1930.

Lorwin, Lewis Levitski. *Syndicalism in France.* New York: Longmans, Green, 1914.

Lorwin, Val. *The French Labor Movement.* Cambridge, Mass.: Harvard University Press, 1954.

Lugan, André. *La Fin d'une mystification. L'Action Française, son histoire, sa doctrine, sa politique.* Paris: Valois, 1928.

Mallet, Alfred. *Pierre Laval.* 2 vols. Paris: Amiot-Dumont, 1955.

Marabuto, Paul. *Les Partis politiques et les mouvements sociaux sous la IVe république.* Paris: Sirey, 1948.

Marcus, John T. *French Socialism in the Crisis Years, 1933–1936.* New York: F. Praeger, 1958.

Maritain, Jacques. *À Travers le désastre.* New York: Éditions de la Maison Française, 1941.

Mathiez, Albert. *La Monarchie et la politique national.* Paris: Alcan, 1917.

Meynaud, Jean. *Les Groupes de pression en France.* Paris: A. Colin, 1958.

Micaud, Charles. *The French Right and Nazi Germany, 1933–1939.* Durham, North Carolina: Duke University Press, 1943.

Mirambel, André. *La Comédie du nationalisme intégral.* Paris: Grasset, 1947.

Montreuil, Jean. *Histoire du mouvement ouvrier en France.* Paris: Aubier, 1946.

Moon, Parker Thomas. *The Labor Problem and the Social Catholic Movement in France.* New York: Macmillan, 1921.

Morazé, Charles. *Les Français et la République.* Paris: A. Colin, 1956.

Moure, Michel. *Charles Maurras.* Paris: Éditions Universitaires, 1958.

Muret, Charlotte Touzalin. *French Royalist Doctrines since the Revolution*. New York: Columbia University Press, 1933.

Naumann, H. *Charles Maurras und die Weltanschauung der Action Française*. Würzburg: Triltsch, 1935.

Néré, Jacques. "La Crise économique et sociale de 1882 et le mouvement boulangiste" and "Les Élections boulangistes dans le Nord." Unpublished doctoral theses, Sorbonne, 1959.

Noble, George Bernard. *Policies and Opinions at Paris. Wilsonian Diplomacy, the Versailles Peace, and French Public Opinion*. New York: Macmillan, 1935.

Osgood, Samuel M. *French Royalism under the Third and Fourth Republics*. The Hague: Martinus Nijhoff, 1960.

Pado, Dominique. *Maurras, Béraud, Brasillach: Trois condamnés, trois générations*. Monaco: Pathé, 1945.

Pawlowski, Auguste. *Les Syndicats jaunes*. Paris: Alcan, 1911.

Pickles, Dorothy M. *France between the Republics*. London: Contact, 1946.

————. *The French Political Scene*. London: Nelson, 1938.

Rémond, René. *La Droite en France de 1815 à nos jours*. Paris: Aubier, 1954.

————. "Droite et gauche dans le catholicisme français contemporain," *Revue Française de Science Politique*, Vol. VIII, Nos. 3 and 4 (Septemper and December 1958).

————. "Le Nouveau régime et les forces politiques," *ibid.*, Vol. IX, No. 1 (March 1959).

Roche, Alphonse V. *Les Idées traditionalistes en France de Rivarol à Charles Maurras*. Urbana, Illinois: The University of Illinois Press, 1937.

Roudiez. Leon S. *Charles Maurras jusqu'à l'Action Française*. Paris: André Bonne, 1957.

Sartre, Jean-Paul. "Portrait of an Antisemite," *Partisan Review*, 13 (1946).

Schnurer, H. "The Intellectual Sources of French Fascism," *Antioch Review* (March 1941).

Sérant, Paul. *Où va la droite?* Paris: Plon, 1958.

————. *Le Romantisme fasciste. Étude sur l'œuvre politique de quelques écrivains français*. Paris: Fasquelle, 1959.

Shattuck, Roger. *The Banquet Years: The Arts in France, 1885–1918*. New York: Harcourt, Brace, 1958.

Siegfried, André. *Tableau politique de la France de l'ouest*. Paris: Plon, 1913.

Simon, Yves. *The Road to Vichy 1918–1938*. New York: Sheed and Ward, 1942.

Bibliography   ❦305

Stern, Fritz Richard. *The Politics of Cultural Despair; A Study in the Rise of the German Ideology.* Berkeley, California: The University of California Press, 1961.

Talagrand, Jacques (pseudonym Thierry-Maulnier). *La France, la guerre et la paix.* Lyon: Lardanchet, 1942.

Tharaud, Jean, and Jérome Tharaud. *Mes Années chez Barrès.* Paris: Plon, 1928.

———. *La Vie et la mort de Paul Déroulède.* Paris: Plon, 1933.

Thibaudet, Albert. *Les Idées politiques de la France.* Paris: Delamain & Boutelleau, 1933.

Touchard, Jean. "L'Esprit des années 1930," in *Tendances politiques de la vie française depuis 1789.* Paris: Hachette, 1960.

———. "La Fin de la quatrième république," *Revue Française de Science Politique*, Vol. VIII, No. 4 (December 1958).

Tournoux, J.-R. *Secrets d'état.* Paris: Plon, 1960.

Tucker, William R. "The Legacy of Charles Maurras," *Journal of Politics*, Vol. XVII (November 1955).

Vialatoux, J., and J. Lacroix. "Le Mythe Pétain," *Esprit*, Vol. XIX (September 1951).

Walter, Gérard. *Histoire du parti communiste français.* Paris: Somogy, 1948.

Weber, Eugen. *The Nationalist Revival in France, 1905–1914.* Berkeley, California: The University of California Press, 1959.

———. "New Wine in Old Bottles: Les Familles spirituelles de la France," *French Historical Studies*, Vol. I, No. 2 (1959).

———. "The Right in France: A Working Hypothesis," *American Historical Review*, Vol. LXV, No. 3 (April 1960).

Weill, Georges. *Histoire du mouvement social en France.* Paris: Alcan, 1924.

Werth, Alexander. *France in Ferment.* London: Jarrolds, 1934.

———. *France, 1940–1955.* New York: Henry Holt, 1956.

———. *The Twilight of France, 1933–1940.* New York: Harper, 1942.

Williams, Philip. *Politics in Postwar France.* Second edition. New York: Longmans, Green, 1958.

Wright, Gordon. *Raymond Poincaré and the French Presidency.* Stanford, California: Stanford University Press, 1942.

———. *The Reshaping of French Democracy.* New York: Reynal and Hitchcock, 1948.

Zirnheld, Jules. *Cinquante années de syndicalisme chrétien.* Paris: Spès, 1937.

Index